EDI LEARNING RESOURCES SERIES

Infrastructure Strategies in East Asia

The Untold Story

Edited by

Ashoka Mody

The World Bank
Washington, D. C.

HC
460.5
.Z9
C35
1997

The Economic Development Institute (EDI) was established by the World Bank in 1955 to train officials concerned with development planning, policymaking, investment analysis, and project implementation in member developing countries. At present the substance of the EDI's work emphasizes macroeconomic and sectoral economic policy analysis. Through a variety of courses, seminars, and workshops, most of which are given overseas in cooperation with local institutions, the EDI seeks to sharpen analytical skills used in policy analysis and to broaden understanding of the experience of individual countries with economic development. Although the EDI's publications are designed to support its training activities, many are of interest to a much broader audience. EDI materials, including any findings, interpretations, and conclusions, are entirely those of the authors and should not be attributed in any manner to the World Bank, to its affiliated organizations, or to members of its Board of Executive Directors or the countries they represent.

Because of the informality of this series and to make the publication available with the least possible delay, the manuscript has not been edited as fully as would be the case with a more formal document, and the World Bank accepts no responsibility for errors. Some sources cited in this paper may be informal documents that are not readily available.

The material in this publication is copyrighted. Requests for permission to reproduce portions of it should be sent to the Office of the Publisher at the address shown in the copyright notice above. The World Bank encourages dissemination of its work and will normally give permission promptly and, when the reproduction is for noncommercial purposes, without asking a fee. Permission to photocopy portions for classroom use is granted through the Copyright Clearance Center, Inc., Suite 910, 222 Rosewood Drive, Danvers, Massachusetts 01923, U.S.A.

The complete backlist of publications from the World Bank is shown in the annual *Index of Publications*, which contains an alphabetical title list (with full ordering information) and indexes of subjects, authors, and countries and regions. The latest edition is available free of charge from the Distribution Unit, Office of the Publisher, The World Bank, 1818 H Street, N.W., Washington, D.C. 20433, U.S.A., or from Publications, Banque mondiale, 66, avenue d'Iéna, 75116 Paris, France.

Ashoka Mody is principal financial economist in the Project Finance and Guarantees Group of the World Bank's Cofinancing and Project Finance Department.

Library of Congress Cataloging-in-Publication Data

Infrastructure strategies in East Asia : the untold story / edited by
   Ashoka Mody.
      p.   cm.—(EDI learning resources series, ISSN 1020-3842)
   "Originally written as background to the World Bank's World
development report 1994"—Pref.
   Includes bibliographical references (p.   ).
   ISBN 0-8213-4027-1
   1. Infrastructure (Economics)—East Asia—Case studies. I. Mody,
Ashoka. II. World Bank. III. Series.
HC460.5.Z9C35   1997
363'.095—dc21
                                               97–34324
                                                 CIP

Contents

Contributors

Morio Kuninori is at the Research Center on Global Warming in Japan.

Cassey Lee is at the University of Malaya in Malaysia.

Ashoka Mody is principal financial economist at the World Bank in Washington, D.C.

G. Naidu is at the University of Malaya in Malaysia.

Tsuruhiko Nambu is a member of the faculty of economics at Gakushuin University in Tokyo.

William Reinfeld is director of strategic services for Greater China, Andersen Consulting.

Kwong Kai Sun is in the Department of Economics at the Chinese University of Hong Kong.

Robert Wade is at the Institute of Development Studies, Sussex University, and Brown University.

Lee Tsao Yuan is at the Institute of Policy Studies in Singapore.

Foreword

In the continuing search for the sources of East Asia's "miraculous" growth, this book highlights the importance of infrastructure development. Focusing on the Republic of Korea, Taiwan (China), Hong Kong, Malaysia, and Singapore—along with selected aspects of Japanese infrastructure strategy—the book documents the high priority and commitment to infrastructure by senior leaders. This commitment reflected itself not only in large amounts of investment but also in a planning and delivery process that was responsive to the evolving needs of the economies. The argument is made that the ability to "keep the eye on the ball" was possible because of a compelling need to meet the requirements of exporters and foreign investors.

Today, the East Asian economies face a number of challenges. With the past focus on trade and production–related infrastructure, environmental infrastructure has not kept pace with the levels of per capita incomes achieved. Also, the basic model of public delivery of infrastructure is being questioned. While Malaysia has moved ahead rapidly towards private delivery, other economies are also surely moving in that direction. In parallel, the old systems of government-mediated financing are coming under strain. To achieve continued growth, these economies will need to demonstrate the organizational adaptability that has been the source of success in recent decades.

Books in the EDI's Learning Resources Series are designed to facilitate self-study by policymakers, researchers, and students. It is my expectation that this book will contribute to our understanding of the economic growth process, the responsibilities of governments, and the mechanisms for ensuring government performance.

> Vinod Thomas, Director
> Economic Development Institute

Preface

The chapters presented in this book were originally written as background papers to the World Bank's *World Development Report 1994: Infrastructure for Development*. The papers were commissioned at an early stage in writing that report when it became evident that vast gaps existed in our knowledge of East Asian infrastructure. This was a source of special concern, because East Asian economies had devoted substantial resources to infrastructure, viewing it as integral to their high growth strategies. Over a period of several months drafts of the background papers became available, and their contributions were reflected in *World Development Report 1994*, but that necessarily brief document could neither reflect the rich detail of the papers nor their broad thematic conclusions adequately. This book, therefore, brings together those papers, as well as an introductory essay.

To the best of my knowledge, this account of infrastructure development strategies in East Asia is the first such comprehensive effort. It should provide valuable insights to policymakers who wish to learn more about successes and failures in the region. Researchers of East Asian development in general, and of infrastructure development in particular, should find here many hypotheses and leads that bear further investigation as the region's massive achievements over the past half-century are assessed.

Some cautionary notes are in order. First, scholars and policymakers are divided on the relevance of East Asian countries' success to other developing countries. First, some investigators continue to believe that the set of initial conditions—low inequality, relatively high education, significant amounts of foreign aid to some of the economies—contributed to an institutional structure and decisionmaking process that is not easy to replicate. Second, factors that contributed to rapid development in the past apply with less force today. Central planning leading to physical targets delivered through government departments and corporations is on its way out around the world. However, the lesson is that mechanisms to coordinate the actions of various arms of a government are important, and alternatives will need to be found. In East Asia, as this book reports, the old institutions are being adapted to the new circumstances. Finally, the title of this book says it is a "story." The authors have focused their energies on describing the sequence of events, sectoral differences, and institutional features. Analysis of options and tradeoffs has been undertaken only to a limited extent.

The volume has two parts. The chapters in part 1 discuss how five East Asian economies renovated and built their infrastructure base to foster their transformation into industrial powers. The chapters discuss how each economy addressed the functional dimensions of infrastructure development: policymaking mechanisms; institutional, regulatory, and financing arrangements; and ownership and service delivery schemes. Because infrastructure development is tied not only to economic transformation, but also to an economy's prevailing social climate, the chapters in part 1 also discuss how these economies balanced their economic and social development. Each chapter highlights changing policy priorities and attempts to identify the challenges ahead. The chapters in part 2 are case studies that illuminate financial, regulatory, organizational, and technological aspects of infrastructure development.

The chapters were discussed and reviewed at two workshops, the first in Tokyo—hosted by the Japan Development Bank—in February 1994, and the second in Singapore—hosted by the Institute of Policy Studies—in June 1994. We thank the many participants at these workshops who provided detailed comments that have helped improve these chapters. I am grateful also to anonymous readers who provided thoughtful and constructive comments that have weeded out some errors and helped provide a better balance in the description of institutions and events. The chapters were edited by Thomas Good and Paul Holtz of American Writing Corporation and Alice Dowsett of The Word Doctor.

We are grateful to the Japanese government, who through the Population and Human Resources Development Fund—administered by the World Bank—supported the writing of these chapters as well as the workshops. Koji Kashiwaya, then vice president of the World Bank's Cofinancing and Financial Advisory Services, and Inder Sud, then director in the same vice presidency, helped secure the funding. Thanks also go to Gregory Ingram, who as director of *World Development Report 1994* viewed this project as a high priority, and who has maintained an interest in its progress even after completion of that report.

Infrastructure Delivery through Central Guidance

Ashoka Mody

Infrastructure development in East Asia remains largely an untold story, despite its impressive—often spectacular—physical achievements and despite its critical contributions to economic growth and social development in the region. As with much of the writing on East Asian growth, one recent account—the World Bank's *The East Asian Miracle* (World Bank 1993)—refers only briefly to infrastructure (pp. 221–23) in its comprehensive survey of macroeconomics policies, human capital investment, export and industrialization strategies, and financial sector institutions and policies. The fascination with East Asian industrialization and the controversies surrounding the degree and success of proactive government strategies have all but eclipsed the more fundamental role of government support in fostering a dynamic infrastructure (see, for example, Amsden 1989; Wade 1990). Thus, by recounting the story of East Asia's infrastructure development during the past five decades, this book fills an important gap in our understanding of the phenomenal economic growth that has occurred in that region.

Infrastructure in East Asia was guided by a strategic vision and propelled by a substantial and sustained drive. A predominantly public sector effort—conceived, financed, regulated, and operated largely by the government or its agencies—infrastructure development often shows the best face of East Asian governments. Yet while the physical achievements are remarkable and their contribution to economic growth is undeniable, some failures were inevitable, including, for example, instances of wasted expenditures, inadequate response to (and sometimes neglect of) growing pressures on the environment, and a disregard for social and political sensitivities. Infrastructure development in East Asia, as elsewhere, continues to test governments' ability to make the right decisions and to balance many competing interests.

This essay highlights the features of infrastructure strategies that are common across the six East Asian economies examined in the book—Hong Kong, Japan, the Republic of Korea, Malaysia, Singapore, and Taiwan (China). At the same time, it recognizes that these economies did not collectively pursue a single, universal infrastructure strategy. Each chose the path best suited to its economic philosophy: witness the emphasis on the private sector in Hong Kong and recently in Malaysia, compared with public sector dominance elsewhere. Strategies varied even within economies, reflecting not only sectoral considerations, such as the subsidization of water as a merit good in otherwise commercially oriented Hong Kong, but also historical inheritance, for instance, the private oligopolistic structure of electric power in Japan.

Three key features help explain successful investment decisions and operations: sustained and powerful government leadership, the nurturing of complex institutions, and adaptability to change.

Government leadership was crucial. Top leaders and senior policymakers in each country were intimately involved in developing comprehensive sectoral strategies, and they guided (and in some cases controlled) how the strategies were implemented and the resources allocated. This sustained commitment to high quality infrastructure was the product of a long-range vision: to maintain the

This paper has benefited from comments by Harinder Kohli, D. C. Rao, Robert Wade, and Shahid Yusuf. The views expressed here are the author's and should not be attributed to the World Bank, its affiliated organizations, or its member countries.

region's competitiveness in export markets, to attract foreign investment to the region, and to support more balanced social development. Compared with an average infrastructure investment of 4 percent of gross domestic product (GDP) among all developing countries, investment in East Asia rarely fell below 4 percent of GDP and was often higher, reaching 7 or 8 percent in several years (World Bank 1994a). On occasion, the commitment to high levels of investment implied a willingness to undertake bold ventures, which often amounted to gambles, in high profile infrastructure projects.

A more subtle achievement—and one this book emphasizes—was the nurturing of a complex and innovative institutional capacity for determining investment priorities, ensuring efficient delivery, maintaining regulatory oversight, and mobilizing domestic financing. Considerable further research will be required to identify the many facets, the country differences, and the strengths and weaknesses of the institutions and decisionmaking processes. My review of the chapters in this book suggests that institutional capacity building efforts shared some common themes, namely:

- Each economy created a strong planning authority for spearheading infrastructure development. The planning agencies became the focal points for interministerial and interagency coordination, as well as vehicles that enabled members of the top leadership echelon to convey their priorities.
- Each government created ownership and service delivery entities that could construct, operate, and maintain the infrastructure most effectively in each sector. In the absence of a market environment, these bodies were largely responsible for ensuring services at fair market prices. Internal incentives for performance were an important determinant of effective service delivery.
- Each economy mobilized domestic sources of financing to fund infrastructure development to avoid relying on external debt or on government subsidies. Infrastructure providers— whether public corporations or private enterprises—were encouraged to adopt cost recovery mechanisms that would enable them to finance their own capital needs.

Despite the tradition of strong institutions that would normally be a source of inertia, East Asian economies displayed an ability to adapt to infrastructure needs as they developed. In this respect, however, their success has been mixed. The sectoral composition of infrastructure has responded to changing economic and social needs, often over short periods of time. Governments in East Asia, as elsewhere, are also increasingly realizing that the private sector must participate more heavily in infrastructure, but the transition to private provision is being undertaken in "East Asian style," in which governments continue to exert a strong influence. For example, the privatization process is being drawn out to a much greater degree than elsewhere, and the commitment to independent regulation has been weak, leading to inefficient and ineffective regulation.

The next section provides an overview of the region's physical achievements, followed by a discussion of the institutions that supported infrastructure, and then an assessment of the adaptive capacities of the economies. Although some new data were gathered for this overview, much of the information is a synthesis of the chapters that follow. Inevitably, given the richness of the papers, only selected themes and examples have been highlighted here.

Infrastructure to Support Growth: Physical Achievements

In any modern society, infrastructure plays a pivotal—often decisive—role in determining the overall productivity and development of a country's economy, as well as the quality of life of its citizens. Infrastructure can be broadly defined as the facilities that provide society with the services necessary to conduct daily life and to engage in productive activities. Defined in this way, the domain of infrastructure can be widened to include, for example, education and health facilities. This book adopts a narrower focus—as did *World Development Report 1994*—encompassing four infrastructure sectors: transportation (roads, railways, ports, and airports); water, sanitation, and irrigation; electric power and other energy sources; and telecommunications. Although even this limited set of sectors exhibits a wide range of characteristics, service facilities in these sectors typically require significant sunk investment outlays and the service providers operate in imperfectly competitive environments, often as natural monopolies (Gramlich 1994).

Infrastructure provision in East Asia has been linked closely to the objective of spurring economic growth. The East Asian economies sometimes invested ahead of the demand for services, but more often they were simply responding to bottlenecks in services as rapid growth outstripped the capacity of existing facilities. Thus infrastructure generally was not a causal factor driving growth, but more a necessary support for sustaining growth. This feature is especially characteristic of Taiwan (China), where the exploitation of existing infrastructure was an important policy objective, but one that led to congestion (chapter 1).

The chapters in this volume do not attempt to estimate regression models to establish a relationship between economic growth and infrastructure availability (Gramlich 1994 demonstrates the inconclusiveness of such studies), but ample evidence links growth and infrastructure in East Asia as follows:

- Sustained infrastructure investment has coincided with rapid economic growth, especially since the mid-1950s. Today, infrastructure endowments in the six East Asian economies are substantial.
- Sectoral priorities shifted as the production structure of the economy changed and as quality of life considerations became more important.
- Concerted efforts were occasionally undertaken in the form of specific, large investments.

Infrastructure Investment and Endowments: Breaking Away from the Developing Country Pack

Obtaining data that are comparable across countries is difficult, and so we must draw on different types of evidence. Here we examine both input—the investments undertaken—and output—the infrastructure installed.

Infrastructure investment by the average developing country is about 4 percent of GDP. In contrast, infrastructure investment by the six East Asian economies has rarely fallen below 4 percent, and has typically ranged from 6 to 8 percent. Japan set the example. After a slow start in the first decade after World War II, the Japanese government accelerated investment in transport infrastructure, quickly exceeding 2 percent of GDP and remaining between 2.0 and 2.5 percent ever since. Even in the early years, however, transport formed only about half of the government's investment in infrastructure. Thus along with private investment—mainly in electric power in the early years and in a wider variety of sectors now—Japan's infrastructure investment has been between 6 and 8 percent of GDP.

Korea and Taiwan (China) have also made large investments in infrastructure (chapter 1). In Korea infrastructure investment rates have been at or above 8 percent in many years in the past few decades, but especially in the 1980s. In Taiwan (China) investment rates have been more than 10 percent in some years, although that economy's more inclusive definition of infrastructure makes this figure an overestimate. If the relevant corrections were made to the data, investment rates would be about the same as or slightly lower than those in Korea. Hong Kong, Malaysia, and Singapore had investment rates of the same magnitude. According to a recent study (Kohli 1994), investment rates in East Asia are likely to remain high, or even to grow.

These large investments are manifested in rapid infrastructure development (table 1). In the early 1970s, Hong Kong, Japan, and Singapore already had extensive electric power and telecommunications capacities. Indeed, capacity in these countries was greater in the early 1970s than are the capacities of many developing countries now. The Malaysian infrastructure of the early 1970s was also substantial when compared with the stock of electric power and telecommunications infrastructure in Ghana and India in the 1990s.

Table 1. Provision of Infrastructure, a Comparison, Selected Years

Economy	Electric power generation (millions of kilowatts per 100 persons)			Telephone connections (number of connections per 100 persons)			Paved roads (meters per 100 persons)		
	1970	1992	Annual growth rate, 1970–92 (percent)	1975	1993	Annual growth rate, 1975–93 (percent)	1970	1990	Annual growth rate, 1970–90 (percent)
Hong Kong	34.0	154.0	13.4	6.7	51.0	11.9	23.0	26.0	0.6
Japan	66.1	165.4	8.0	30.8	46.8	2.4	146.1	630.7	7.6
Korea	8.8	61.7	17.6	4.0	37.8	13.3	11.5	79.9	10.2
Malaysia	8.7	36.0	12.5	1.6	12.6	12.2	143.1	156.1	0.4
Singapore	31.0	126.8	12.4	12.3	43.5	7.3	58.3	101.9	2.8
Thailand	3.7	22.1	16.0	0.6	3.7	10.9	27.0	70.9	4.9
Brazil	11.8	35.8	9.7	2.2	7.5	6.9	53.1	108.4	3.6
Chile	22.9	35.4	3.7	3.0	11.0	7.5	79.1	83.4	0.3
Ghana	7.7	7.5	-0.2	0.3	0.3	-0.7	53.6	55.5	0.2
India	3.0	9.2	9.9	0.2	0.9	7.6	59.3	89.4	2.0

Source: ITU (1992); United Nations (1992); World Bank (1994a, b).

Moreover, despite its initial advantage in power and communications, growth in these sectors was substantially greater, widening the gap between East Asia and other developing economies over time. Korea, which started with a relatively underdeveloped power and telecommunications infrastructure, experienced the most rapid growth in the region. Another East Asian economy, Thailand, had low levels of infrastructure capacity throughout, but was clearly catching up, experiencing growth rates just below those in Korea. However, the impact of high growth is particularly visible when one compares Malaysia and Chile, two economies of similar size that were both dependent on exports of primary goods in the early 1970s. Although Chile had a more advanced infrastructure in 1970, Malaysia's infrastructure had surged ahead by the early 1990s, even though Chile is Latin America's star performer and in the vanguard of market-oriented reforms. The contrast with Ghana and India is more sobering, for in those countries both initial levels and growth rates have been low. Ghana actually experienced a decline in per capita capacity from 1970 to 1990.

The story with regard to road infrastructure is less clear cut. As noted, some of the East Asian economies made large investments in this sector. Japan increased the length of its paved roads substantially, and at 631 meters per 100 persons, it now has the highest road density in the world. Korea's road density grew by 10 percent a year, the highest growth rate of all the countries reported in table 1. The city economies of Hong Kong and Singapore increased their road capacity only modestly, while the growth of roads in Malaysia barely kept pace with population growth. Elsewhere, road investment has been substantial only in Brazil, but despite its comparatively rapid growth in per capita length of roads (3.6 percent a year), it is still slower than in Korea (10.2 percent), Japan (7.6 percent), and even Thailand (4.9 percent).

The high investment rates in infrastructure have generated a substantial accumulation of infrastructure stocks in the East Asian economies. Evidence suggests that the pace of infrastructure investment in East Asia will not slow down in the next several years; indeed, it may accelerate (Kohli 1994). In particular, the newly industrialized East Asian economies must still do some catching up with the more advanced Western economies. In doing so, they will widen the gap between East Asia and much of the developing world.

Sector Priorities: Facilitating the Movement of Goods and Information

As in most economies, transportation received substantial resources early on, typically accounting for between one-third and one-half of all infrastructure investments. Railways rapidly lost ground to roads, which have since dominated investment in the transport infrastructure. However, recent technological developments, the more benign environmental consequences of railways, and their greater efficiency in long-haul freight traffic have revived investments in railways in many of the East Asian economies.

Priorities within the road sector have varied. Japan embarked on an extensive toll road program early on. Toll roads are less common elsewhere in the region, although the emphasis on connecting key urban centers has been an important determinant of road development. Experience with road development in rural areas has been mixed. In Taiwan (China) rural road development sustained industrialization, generating rural economic activity and reducing pressures on the urban infrastructure (chapter 1). In contrast, a massive rural road program in Malaysia proved to be a significant waste of resources when the expected economic activity did not materialize (chapter 2).

Another high priority element of the transport sector pertains to the international movement of goods and people via ports and airports. In all East Asian economies the drive toward nurturing international commerce and investment made ports and airports critical to the overall economic strategy. Trade links were often direct, as when a port was made an integral component of an industrial estate that exported manufactured goods. A city economy geared toward international transactions, Singapore most strongly exemplifies the link between trade and its supporting infrastructure.

Singapore's port and airport are among the best in the world and have successfully kept pace with growing demands and technological developments, for example, with the rapid expansion of containerization facilities and increased reliance on advanced information technology (chapter 4). The other economies also embarked on extensive port and airport development.

The highly international orientation of the East Asian economies is also reflected in their investment in telecommunications. Telecommunications investments of between 1.5 and 2.0 percent of GDP in the late 1970s and early 1980s were a function of the demand for high quality, relatively inexpensive communications by international buyers, sellers, and investors. Although the East Asian economies have not sustained such high levels of investment, they have continued to place a high priority on expanding the physical network and extending the range of services as they seek to differentiate themselves on the basis of advanced information technology (chapter 8).

Finally, electric power generation has been a constant concern for every East Asian economy. Although each has allocated substantial resources to the sector (second only to road development), power generation capacity has often threatened to fall short of economic growth, with declines in energy reserve margins. The governments have responded by increasing investments in generation, transmission, and distribution capacities. Today, concerns about the environment are prompting the governments to increase their investments in pollution prevention.

Taking Gambles: The Payoffs

Inevitably, certain large investments amounted to gambles. In some cases strong indicators of latent demand tempered the extent of the gambles, but the caution international advisers expressed at the time of the investment and the subsequent huge impact of the investment on the economy indicate the boldness of these initiatives. Given the dominance of the transport sector, these bold schemes were implemented primarily in the highway subsector, and the largest gambles were made with the construction of major arterial roads. The Kobe-Nagoya Highway in Japan and the Seoul-Pusan Highway in Korea are examples of these gambles.

The Kobe-Nagoya route connected several important economic centers in Japan, with one end—Nagoya—being the headquarters of the Toyota Motor Company. It was also a major element of a planned network of toll roads. The Japanese government requested financial assistance from the World Bank to fund a portion of the anticipated US$260 million in construction costs, and at the Bank's suggestion invited a mission to assess the road's economic feasibility (Uzawa 1994). Although the mission supported the planned toll network and recognized the economic importance of the Kobe-Nagoya Highway, it advised against constructing the road as planned, partly on the grounds that the tolls would be insufficient to cover costs. Japan constructed the highway anyway, and it became operational in the mid-1960s. Besides using tolls to fund construction, the government used resources from a special account funded by earmarked gasoline taxes, as the mission had suggested. The road's economic contribution has been substantial.

The Seoul-Pusan Highway was a riskier enterprise, at least from the perspective of the late 1960s (chapter 1). This project to connect the capital, Seoul (on the northwest coast), with a major port, Pusan (in the southeast), was an attempt to drive economic activity rather than a response to overwhelming demand. Once again the World Bank and other development agencies advised against building the road on the grounds that the economic costs would outweigh the benefits. Today, the artery between Seoul and Pusan serves an extended industrial community. Moreover, the project launched a construction industry that is a major force internationally and served as a symbol of Korea's emerging self-confidence. As the highway is no longer able to support the heavy traffic that it has spawned, there are plans to build a high-speed rail link between the two cities.

Institutions for Infrastructure: Key to Successful Delivery

The governments of the six East Asian economies established sophisticated institutions to determine infrastructure priorities and guide construction, financing, operations, and maintenance. These institutions substituted for the market by allocating resources and providing feedback to policymakers about the outcome of investment decisions. Of equal, or perhaps greater, importance, the institutions accomplished tasks that markets could not, that is, setting strategic agendas and ensuring private sector participation and input in the face of emerging externalities. It is a tribute to the ingenuity of East Asian leaders that, by and large, these institutions functioned effectively: their performance was central to the successful delivery of infrastructure services.

In establishing these institutions, the governments demonstrated an active commitment to infrastructure development, but viewing the commitment as a big push strategy would be a mistake. True, the governments did make substantial investments and, on occasion, promoted risky projects. For the most part, however, East Asian infrastructure was trying to keep pace with the tremendous growth that was occurring in the region. As such, despite the absence of the discipline of market forces, the governments made decisions in the face of emerging demands and subject to varying degrees of commercial discipline. This section discusses the traditional institutions that set the agenda, delivered the infrastructure, and financed the capital expenditures.

Setting the Agenda: Infrastructure Development Starts at the Top

The infrastructure agenda in each East Asian economy—its goals, resource allocation mechanisms, and delivery institutions—was determined by top leadership, who maintained close involvement in infrastructure development by using the planning process as a coordinating and feedback device. Infrastructure agenda setting in each economy is described in the country-specific chapters in part 1 of this volume, but is articulated most forcefully in chapter 4, which describes the decisive role of Singapore's senior leadership in determining the basic strategy for development (box 1). Similarly, chapter 2 describes the powerful role of Malaysia's prime minister's office in determining priorities and serving as an information clearinghouse.

However, setting the agenda was not enough, especially in the larger economies. The centralization of goal setting had to be balanced by effective decentralization to obtain the necessary information and to provide local incentives to perform. Two interrelated themes are noteworthy. Given the sector and location specificity of infrastructure, decisionmaking must be delegated, but coordination is also important, not only for meeting physical logistics, but also for ensuring that various, often competing, interests are represented. This mix of effective central coordination and oversight and a more decentralized approach to implementation characterizes East Asia's infrastructure.

Box 1. Singapore's Commitment to a Vision Bred Successful Infrastructure

Singapore's political leaders launched a three-part economic growth strategy: pursuing export-oriented industrial activity that was led by foreign investors and the domestic private sector; creating a robust trade-related infrastructure (the port and the airport), a durable industrial infrastructure (industrial estates), and a world-class telecommunications infrastructure; and investing in human capital.

Singapore built a physical infrastructure that has an enviable reputation worldwide. Now the country is beginning to export its expertise in developing and managing industrial estates and townships to other developing countries. The primary reason for the government's successful implementation of its policy strategy was its sustained commitment to excellence. The government articulated its broad national policy of economic expansion and facilitated the development of the required institutional structures. Infrastructure projects were largely permitted to operate commercially and thus to generate operating surpluses that funded the necessary investments.

Source: Chapter 4.

In Japan policymaking control in specific sectors has rested with the various ministries, which in turn created public corporations as channels for implementing ministerial policy. The government has also appointed advisory boards composed of government officials, academics, and private consultants to monitor each sector and convened commissions to arbitrate disputes about the direction of infrastructure development. In Korea and Taiwan (China) the governments created high-level coordinating bodies under ministerial control. Each body has formed commissions or implemented other monitoring mechanisms to respond to problems. In Singapore the government established the Economic Development Board to spearhead industrialization and infrastructure development and created autonomous statutory boards that ultimately proved crucial to the success of major infrastructure projects. In Hong Kong the government has retained almost exclusive institutional control for planning infrastructure development, but it has delegated investment and operations to private parties. In Malaysia a dynamic central planning agency and a high-powered policymaking body in the prime minister's office provide an effective administrative mechanism for implementing the government's economic and infrastructure policy, but both entities seek substantial input from state and local bodies (box 2).

The intriguing question, which cannot be answered without more research, is why this top-driven process, mediated by elaborate planning mechanisms, successfully developed an expanding infrastructure of generally sound quality. Why were more mistakes not made? Why did the coordination function work when similar attempts in other economies have generally led to poor results? Why did incentives reinforce positive outcomes, rather than create confusion, or even downright subversion? The answers are found in three complementary hypotheses. First, the goal of infrastructure development was simple: the emphasis was on production and trade-related infrastructure to support economic growth. Equity considerations and environmental concerns received less attention, no doubt along with costs that must now be dealt with. Second, the number of competing "voices" or competing claims were limited, allowing the focus on growth to proceed. Third, the elixir of growth itself is a powerful reinforcement mechanism, where positive outcomes engender socially responsible behavior.

Organizing for Delivery: Creating Incentives in Nonmarket Settings

Across countries and sectors, the public corporation has been the most common service delivery mechanism, but delivery mechanisms have also varied substantially, including different forms of

---

Box 2. Malaysia's Planning Is Top Down and Bottom Up

Several public institutions are involved in planning infrastructure development and implementing infrastructure projects in Malaysia—from government departments to ministries, to state-level and local government authorities. National development planning consists of two processes. The National Economic Council, a ministerial council chaired by the prime minister, and the National Development Planning Committee, which comprises top civil servants from various ministries, formulate top-down planning. Bottom-up planning captures the policy needs and interests of ministries, statutory boards, and state governments, which are required to submit programs for five-year economic plans.

Both processes lead to the formulation of national development objectives and targets. The Economic Planning Unit, which is under the aegis of the prime minister's department, coordinates project proposals from the top down and bottom up. Responsible for drafting the rationale for and logistics of medium- and long-term sectoral projects, the Economic Planning Unit is one of the most influential agencies in the development planning process. At the culmination of the two linked processes, the National Economic Council and the National Development Planning Committee produce the country's five-year plans, with targeted strategies for achieving economic and development targets. This institutional process has helped Malaysia create a robust infrastructure.

Source: Chapter 2.

private participation, especially in Hong Kong. Of the many variations, a case study of Korean irrigation demonstrates the capacity for innovative institutional design in East Asia.

The public corporation is a mechanism that introduces commercial discipline to publicly supplied services. By insulating operations through a legislative charter, the goal is to give managers autonomy to make decisions based largely on commercial considerations, autonomy that ideally extends to both financing and operational decisions. Because the corporation is public, however, its charter often requires social obligations that circumscribe the range of permissible actions. In particular, where pricing does not reflect costs, reliance on general government revenues limits independence.

Public corporations have been relatively successful in East Asia. Pioneered in Japan in the mid-1950s, early applications included a public corporation to run the toll road system. This example is interesting, because even though it was financed partly by tolls, the road system was also financed by a special account funded with gasoline taxes, with the rest coming from the general budget. Yet despite relying on the government for its revenues, the corporation operated and maintained the toll road system efficiently. Korea also used public corporations successfully. For example, although the Korean Electric Power Company charged rates below its long-run marginal costs in accordance with government policy, it was still able to increase its capacity and to deliver high quality services. The inference from these examples is that financial support from the government does not necessarily interfere with investment and operations.

The chapters in this volume have not probed the incentive structures of public corporations, which permitted efficient action despite scope for government interference. However, a case study of canal irrigation (chapter 7) highlights the keen attention public organizations have devoted to individual and team incentives (box 3). The study, drawn from Korean irrigation, but reflecting conditions in Japan and Taiwan (China), also describes how institutions structure themselves to deal with complex situations, where both centralized design and construction and decentralized operations and maintenance are required to ensure efficient service delivery.

A variety of other delivery mechanisms exist in East Asia, conditioned partly by history. For example, Japan's electric power sector has always been privately owned, even during periods when the government has intervened heavily in other sectors. Hong Kong has also used private enterprises in many sectors, and Malaysia has taken big steps toward privatization. However, Hong Kong's central government also delivers services directly, particularly in sectors that the govern-

---

Box 3. Korea's Canal Irrigation Agency: A Model of Institutional and Social Efficiency

Water is scarce in Korea. Farmers rely on the Canal Irrigation Agency—specifically the canal patrollers who distribute water in the field and collect fees from farmers—to meet their needs. The canal patrollers, whose responsibilities often remove them physically from the bureaucracy of the agency, must be motivated to perform their jobs well, so that the agency can meet its fiduciary obligations. Korea's canal irrigation agency and its patrollers are models of institutional efficiency for a number of reasons.

First, the agency's organizational structure and worker incentive system foster individual and team dedication to job performance through salary and promotional incentives, job stability, and efforts to cultivate organizational loyalty and a sense of teamwork. Second, the agency's operations and maintenance functions are decentralized from its design and construction functions. This separation of responsibilities facilitates field monitoring and makes the relationship between workers and farmers more dynamic. Farmers are willing to pay water fees regularly, and workers are motivated to meet the organization's goals. Third, despite the absence of independent farmer advocates, independent media, and locally elected politicians, the canal irrigation agency has not become a cozy haven in which workers share the spoils. What checks this tendency in Korea is monitoring from above by multiple independent agencies and dependence on farmers' water payments as a source of revenue—in effect, discipline from above and below. The contrast with India's organization for maintaining and operating irrigation canal systems is striking: India's system has virtually no incentives for conscientious work, while Korea's organization is full of both individual and collective incentives.

Source: Chapter 7.

ment views as strategic (chapter 3). Indeed, the government is the largest infrastructure investor, given its exclusive control over the provision of roads and water. In the road sector, the government has consistently generated surplus operating funds from a gasoline tax, road tolls, and car registration fees. Despite spending billions each year on road construction, it actually receives more from the road sector than it puts back. In the water sector, the government sets charges below average costs, subsidizing consumers heavily. Nevertheless, the government has contracted out services to the private sector—including those for construction and maintenance—in both the road and water sectors. Methods of contracting out have come under criticism because they lack transparency and are not disclosed publicly, but they are monitored by an independent commission on corruption, backed by the government's auditing department and the judicial system.

Using Domestic Resources for Capital Investment

Reflecting their heavy involvement in infrastructure, the governments of the six East Asian economies have been central to its financing. Direct funding from government budgets has played a major role in every economy, but the governments have also established mechanisms for bringing commercial discipline to the financing and operations of infrastructure enterprises. Early on, the governments stipulated that consumers be charged service fees, a principle that was a corollary to the formation of public corporations or statutory boards and was an important source of financing. Where relevant, especially in transport services, earmarked taxes supplemented user fees.

For long-term financing, all governments tried to minimize their reliance on external sources of funding for infrastructure projects, which generate revenues primarily in local currency. At the same time, each government cultivated domestic sources of financing for capital investment in infrastructure; in particular, long-term investments were supported through funds drawn from long-term private savings. Today, all governments are increasingly ceding their deep financial involvement to private sources of finance.

Malaysia is illustrative. In Malaysia infrastructure financing was once the strict domain of the central government. The government funded infrastructure projects directly and provided grants and loans to state and local governments. It also guaranteed the domestic and foreign borrowings of various statutory bodies and borrowed extensively from domestic sources (social security, provident, pension, and insurance funds) and foreign development agencies. Earmarked taxes played virtually no role in infrastructure financing, in contrast to the situation in Hong Kong, Japan, Korea, and Taiwan (China). When budgetary constraints restricted the ability of government-funded public enterprises to improve and expand services to any significant extent in the mid-1980s, the government privatized the delivery of many infrastructure services. Besides holding equity, domestic sources of funding (banks, capital markets) provide private ventures with some of their financing needs, but the government continues to supply soft loans to enterprises and guarantees foreign loans contracted by private projects. It also continues to be the largest investor in infrastructure development. This mix of public-private financing will probably continue in the near future.

In Korea and Taiwan (China) the central government provides the bulk of infrastructure financing, mostly from tax revenues, user fees, and earmarked taxes. Current and projected financial needs for infrastructure are enormous, and both economies are proposing innovative strategies for generating the necessary resources. Both economies are expected to reduce their levels of support and will rely increasingly on user fees, earmarked taxes, the liquidation of government enterprises, and private sector investment.

In Singapore a substantial proportion of financing comes from revenue generated by the public sector. Quasi-public statutory boards are required to charge for services rendered. These boards have consistently generated operating surpluses that they use to fund their development expenditures. The government also uses a percentage of compulsory savings by employers and employees to fund infrastructure projects.

In Japan public corporations assumed the burden of financing by charging user fees, floating corporate bonds, and borrowing from government financial institutions. The government also established several special accounts funded with user fees and earmarked taxes. Although the government is legally forbidden to issue deficit financing bonds, it is allowed to issue bonds for public works (as construction bonds) as long as the amount of the bonds does not exceed the expenditures required for the public works.

Beyond these domestic sources of capital investment, Japan's government has created a mechanism for transferring money from private (postal) savings, the general account, and bond issues to the Japan Development Bank, which makes interest bearing, policy-based loans to public corporations and the private sector. This scheme—the Fiscal Investment and Loan Program (FILP)—is the most intriguing innovation in infrastructure financing in East Asia and has been imitated by the other economies (box 4). The FILP served the Japanese economy well during its urgent drive to expand physical infrastructure. Today, its value is being questioned for several reasons. Most important, the system involves a substantial subsidy, because the rates at which it lends money are often significantly lower than the rates paid to postal savings depositors. Critics also argue that by channeling funds in this manner, the government is inhibiting the development of the private financial sector.

Most infrastructure development in Japan has been financed directly or indirectly by the national government, local governments, or public corporations. Even private sector investment has been directed by government policy. But current debate is focusing on whether government control over financing is still necessary for ensuring that the government can implement its economic policy. Recent evidence of successful private financing of infrastructure operations and maintenance suggests that private financing will become increasingly important in Japan. Nevertheless, as elsewhere in the region, the government's role will continue to be significant.

Managing Change: Success and Its Emerging Limits

Infrastructure facilities in East Asia have been built at a strong rate, supported by the virtually single-minded goal of sustaining the region's unprecedented growth rates. Several pressures have built up, partly from within the system as governments' resource constraints have increased. In

---

Box 4. The FILP: An Innovative Mechanism for Controlling Infrastructure Financing

The FILP is a financial intermediation mechanism that obtains money from private savings, the general account, and bond issues and channels them to the Trust Fund Bureau. The bureau, in turn, lends to public corporations or transfers the funds to government financial institutions for private sector lending. Because the FILP is backed by state credit, the government can control its policy agenda.

The largest contributor to the FILP is the postal savings system, which has been collecting savings and deposits from households for more than 100 years. Mobilizing small-scale funds, the postal savings system generated more than ¥ 155 trillion in outstanding balances by the end of fiscal 1992, which represented about 30 percent of private household savings in Japan. As such, it is the largest savings institution in the world.

Alternative mechanisms for mobilizing savings for infrastructure investment could have been used. However, the FILP's merit lies not in its being the best mechanism to address the financing needs of infrastructure. The FILP has enabled the government to construct a massive and diverse infrastructure while limiting tax increases. It has also enabled the government to monitor accountability: because public corporations have to repay the loans with interest, they are forced to pursue profitability. In today's context, the FILP gives the government a vehicle for monitoring the priorities of private investment in infrastructure. The system of channeling household savings through a government program may be dated, but for other channels to be effective, extensive financial sector reforms (including reforms of the banking, pension, and insurance systems) will be required.

Source: Chapter 5.

addition, technological changes—especially in telecommunications, but also in railways and electric power—have diminished the traditional justification for public provision of services. Governments are being forced to assume a new role as regulator, a role they have thus far been unable to perform successfully. Similarly, environmental concerns pose a serious challenge, including both the provision of environmental infrastructure (water, and especially sanitation services) and the construction and operation of infrastructure that is sensitive to environmental degradation.

Private Delivery of Services the East Asian Way

For the most part, privatization is occurring slowly and grudgingly in East Asia. Even where governments allow private entry, they retain their hold in many ways. With the public corporations, governments are maintaining their stake in shareholding. Where new, stand-alone projects are being constructed, governments are providing substantial support through loans and guarantees. This is in sharp contrast to Latin America, where privatization has been extensive and the process less protracted. We may well be witnessing a pragmatic evolution of the East Asian model to accommodate public-private partnerships as an integral element of the long-term growth strategy, but the sustainability of such partnerships cannot be assured.

In Malaysia, for example, the government decided to privatize many of its infrastructure services in the mid-1980s in response to resource constraints and the poor performance of some of its state-owned enterprises. In 1989 the government formulated a master plan that prioritized sector-specific privatization in two-year action plans. By 1994 the government had privatized eighty-five infrastructure projects, with water and sanitation projects leading the way. All indications are that the projects are providing improved, more responsive services.

The country's 869-kilometer North-South Highway, from Bukit Kayu Hitam on the Thai border to Johor Bahru at the southern tip of the Malaysian peninsula, exemplifies some of these trends. Long planned to ease congestion along existing and heavily traversed routes, the highway languished because of cutbacks in funding for the highway authority. To prevent delays in the road program, the government awarded a build-operate-transfer concession in 1988, including the right to collect tolls from expressway users for thirty years. The government provided a soft loan, as well as guarantees against shortfalls in forecast traffic volumes and losses from adverse movements in exchange rates. The project became operational in 1994, fifteen months ahead of schedule.

In Malaysia, as in the rest of the region, public corporations are being privatized gradually; the government continues to hold on to substantial stakes. Moreover, even when government shareholding has fallen below majority, it has relied extensively on the "golden share" mechanism, retaining the right to veto decisions that affect public policy. For the most part, however, the government has tried to benefit from private initiatives rather than use its control to influence decisions. In the telecommunications sector, for example, where the government continues to hold a golden share in the dominant carrier (Jabatan Telekom Malaysia), management has significant autonomy in its efforts to increase telephone penetration.

Privatization has proceeded at a slower pace in the rest of East Asia. In Korea the electric power and telecommunications sectors have been partially privatized. In 1989, 21 percent of the Korean Electric Power Company's stock was sold to the public as a first step toward privatization. Power generation by private parties is also being allowed. Private initiatives could be an important element of an ambitious plan to meet Korea's growing power needs. In telecommunications, Korea Telecommunications has also been partly privatized and limited competition has been allowed. In Singapore and Taiwan (China) privatization is in its infancy.

Will the emerging public-private balance in East Asia be sustained? As always, the rapidly growing, newly industrializing economies of East Asia are looking to the Japanese experience. Japan is developing a fluid mix of public-private participation in infrastructure ownership and service delivery. Infrastructure arrangements have evolved interactively: the government has allowed private entry in most sectors, and the private sector has relied on government policy and guidance to resolve nettlesome issues that have sometimes threatened effective service delivery. Much of the success of this arrangement stems from the private sector's response to the government's economic and social policy. However, ministerial policy has clearly sometimes stifled the service efficiency benefits of privatization by over-regulating profit margins. Nowhere is this shuffling between fluidity and constraint in public-private ownership and delivery more evident than in the privatization of Japan National Railways and Nippon Telegraph and Telephone (box 5).

Regulating Service Pricing and Quality: Government Limits

Each government exerts some degree of regulatory control over its infrastructure providers, whether to ensure that suppliers do not exploit their market position or that they have sufficient incentives to perform efficiently. Regulation has acquired greater importance with privatization, but it is one area that the governments of East Asia have not yet mastered; the learning process is ongoing.

Traditionally, most economies (other than Hong Kong) have used regulatory measures to determine the prices of publicly provided services. Korea has regulated pricing heavily, using a national price index that often sets prices at levels that are lower than the costs of providing services. At the other end of the regulatory spectrum is Taiwan (China), which has liberalized its regulatory environment and allowed prices to reflect the profit-making autonomy of its service providers—even though its infrastructure has not yet been privatized to any significant extent. In Singapore the quasi-government statutory boards have been given regulatory autonomy. They have used market forces to establish service pricing. The liberalized environment has enabled them to generate operating surpluses and thus to finance their own capital expenditures.

In Hong Kong, with its tradition of private provision, the government has exercised regulatory control with franchises and other mechanisms to regulate profit margins and to protect consumers. One important mechanism—used in the electric power, telecommunications, and public transportation sectors—is the control scheme, which dictates the operations and prices of service providers (box 6). However, private providers who operate under control schemes have consistently been able to generate surpluses for their development funds.

Box 5. Privatizing Japanese Giants

Both Japan National Railways (JNR) and Nippon Telegraph and Telephone (NTT) started out as public corporations with monopoly status. In the 1960s, however, competition from private vehicles severely reduced the demand for JNR's services, and when the government froze railway fares in the 1970s, JNR became financially unviable. In telecommunications, the introduction of new technology threatened NTT's existence, as the business community began clamoring for cheaper, more modern services. The government decided to privatize both these huge public corporations, but with differing success.

JNR was broken into six regional companies and one freight company. The legal and institutional arrangements governing how the transport infrastructure was implemented were also restructured extensively and institutionalized by the new Railway Enterprise Act. The results of the breakup have been far more successful than expected, because the government, in response to economic and social needs, found the arrangement that was best suited to the financial and operational success of the railway system.

NTT's privatization has not been successful, largely because the Ministry of Posts and Telecommunications continues to over-regulate the company. When NTT was privatized, it inherited the obligation to provide universal service, and it was not allowed to compete effectively in the market for long distance services, because new common carriers were given access to the NTT network at highly subsidized prices. Thus the ministry's policy suppresses the NTT's revenue-generating incentives, and hence the services that it can effectively offer to consumers.

Source: Chapter 6.

Box 6. Hong Kong's Central Government Maintains Regulatory Control

Hong Kong has been flexible enough to allow private activity and investment in some sectors, but it has been reluctant to relinquish regulatory control fully and allow competitive forces to flourish. With scarce natural resources, a small geographic area, and a densely concentrated population, the government feels obligated to protect consumers' rights by regulating profit margins. It uses two mechanisms to maintain regulatory control.

The government grants franchises to certain infrastructure monopolies—either for specific services or for entire networks of services—to protect them from the entry of competitors and from the expansion of other monopolies into certain service areas. These franchises cover specified lengths of time, usually twenty-five to thirty years, but the government monitors the franchises rigidly to ensure that they maintain delivery and production standards and to ensure that they do not collude in setting prices.

The government also uses control schemes to limit profit maximization by infrastructure providers, thereby protecting consumers from high prices. The government negotiates with franchises and other monopolies to set a rate of return that is tied to fixed assets and that take the price of production inputs into account. Profits beyond a certain threshold are either rebated to customers or go into a development fund. The fund bails out a franchise or monopoly if its profits are below the threshold. These control schemes are not static. The government has adapted them as necessary to maintain a balance between consumers' concerns about costs and service providers' concerns about profits.

Source: Chapter 3.

Experience with regulation has been mixed. Even in Hong Kong, which has long practiced it, the regulation of urban transportation aggravated rather than alleviated congestion (chapter 3). Recent efforts at regulation in Japan have been inefficient, because bureaucratic units within the government continue to serve competing interests (chapter 6). Meanwhile Malaysia has flouted the precept that regulation must precede privatization. Privatization is proceeding with only a rudimentary regulatory framework for sectoral pricing and performance, and the government continues to exercise its influence directly with ad hoc regulatory control (chapter 2).

Infrastructure and the Environment: Meeting New Challenges

Each economy's environment has suffered from relative neglect: water and sanitation infrastructure have suffered from limited investment, especially in rural areas; efforts to increase water supply have led to water pollution and environmental disruption; and electric power generation, highway construction, and heavy traffic have also contributed to pollution. Today, however, the problem is widely recognized. Governments are adopting a variety of solutions and have remedied some of the problems, especially in Japan.

The buildup of infrastructure facilities has generated many social and environmental problems in Japan. Japan is densely populated, with uncontrollable rivers and mountainous regions that occupy a substantial portion of the land. This configuration creates a sensitive ecological environment of forests and wetlands near densely populated areas. Construction of the extensive highway network and several thermoelectric power plants destabilized the subtle ecological and environmental equilibrium in many parts of Japan. Environmental disruption was particularly rampant in the 1960s and early 1970s (Uzawa 1994).

In 1971 the government established the Environmental Protection Agency to implement legal and administrative standards governing environmental pollution. The agency has played a pivotal role in restoring environmental equilibrium, for example, atmospheric concentrations of sulfur dioxide dropped by a third over twenty years; however, this dramatic reduction was also partly due to the Pollution Injuries Compensation Act of 1973. As a result of this act, 112 "pollution patients" or their heirs brought litigation in the Nishi-Yodogawa district against the national government, the Hanshin Road Public Corporation, and 10 companies with establishments in the district. This litigation and other litigation like it led to the Pollution Injuries Compensation Program, which became both an effective remedy for compensating the victims of environmental pollution and an instrument for ensuring that production and infrastructure facilities would take social costs into account during the planning phase of projects.

Other economies in the region are also aware of the environmental imperatives. Korea and Taiwan (China) face difficult challenges as emerging externalities force them to take a new look at infrastructure development. Their primary concerns are the relatively small stock of housing, environmental degradation from industrial accumulation, and immense traffic congestion despite high levels of investment during the past three decades. Although the governments' priorities shifted toward satisfying social rather than economic objectives during the 1980s, investment was still inadequate relative to what one would expect for economies of Korea's and Taiwan's (China) size and record of economic development. Both governments will have to invest enormous amounts to respond to consumers' demands as they concern the environment.

Malaysia has encouraged private investment in water and sanitation, awarding rights for the construction of water treatment plants to private parties on a build-operate-transfer basis. These plants sell water to local water authorities. The government has also privatized the management of a number of state-owned water treatment plants. Nevertheless, water shortages persist, and the authorities are beginning to realize that piecemeal privatization—or privatization of parts of the water and sanitation system—will not be sufficient. As a first step toward full privatization, the Johor and Pulau Pinang water authorities were corporatized in 1994. Others are expected to follow suit.

Lessons Learned

Infrastructure development in East Asia occurred within an essentially centrally controlled economic framework, where the role of senior policymakers—mediated through public sector planning, regulatory, and delivery agencies—was critical. This framework coordinated the different agencies and levels of government effectively, responded to evolving requirements with flexibility, and developed new approaches when mistakes were made. In a curious turnaround, the market-oriented processes the governments are currently adopting may actually reduce the flexibility of these systems (chapter 1).

The current global trend in infrastructure development is to shift responsibility for service delivery to the private sector. This trend is largely merited, because in many countries the public sector has failed to deliver necessary services and is unable to mobilize the resources required to finance needed investment. The direction of change is clear even in East Asia: privatization is emerging in response to technological change and the limits of public delivery systems.

What lessons can we learn from a half century of spectacular infrastructure development in the world's most dynamic region? Were the decades after World War II unique, and was the constellation of economic and political systems in East Asia sufficiently distinctive that developing countries today cannot look to that experience for guidance?

In some ways the world has changed. Today—despite the East Asian experience—relying entirely, or even primarily, on public ownership and delivery in the telecommunications and power sectors would probably be a mistake. Not only have technologies changed, but much has been learned about the institutional arrangements needed to deliver services through private, competitive systems. These emerging forms are not perfect, but where implemented with due care they have generated substantial benefits (World Bank 1994a; Mody 1997). Even in the traditionally public sector-dominated transportation sector, the opportunities for market-oriented methods are increasing. In this connection, remember that toll roads in Japan, even though they are run by a public corporation, have relied heavily on user tolls and indirect user payments through gasoline taxes.

Thus a debate on the relative merits of public and private delivery systems would not be the best way to learn from the East Asian experience. Nevertheless, some fundamental lessons are relevant regardless of the specific mode of infrastructure delivery. Public corporations have been relatively successful in East Asia. Pioneered in Japan in the mid-1950s, early applications included a public corporation to run the toll road system. This example is interesting, because even though it was financed partly by tolls, the road system was also financed by a special account funded with gasoline taxes, with the rest coming from the general budget. Yet despite relying on the government for its revenues, the corporation operated and maintained the toll road system efficiently. Korea also used public corporations successfully. For example, although the Korean Electric Power Company charged rates below its long-run marginal costs in accordance with government policy, it was still able to increase its capacity and to deliver high quality services. The inference from these examples is that financial support from the government does not necessarily interfere with investment and operations.

Second, policy prioritization must reflect prevailing conditions. In East Asia growth-oriented infrastructure was given primacy, while equity and environmental concerns suffered from relative neglect. The East Asian experience shows the limits of using infrastructure as an instrument for redressing income inequalities. While Taiwan's (China) rural roads program supported rural industrialization, Malaysia's effort to create a new class of rural entrepreneurs was less successful. Similarly, the East Asian economies eschewed subsidies to the extent possible. Most developing countries, in contrast, provide subsidies so that the poor can afford infrastructure services, yet the services rarely reach the poor, while providers suffer from undercapitalization (World Bank 1994a; Swaroop 1997). In one respect, however, priorities in developing countries today will have to differ from priorities in East Asia in the past: increasing urbanization is placing immediate pressures on governments to develop environmentally sensitive infrastructure.

The final lesson from East Asia is the value of sophisticated consumers. The export drive and the attention to the interests of foreign investors implied that the quality of infrastructure was being continuously tested against international benchmarks. Thus the public agencies that provided the infrastructure were under pressure to deliver services that promoted the overall growth strategy. This factor also raises a cautionary note about current efforts in many developing countries to make infrastructure delivery more market-oriented: greater market orientation will not result if consumers are not sophisticated.

References

Amsden, Alice. 1989. *Asia's Next Giant: South Korea and Late Industrialization*. New York: Oxford University Press.

Gramlich, Edward M. 1994. "Infrastructure Investment: A Review Essay." *Journal of Economic Literature* 32 (September): 1176–96.

ITU (International Telecommunications Union). 1992. *Statistical Yearbook, 1985–92*. Geneva, Switzerland.

Jacobson, Charles D., and Joel A. Tarr. 1997. "No Single Path: Ownership and Financing of Infrastructure in the Nineteenth and Twentieth Centuries." In A. Mody, ed. *Infrastructure Delivery: Private Initiative and the Public Good*. EDI Development Studies. Washington, D.C.: World Bank.

Kohli, Harinder. 1994. *Infrastructure Development in East Asia and Pacific: Towards a New Public-Private Partnership*. Washington, D.C.: World Bank.

Mody, Ashoka, ed. 1997. *Infrastructure Delivery: Private Initiative and the Public Good*. EDI Development Studies. Washington, D.C.: World Bank.

Swaroop, Vinaya. 1997. "The Public Finance of Infrastructure: Issues and Options." In A. Mody, ed. *Infrastructure Delivery: Private Initiative and the Public Good*. EDI Development Studies. Washington, D.C.: World Bank.

United Nations. 1992. *Energy Balances and Electricity Profiles*. New York.

Uzawa, Hirofumi. 1994. "Infrastructure in Japan: Issues and Lessons." Background paper prepared for the *World Development Report 1994*. World Bank, Washington, D.C.

Wade, Robert. 1990. *Governing the Market: Economic Theory and the Role of the Government in East Asian Industrialization*. Princeton, New Jersey: Princeton University Press.

World Bank. 1993. *The East Asian Miracle: Economic Growth and Public Policy*. A World Bank Policy Research Report. New York: Oxford University Press.

————. 1994a. *World Development Report 1994: Infrastructure for Development*. New York: Oxford University Press.

————. 1994b. *World Tables*. Baltimore, Maryland: Johns Hopkins University Press.

Part I
Country Studies

1

Tying Infrastructure to Economic Development: The Republic of Korea and Taiwan (China)

William Reinfeld

The Republic of Korea and Taiwan (China) have amassed impressive records of economic performance since the early 1960s. Much of their success stems from a commitment to infrastructure development. Several factors enabled Korea and Taiwan (China) to realize sizable economic benefits from their infrastructure investments between the early 1960s and the late 1980s, namely:

- A strong infrastructure base and external support. Korea and Taiwan (China) both had solid infrastructure bases to start with that they inherited from the Japanese occupation during World War II and both received valuable support for rebuilding and modernizing their infrastructure after the war.
- Strong leadership and good coordination. Korea and Taiwan's (China) ability to install the infrastructure necessary to spur economic performance was due largely to strong political leadership and the coordinated efforts and resources of relevant institutions. In Korea, the Economic Planning Bureau played the coordinating role; in Taiwan (China) it was the Council on Economic Planning and Development.
- Defined focus and priorities. Both economies tied infrastructure development to economic expansion, which itself had well-defined priorities. Both governments undertook substantial investments, often in the range of 6 to 8 percent of gross national product (GNP) per year, but almost never below 4 percent of GNP per year. Bold investments, such as the Seoul-Pusan Highway in Korea and the Ten Major Projects in Taiwan (China), were attempts to forge a symbiotic relationship between infrastructure and economic growth, but infrastructure development was often unable to keep pace with virtually unabated growth.
- Willingness and flexibility. Both economies "made do" with the infrastructure they had and found ways around shortfalls. In addition, citizens were willing to forgo the comforts normally associated with improved economic well-being. These choices were not necessarily based on consensus or made in a democratic manner, however.

Both economies now face the challenges inherent in upgrading their infrastructure to the standards common to economies at their level of economic development, especially in connection with meeting growing social objectives.

The author wishes to thank Ashoka Mody for the valuable insights and guidance he provided. Special thanks are also extended to the numerous people in Korea and Taiwan (China) who provided valuable input during extensive interviews. In Korea they included Dong-Duk Cha, Sung-Woong Hong, Jin-Kwon Hyun, Eung-Seon Kang, Jong-Gie Kim, Song-Jin Kim, Yun-Kwang Kim, Soo-Seong Lee, Ju-Young Lim, Sang-Wu Nam, Dongshik Shin, and Eui-Young Shon. In Taiwan (China) they included Louis S. Chou, Shu-Cheng Chuang, Sam C. Hsieh, C.Y. Hu, K.T. Li, Hsung-Hsiung Tsai, T. K. Tsui, and Rong-I Wu.

Infrastructure Keeps Pace with the Economy's Drumbeat

Infrastructure projects played an important role in supporting Korea and Taiwan's (China) economic goals from the 1960s through the 1980s. Infrastructure investments were large relative to those in other economies at similar stages of development, an approach that was required to maintain rapid growth. However, when infrastructure development faltered, both economies were able to avoid major disruptions while they corrected deficiencies.

Korea: The Effect of Industrial Development Priorities on Infrastructure

Japan's occupation of Korea left the country with a good education system; an understanding of the Japanese way of doing business; and a relatively sound infrastructure for supporting production and exports, including irrigation systems, an electric power network, the Seoul-Pusan railroad, and ports (Song 1990). Nevertheless, World War II also damaged Korea's infrastructure considerably. After the war, Korea was partitioned into two parts, the Republic of Korea and the Democratic People's Republic of Korea. The economy was in chaos, and unfavorable political and administrative factors exacerbated the situation. The Korean War (1950–53) wreaked further havoc by destroying nearly two-thirds of the Republic of Korea's productive capacity. By 1953 total industrial output had fallen to less than one-third its 1940 level (Sakong 1993).

Immediately after the Korean War, the Korean economy began making a solid recovery, largely with the support of foreign aid, which remained the primary source of foreign capital during the 1960s. In May 1961 a military coup led by General Park Chung Hee gave Korea strong political leadership that was committed to economic development. Korea's first Five-Year Development Plan (1962–66) focused on developing light industry and import substitution capacity. Infrastructure to support these activities included the construction of 275 kilometers of railways and several highway projects.

The second Five-Year Development Plan (1967–71) sought to stimulate exports, which grew by nearly 50 percent per year during this period. Investment in railways continued, and highway construction was accelerated. Korea's first major highway project was a road that connected two major cities, Seoul in the northwest and Pusan in the southeast. This project was particularly significant because not only did it establish a vital industrial corridor in Korea, it was also a symbol of Korea's emerging self-confidence (box 1–1).

Box 1–1. Using Infrastructure to Develop Industry: Construction of the Seoul-Pusan Highway

In the mid-1960s, after deciding that a highway between Seoul and Pusan was needed to link the economies of the two cities, the Korean government asked the World Bank and other sources of development funds for assistance. The government was turned down for various reasons, including the belief that the project was not justifiable on a cost-benefit basis.

Korea proceeded to build the road on its own. Lacking the funds to contract the project to qualified foreign construction companies, the project was undertaken entirely with domestic efforts. Most of the equipment used was re-engineered from that left behind by the U.S. military after the Korean War. Small, inexperienced Korean companies joined together to meet the challenge. The project was successfully completed in just twenty months—far less time than anyone had expected—and at virtually no cost in foreign exchange. Moreover, this undertaking launched a construction industry in Korea that eventually became a major player in infrastructure projects throughout the world. The Seoul-Pusan Highway has become the cornerstone of Korea's industrial corridor and has been a key determinant of how the economy has evolved since.

Source: Interview with Shin Dong Shih, former minister of finance, 1993.

Nevertheless, Korea invested too little in infrastructure during the 1960s, and as the economy approached full employment in the early 1970s, the country began experiencing major bottlenecks in services. Moreover, finding it increasingly difficult to remain competitive in labor-intensive light industries, Korea shifted its focus to heavy and chemical industries. Beginning with the third Five-Year Development Plan (1972–76), the government identified new priorities, policies, and infrastructure needed to support such industries as petrochemicals, steel, and shipbuilding and undertook comprehensive programs to develop the country's airports, seaports, highways, railways, and telecommunications systems to serve these industries.

To support its efforts to promote physical and regional planning, Korea issued its first Ten-Year Comprehensive National Physical Plan in 1972. During this period the government also decided to develop major industrial estates with new deepwater harbors, primarily along the southeast coast near the ports of Pohang, Ulsan, and Masan. These areas experienced rapid growth during the 1970s. In addition, the authorities initiated major port projects in Inchon and Pusan, added 487 kilometers of highways in the south, and built a subway system in Seoul. Government investment rose sharply, but even as the physical capacity of Korea's infrastructure increased significantly between 1973 and 1978, so did demand (table 1–1). For instance, paved road capacity grew by 11.5 percent a year, but the number of vehicles grew by 18.4 percent a year.

During the first half of the 1980s Korea introduced policies that favored stabilization, private sector development, and deregulation. The government placed less emphasis on the heavy and chemical industries program and paid more attention to high quality consumer goods and to containing government spending. Infrastructure investment remained high, however, reaching 8 percent of GNP in 1983. Spending on both transport and electric power was more than 2 percent of GNP (table 1–2) that same year, and investment in telecommunications surged to just under 2 percent of GNP, which, though lower than the level of investment in transport and electric power, was almost twice the 1 percent of GNP typical in other developing countries.

In 1985, confident that inflation was under control, the government initiated several measures to stimulate the economy and established a supplementary budget to stimulate demand and increase investment in infrastructure. These measures, along with the economic windfall from the Seoul Olympics, pushed economic growth to unprecedented double-digit levels. Although the share of infrastructure in GNP fell to about 5 percent, absolute amounts of spending on infrastructure rose briskly.

Taiwan (China): The Drive toward Infrastructure Development

Taiwan's (China) readiness for an economic takeoff after the Japanese occupation was based on infrastructure that supported agricultural development. As Ranis (1979, pp. 208–209) points out: "The transport network [and] all electrification works were, from the beginning, directed not to the narrow purpose of extraction and export of primary materials . . . but to the purpose of a broad agricultural mobilization, especially on the West Coast." A modern agricultural sector was, in turn, an important factor behind Taiwan's (China) considerable head start in its efforts to industrialize (Ho 1978).

In contrast to Korea, Taiwan (China) was able to pull itself together relatively quickly after World War II, despite formidable challenges. As in Korea, Allied bombing had inflicted substantial damage, destroying three-quarters of the industrial sector, two-thirds of power generation capacity, and half of transport and communications capacity. Moreover, about 30,000 Japanese technicians, administrators, and professionals had left Taiwan (China) by 1945.

In addition to the physical destruction, Taiwan (China) had to cope with the impacts of its retrocession to China in 1945 and, shortly thereafter, a civil war and the evacuation of the Nationalist Chinese government and its armed forces to Taiwan (China) in 1949. Nevertheless, by the early 1950s industrial output had recovered to its prewar levels. By 1953, while still poor (annual per capita income was less than US$100), Taiwan (China) had sufficient infrastructure to embark on the steps to economic growth.

Table 1–1. Physical Capacity and Infrastructure Use in Korea, 1973–92

Type	1973	1978	1983	1988	1992	Average increase, 1973–78 (percent)	Average increase, 1978–83 (percent)	Average increase, 1983–88 (percent)	Average increase, 1988–92 (percent)
Road transport									
Paved roads (thousands of kilometers)	7.8	13.5	21.3	34.2	47.6	11.5	9.5	9.9	8.6
Motor vehicles (thousands)	165.0	384.0	785.0	2,035.0	5,230.0	18.4	15.3	21.0	26.6
Passengers (billions of kilometers)	32.0	57.0	74.0	85.0	83.0	12.2	5.3	2.8	-1.0
Freight (billions of ton kilometers)	3.1	6.8	5.9	8.6	11.4	17.0	-2.8	7.8	7.3
Rail transport									
Track (thousands of kilometers)	5.5	5.8	6.1	6.4	6.5	1.1	1.0	1.0	0.0
Passengers (billions of kilometers)	10.7	20.1	21.7	26.0	34.8	13.4	1.5	3.7	7.6
Freight (billions of ton kilometers)	8.6	10.9	11.6	13.8	14.3	4.8	1.3	3.5	0.8
Subways									
Length of system (kilometers)	n.a.	n.a.	42.3	138.1	155.8	n.a.	n.a.	26.7	3.0
Passengers (millions of kilometers)	0.14[a]	0.78	1.6	8.6	13.0	53.6	15.4	40.0	10.9
Ports									
Port freight[b] (millions of tons)	49.0	95.0	147.0	246.0	371.0	14.1	9.1	10.8	1.8
Air transport									
Passengers (millions)	2.7	4.2	6.1	12.6	25.8	9.2	7.7	15.6	19.6
Freight (thousands of tons)	67.0	153.0	309.0	619.0	1,079.0	18.0	15.1	14.9	14.9
Utilities									
Telephone (millions of subscribers)	0.7	1.9	4.8	10.3	15.6	22.1	20.4	16.4	10.9
Coverage (sets/100 people)	0.4	5.4	13.3	26.7	44.1	68.2	19.8	15.0	13.3
Electricity capacity (gigawatts)	3.8	5.5	10.1	16.2	21.7	7.6	12.9	9.9	7.6
Generation (thousands of gigawatt hours)	12.4	27.3	42.6	74.3	115.2	17.0	9.3	11.8	11.6
Water (million tons/day)	2.8	4.8	8.1	12.6	16.9	11.4	11.0	9.2	7.6
Coverage (percentage of population)	36.0	51.0	59.0	71.0	80.0	n.a.	n.a.	n.a.	n.a.
Sewerage (million tons/day)	—	—	0.8	4.6	5.1[c]	—	—	41.8	5.3
Coverage (percentage of population)	—	—	8.0[d]	39.0	36.0[e]	—	n.a.	n.a.	n.a.

— Not available.
n.a. Not applicable.
a. 1974.
b. Includes coastal and ocean shipping.
c. 1990.
d. 1985.
e. 1991.
Source: National Statistical Office (1993).

Table 1-2. Infrastructure Investment in Korea, 1983–91

Year	Transportation Won (100 billions, current prices)	Transportation Percentage share of GNP	Telecommunications Won (100 billions, current prices)	Telecommunications Percentage share of GNP	Dams, flood control, water and sewerage Won (100 billions, current prices)	Dams, flood control, water and sewerage Percentage share of GNP	Industrial parks Won (100 billions, current prices)	Industrial parks Percentage share of GNP	Electricity Won (100 billions, current prices)	Electricity Percentage share of GNP	Total Won (100 billions, current prices)	Total Percentage share of GNP
1983	18.00	2.9	11.21	1.8	8.11	1.3	0.85	0.1	13.09	2.1	51.26	8.2
1984	21.70	3.0	10.14	1.4	10.39	1.5	0.96	0.1	11.31	1.6	54.50	7.6
1985	22.80	2.9	11.66	1.5	11.51	1.5	1.85	0.2	10.60	1.4	58.42	7.5
1986	23.70	2.4	15.03	1.7	10.48	1.2	2.24	0.2	7.99	0.9	59.44	6.7
1987	23.00	2.2	11.57	1.1	12.08	1.1	3.21	0.3	5.59	0.5	55.45	5.2
1988	27.10	2.1	13.04	1.0	14.03	1.1	3.60	0.3	4.07	0.3	61.84	4.8
1989	32.50	2.3	20.21	1.4	14.39	1.0	2.94	0.2	4.51	0.3	74.55	5.2
1990	45.55	2.7	21.00	1.2	12.66	0.8	3.50	0.2	8.01	0.5	90.72	5.3
1991	—	—	23.83	1.2	14.77	0.8	3.76	0.2	20.87	1.1	—	—

— Not available.
Note: Includes central and local governments and private investment.
Source: Bank of Korea data.

Several reasons explain the rapid recovery: the substantial inflow of human capital from mainland China (more than 1 million civilians, plus another 600,000 members of the armed forces) to fill managerial, administrative, entrepreneurial, technical, and labor gaps; the adoption of progressive policies toward land reform, monetary reform, import substitution, investment, and savings; and the restoration of the infrastructure base, which was greatly assisted by foreign aid, particularly from the United States.

Taiwan's (China) economic development planning began in the 1950s with two Four-Year Economic Development plans (1953–60) targeted at import substitution, agricultural production, stability, and employment. Social overhead capital projects in the plans called for reconstructing basic infrastructure and improving agricultural infrastructure, that is, irrigation systems, access roads, and marketing systems. Beginning in 1961 with the third Four-Year Economic Development Plan, the government paid greater attention to developing an export-oriented industrial base and the infrastructure needed to support it. Communications projects were separated from industrial projects, thereby creating a separate sectoral program.

In the 1960s Taiwan (China) constructed seventeen rural industrial estates, which allowed private industry to grow and develop in areas where labor and living expenses were relatively cheap. The efficient road and railway network developed during the Japanese colonial period made this strategy possible. Rural industrialization contributed to the broader government policy of promoting light industries, such as textiles and plywood, that required limited skills and little capital. Light industrial growth fueled exports, which rose from 9 percent of GNP in 1960 to 36 percent in 1972. As its export-oriented manufacturing sector evolved, Taiwan (China) invested in projects not only to expand and upgrade harbor facilities and road and rail networks, but also to develop export processing zones, the first of which the authorities established in Kaohsiung in 1966. This zone proved to be a highly successful vehicle for stimulating exports: by 1969 it was fully occupied, and in the next ten years its exports increased exponentially.

Like Korea, Taiwan (China) entered the 1970s with its infrastructure lagging behind its economic growth. By 1973 bottlenecks were common, for example, ships calling at the ports of Keelung and Kaohsiung had to wait for more than twenty hours, compared with eight to twelve hours in the late 1960s; railway and highway jams increased travel times by as much as 50 percent in some areas; and electricity shortages were regular occurrences (Yeh 1979).

Taiwan (China) also had to learn to contend with another difficulty during this period, the loss of formal diplomatic relations with many of its leading trade partners, including Japan, the United States, and the other countries of the Organization for Economic Cooperation and Development. Taiwan (China) was also removed from membership in many international organizations, including the United Nations and the World Bank. Nevertheless, the government proceeded with efforts to develop more sophisticated heavy industry and in 1973 initiated a large-scale infrastructure development program. This program, known as the Ten Major Projects, was largely a response to the transportation bottlenecks that had become apparent by the late 1960s (box 1–2). The program also included a nuclear power plant as Taiwan (China) sought to protect itself from another oil crisis.

The Ten Major Projects provided both much needed infrastructure improvements and economic stimulation for the sagging economy. While the recession forced private manufacturers to cut back on their investments, the projects took up the slack and laid the groundwork for better infrastructure. The projects cost US$8 billion by the time they were completed in 1979. Like Korea's Seoul-Pusan Highway, the projects were an important symbol of Taiwan's (China) economic self-confidence and were so successful that the government announced plans for twelve additional projects that would provide transportation links to the less developed areas of eastern and central Taiwan (China), as well as important social and cultural facilities. These projects began at the end of the 1970s and were completed by the late 1980s.

Box 1–2. Investing in Infrastructure to Secure the Future: Taiwan's (China) Ten Major Projects

In 1973 the Taiwanese (China) government announced that it was launching seven infrastructure projects and three industrial development initiatives deemed vital for "coordinating" development. While their primary purpose was to address deficiencies in Taiwan's (China) infrastructure, they also proved to be an important economic stimulus.

The projects were initially criticized on the grounds that they would create inflationary pressure, but as economies around the world began to feel the impact of the oil crisis, Taiwan's (China) exports and private investment fell off dramatically. In this climate, the projects proved to be an important boost to employment and economic growth, particularly in 1974 and 1975.

The Ten Major Projects included the following infrastructure projects:

- North-South Freeway. A 373-kilometer freeway between Keelung and Fengshan that was completed in 1978 for NT$ 45 billion. The freeway halved travel time between the two cities.
- Railway electrification. This project electrified 1,153 kilometers of track between Keelung and Kaohsiung and introduced several other operational improvements at a cost of NT$ 22 billion, thereby reducing travel times significantly.
- North Link Railway. Linked existing railway lines in the north and east with 82.3 kilometers of track. Completed in 1979 at a cost of NT$ 5 billion.
- Taichung Harbor. An artificial harbor (3,970 hectares, 9-kilometer shoreline) built to offset the traffic burden at the Keelung and Kaohsiung harbors.
- Suao Harbor. A natural harbor in the northeast built to offset traffic at Keelung harbor and help develop the Lanyang area.
- Chiang Kai-Shek International Airport. Built to shift international passenger and cargo flow out of Sungshan Airport in Taipei. Opened in 1979.
- Nuclear power plant. A 636,000-kilowatt plant built to diversify Taiwan's (China) sources of electric power and reduce its dependence on imported energy sources. Opened in 1977.

These seven projects significantly upgraded the capacity of road, rail, port, and power generating facilities on the west coast. Whereas cargo had once accumulated at seaports because of congestion on the various road and rail distribution networks, the projects helped alleviate these problems. They also generated 40,000 new jobs at a time when unemployment had been rising, enabling Taiwan (China) to show positive economic growth in 1974 and 1975.

Yet, as in Korea, Taiwan's (China) infrastructure capacity did not expand as fast as demand. For instance, paved road capacity expanded by 7.6 percent a year during 1973–78 and 5.9 percent a year during 1978–83, but the number of vehicles grew roughly two-and-a-half times faster, and highway freight traffic grew by 26.6 percent a year. Although road length generally does not keep pace with vehicle growth, the differential was large enough to create many points of serious congestion. Demand for other infrastructure also grew rapidly during this period (table 1–3).

During the 1980s rapid growth continued unabated in Taiwan (China), largely because of the economy's ability to shift the focus of its industrialization from labor-intensive and mid-level technology markets to more capital-intensive and higher-level technology markets. Again, the shift in focus was accompanied by corresponding shifts in policy and infrastructure. The 1980–89 Ten-Year Plan emphasized telecommunications, computers, and robotics as strategic industries. The government planned to invest US$8.5 billion—four times what it had spent during the 1970s—to upgrade and improve telecommunications facilities (table 1–4). In 1980 the government also opened Hsinchu Science Park. By providing low-cost engineers and easy access to technical universities and state-sponsored research organizations, Hsinchu attracted high-tech firms that invested in sophisticated research and development projects and upgraded the manufacturing output of industry.

The Current Situation

Now that Korea and Taiwan (China) have become industrial economies, they have established new sets of development goals. Moreover, the relationship between their infrastructure and their economies has

Table 1–3. Physical Capacity and Infrastructure Use in Taiwan (China), 1973–92

Type	1973	1978	1983	1988	1992	Average increase, 1973–78 (percent)	Average increase, 1978–83 (percent)	Average increase, 1983–88 (percent)	Average increase, 1988–92 (percent)
Paved roads (thousands of kilometer)	8.1	11.7	15.6	16.5	16.9	7.6	5.9	1.1	0.6
Motor vehicles (millions)[a]	1.3	3.2	6.7	8.9	13.9	19.7	15.9	5.8	9.7
Passengers (billions of kilometers	9.6	16.6	20.5	16.9	15.6	11.5	4.3	–3.8	–2.0
Freight (billions of ton kilometers)	1.9	6.2	8.9	11.3	12.2	26.6	7.5	4.9	1.9
Railroads (thousands of kilometers)	2.1	2.2	2.6	2.6	2.8	0.9	3.4	0	1.9
Passengers (billions of kilometers)	7.9	7.9	8.5	8.2	9.3	0	1.5	–0.8	3.2
Freight (billions of ton kilometers)	2.7	2.5	2.5	2.2	2.0	–1.6	0	–2.6	–2.5
Port freight (millions of tons)	49.0	84.0	151.0	283.0	345.0	11.4	12.4	13.4	5.1
Airports passengers (millions)	4.9	10.9	10.0	14.7	26.7	17.3	–1.8	8.0	16.1
Freight (thousands of tons)	105.0	183.0	308.0	542.0	812.0	11.8	11.0	11.9	6.3
Telephones (millions of subscribers)	0.5	1.5	3.6	5.3	7.4	24.5	19.1	8.0	8.7
Coverage (sets/100 people)	4.8	12.3	25.8	35.9	48.6	20.7	16.0	6.8	7.9
Electric capacity (gigawatts)	4.1	7.7	12.4	16.6	19.2	13.4	10.0	6.0	3.7
Generation (thousands of gigawatt hours)	21.7	36.8	45.9	71.4	96.0	11.1	4.5	9.2	7.6
Water coverage (percentage of population)[b]	46.3	61.6	74.5	81.7	88.3	15.3	12.9	7.2	6.6

a. Includes buses, sedans, trucks, motorcycles, and vehicles for special purposes.
b. The average increase is in percentage points.
Source: Council for Economic Planning and Development (1993).

changed. Although their levels of infrastructure are advanced compared with those of other emerging industrial economies, they lag far behind the infrastructure of fully industrial economies (table 1–5).

Major infrastructure bottlenecks are appearing as the economies continue to expand. However, many critically needed programs and projects are being held up for a number of reasons, including resistance by determined environmentalists and other interest groups, sharply divided political opinions, calls for radical policy changes, exposure of contract-related scandals, and unprecedented budgetary requirements.

As citizens' lifestyles and preferences change and the political processes of the two economies become more democratic, their governments are increasingly emphasizing the infrastructure needed to improve the quality of life, for example, urban mass transit, pollution control, and high-speed rail projects. Development goals now focus on restructuring, liberalization, and private sector development.

Table 1–4. Infrastructure Investment in Taiwan (China), 1955, 1960, 1965, 1970–92

Year	GNP (NT$ billions, current prices)	Transportation and telecommunications		Electricity, gas, and water		Other public services [a]		Total	
		NT$ billions, current prices	Percentage share of GNP	NT$ billions, current prices	Percentage share of GNP	NT$ billions, current prices	Percentage share of GNP	NT$ billions, current prices	Percentage share of GNP
1955	30.0	0.2	1.5	0.6	2.0	0.6	2.0	1.4	4.6
1960	63.0	1.5	2.4	1.1	1.7	1.4	2.2	4.0	6.3
1965	112.0	2.4	2.1	1.8	1.6	2.4	2.1	6.6	5.9
1970	226.0	7.2	3.2	4.7	2.1	6.3	2.7	18.2	8.1
1971	263.0	9.2	3.5	7.2	2.7	7.3	2.8	23.7	9.0
1972	316.0	8.2	2.6	11.3	3.6	8.2	2.6	27.7	8.7
1973	410.0	10.6	2.6	14.8	3.6	9.7	2.4	35.1	8.6
1974	549.0	13.3	2.4	25.2	4.6	18.3	3.3	46.8	8.5
1975	586.0	17.1	2.9	25.8	4.4	25.5	4.4	68.4	11.6
1976	702.0	21.1	3.0	21.0	3.0	32.8	4.6	74.9	10.7
1977	824.0	27.6	3.3	22.4	2.7	43.9	5.3	93.9	11.4
1978	989.0	39.1	4.0	36.6	3.7	41.0	4.1	116.7	11.8
1979	1,196.0	46.3	3.9	48.0	4.0	47.5	4.0	141.8	11.8
1980	1,489.0	58.1	3.9	69.3	4.7	67.0	4.5	194.4	13.0
1981	1,764.0	53.5	3.0	71.1	4.0	75.5	4.3	200.1	11.3
1982	1,899.0	59.0	3.1	84.9	4.4	84.4	4.4	228.3	12.0
1983	2,103.0	60.3	2.9	82.7	3.9	78.2	3.7	221.2	10.5
1984	2,368.0	50.0	2.1	62.0	2.6	82.7	3.5	194.7	8.2
1985	2,515.0	50.1	2.0	50.7	2.0	88.5	3.5	189.4	7.5
1986	2,925.0	45.7	1.6	41.2	1.4	98.2	3.4	185.1	6.3
1987	3,289.0	58.8	1.8	49.8	1.5	106.9	3.3	215.5	6.5
1988	3,585.0	68.2	1.9	51.3	1.4	132.6	3.7	252.1	7.0
1989	3,969.0	82.0	2.1	72.1	1.8	170.0	4.3	324.1	8.2
1990	4,327.0	99.6	2.3	94.6	2.1	222.5	5.1	416.7	9.6
1991	4,821.0	122.0	2.5	86.8	1.8	281.3	5.8	490.0	10.2
1992	5,307.0	128.6	2.4	95.1	1.8	344.9	6.5	568.6	10.7

a. Investment in fixed capital in government services not covered in the other categories.
Source: Data from the Directorate-General of Budget, Accounting and Statistics, Taiwan (China).

Table 1–5. Infrastructure Indicators, Selected Economies and Years

Sector	Korea	Taiwan (China)	Holland	Italy	Japan	Singapore	United States
Highways							
(kilometers/1,000 people)	1.26	1.01	6.73	5.32	9.19	1.02	27.02
Cars (per 100 people)	13.0	13.1	36.5	42.4	39.1	11.6	69.7
Telephones (sets/100 people)	44.1	48.6	61.8	46.9	54.3	42.9	71.6
Electricity demand							
(megawatt hours/person)	1.64	2.99	4.73	3.69	5.48	4.07	10.64
Electricity supply							
(kilowatt hours/US$ GNP)	0.47	0.48	0.33	0.28	0.26	0.44	0.54
Gross fixed capital formation							
(percentage of GNP)	38.0	23.2	20.8	19.8	31.7	40.1	15.3
GNP/capita (1991 US$)	6,493	8,788	19,032	19,768	27,196	14,818	22,537

Note: Figures refer to different years between 1985 and 1992 based on data available.
Source: Chou (1990); data from the National Statistical Office, Republic of Korea; data from the Council for Economic Planning and Development, Taiwan (China).

Korea: Infrastructure Problems

Major bottlenecks have started to affect Korea's economic performance, particularly in road and highway transportation. Because of the unusually rapid growth of automobile use, which the government encouraged to support the domestic automobile industry, Korea is now caught in a vicious circle of highway-oriented, rail-retarded demand. A recent study estimated that total highway congestion costs have reached US$6.5 billion, or about 20 percent of total highway user costs. A special commission on social overhead capital has recommended that railroads be used more extensively to relieve the pressures on the highway sector (Cha 1993). During the 1990s Korea plans to spend about US$100 billion on transportation infrastructure alone, about half of it on roads, 40 percent on rail (including a high-speed rail from Seoul to Pusan), and the rest on airports and seaports.

Korea's infrastructure is encountering other problems as well: rapidly rising costs (particularly for land acquisition and domestic labor) and greater concern about government budget deficits have placed proposed projects under greater scrutiny. For instance, land speculation increased the cost of adding to the highway network from US$4 million a kilometer in 1985 to roughly US$26 million a kilometer by 1990. The 1993–97 Five-Year Economic Development Plan mapped out an ambitious program targeting improved living conditions (housing, the environment, urban traffic) and expanded social overhead capital (transportation and distribution, including the development of communications standards) in an attempt to address society's infrastructure needs. For the energy sector the plan called for lowering entry barriers for energy-related industries and improving market mechanisms for determining energy prices. The success of these and future infrastructure investments will depend increasingly on how the investments are financed and, more precisely, on how private funding can be mobilized most effectively.

Taiwan (China): Facing Challenges

The situation in Taiwan (China) is similar to that in Korea. The economy's infrastructure lags far behind that of industrial economies in terms of road length per 1,000 people (or per square kilometer) and telephone coverage. The number of cars per kilometer of roads, by contrast, is high and rising. Electricity capacity has not kept up with demand, and shortages are occurring more frequently.

However, the most serious deficiencies are in environmental infrastructure, which has suffered from neglect, and the public is now demanding amenities commensurate with the economy's advanced stage of development. For example,

- Potable water and sewerage systems are highly inadequate. Less than 5 percent of the population is served by sanitary sewer systems, and a little more than half is served by storm sewer systems.
- Environmental shortcomings are occurring in all sectors and in all forms because of the authorities' neglect of the environment in favor of economic development until about eight years ago, when the Environmental Protection Administration was established. The environmental indexes most out of line include the following:
- Air pollutant emissions are greater than in Holland by a factor of 2.5, than in the United States by 12.0, and than in Canada by 80.0.

The pollution of groundwater is steadily increasing. More than 25 percent of major rivers are classified as either highly or moderately polluted.

Only 61 percent of garbage is treated satisfactorily (nearly all goes to landfills). Thirty million tons of industrial waste is produced each year, and most of it is disposed of improperly (Tsai 1993b).

As in Korea, financing projects to overcome these shortcomings will be a great challenge for Taiwan (China). In 1991 the government launched a plan consisting of 775 environmental protection, transportation, electricity generation, housing, agriculture, and recreation projects to alleviate infrastructure problems; however, a number of problems have surfaced, forcing major revisions of cost estimates and scaling back of the plan (box 1–3).

Sector Analysis

Korea and Taiwan (China) have faced similar challenges in the principal infrastructure sectors. Their governments have emphasized transport to facilitate the movement of goods and services, especially for exports. Taiwan (China), however, has had a more balanced investment strategy between rail and roads and between urban and rural networks. In both economies a public supplier dominates telecommunications services, but both are under pressure to liberalize, with Korea a step ahead. Korea has also used an aggressive approach toward developing switching technology. Despite continued improvements, reserve margins in the power sector are declining in both economies; however, both are in the early stages of liberalizing the entry of independent power producers. Other challenges include controlling pollution and dealing with public concerns about the location of power plants.

Korea: Insufficient Transportation Systems

During the 1950s and 1960s the authorities emphasized rebuilding what had been destroyed or neglected for the previous twenty years; during the late 1960s and the 1970s their priorities shifted to expansion and integration. Priorities among modes also shifted from rail transport to highways, because the government viewed investment in new rail capacity as too expensive. As a result, the share of railways in passenger transport fell from 43 to 25 percent between 1968 and 1990 and the share of railways in freight transport fell from 87 to 60 percent during the same period (Cha 1993).

Although the Seoul-Pusan Highway marked a high point in the development of road transport, investment typically did not keep pace with demand given the unabated economic growth and rapid increase in vehicles prompted by the government-led initiative to build a domestic automobile industry. During 1972–92 GNP grew by 8.6 percent a year and vehicle registration grew by nearly 20 percent a year. In contrast, arterial road length grew by 10 percent per year and railroad track length by less than 1 percent a year during this time. Current plans for inland transport call for

Box 1–3. Revising Development Plans to Achieve Objectives in Taiwan (China)

The original Six-Year Development Plan (1991–96) for 775 projects at an estimated cost of US$310 billion did not get off to a good start. By June 1993 only US$48 billion had been spent, and most projects had not passed the approval process. Many problems were cited as reasons for these delays, including:

- Land acquisition
- Absorptive capacity, for example, labor, engineering, and materials shortages
- Scandals, which made those selecting contractors excessively cautious to avoid being accused of improper behavior
- Slow progress in creating a proper environment for private participation
- Slow response by the private sector
- Politically motivated debates surrounding the projects
- Debates about technology
- Social and environmental opposition
- A protracted approval process with unacceptable contract terms and conditions
- An unrealistic program that included many projects that had not been studied.

Following controversy about whether the government should prioritize projects, how active it should be in planning, whether the economy could absorb the proposed US$310 billion in projects over six years, and so on, the premier asked the Council for Economic Planning and Development to review the plan. A special task force of government officials and academics was asked to participate in this process and to prepare a revised plan. The revised plan focused on 1993–97, although it was generally acknowledged that many of the projects would take longer to complete. The plan included 479 projects, most of which are for infrastructure development as shown in the table. Although some of the large and controversial projects are still under review, many have been approved, including the high-speed train from Taipei to Kaohsiung.

Investment under the Six-Year Development Plan

(billions of U.S. dollars)

Sector	1991–93	1994–97	Total
Transport and communications	28.9	44.7	73.6
Energy	8.5	13.3	21.8
Environmental protection	3.9	5.9	9.8
Water and sewerage	5.6	10.3	15.9
Housing and urban development	14.7	21.7	36.4
Total	61.6	95.9	157.5

spending US$55 billion on highways and roads, which includes paving all remaining unpaved roads and adding 1,500 kilometers of new secondary roads. Another US$40 billion is to be spent on railways and subways, which includes upgrading railroad electrification and constructing a high-speed railroad from Seoul to Pusan.

During the 1970s the focus was on developing cost-effective systems for handling trade. To that end, the government assigned higher priority to building up a national port network and successfully prepared and implemented two major national port plans. It neglected airport expansion and modernization until the 1980s, when investments were made in anticipation of the 1988 Olympics. Until recently the airports were adequate and operationally efficient, but now they are less efficient than others in the world and elsewhere in the region, where more advanced infrastructure services, such as information technology and interconnections with global networks, are available. Failure to provide more advanced services stems largely from the limitations the government has placed on private participation, particularly by foreign-invested service companies.

Except for the initiation of the Seoul subway system in the 1970s, urban transport did not receive much attention until the 1980s. Although priorities shifted in the 1980s to satisfy social rather than economic objectives, the priority level was not high, and investment was inadequate relative to what one would expect for an economy of Korea's size and record of economic development. Between 1971 and 1975, 80 kilometers of urban rail and 10 kilometers of subways were built in Seoul; another

34 kilometers of urban rail and 113 kilometers of subways were added in the 1980s. Pusan, the only other city with an urban rail transit system, built 26 kilometers of subway in the 1980s. To alleviate the severe congestion in Seoul and Pusan, the authorities have decided to expand both cities' subways, provide networks for new satellite cities, and create new lines in four other cities.

Taiwan (China): Exports Stimulate Transportation Infrastructure

Whereas the primary goals during the 1950s and 1960s were the rebuilding of destroyed and neglected infrastructure, during the 1970s the government gave the highest priority to export-related transport. Then during the 1980s it largely ignored transportation services, as the ambitious projects of the 1970s seemed to remove the sense of urgency to build up this sector.

For inland transport, railroads initially had the highest priority, because they were the main means of transporting goods and people. Until the 1980s Taiwan (China) had one of the few profitable rail transport systems in the world. Even though the rail sector eventually lost its preeminence as highway transport became more important, the government continued to strengthen its railroads, electrifying them in the 1970s and expanding capacity and improving services. This more balanced approach to rail and road development—in contrast to Korea—took pressure off total investment requirements in the 1970s and early 1980s.

Ports in Taiwan (China) have always been accorded high priority, keeping pace with economic growth and staying competitive with other ports in the region. Several factors explain the soundness of the port system, namely: good ports were inherited from the earlier period of Japanese occupation; planners recognized the critical role that ports play in supporting the economy; and although the government runs them as monopolies, it recognizes that the ports must compete with highly efficient ports in the region's other dynamic economies. Consequently, the Port of Kaohsiung has been developed to be the third largest container port in the world, and many transport companies are considering Taiwan (China) as their hub for the Asia-Pacific region (see chapter 4 for a similar and, indeed, more aggressive approach in Singapore).

The government did not expend the same sustained effort on airports (unlike Singapore, where the airport also received high priority). When Chiang Kai Shek International Airport was planned in the 1970s, many argued that the capacity of the existing airport would be adequate, at least through the 1990s. This proved to be another example of underestimating the growth in demand— the airport is unable to handle present traffic levels. Expansion plans are under way, although they are fraught with seemingly almost insurmountable obstacles, including difficulties associated with cost, land acquisition, and the environment.

Urban transportation did not receive any recognition in planning until recently. Hence, it is the most neglected of the transport sectors. The demands of the rapidly growing and increasingly affluent urban population are far greater than what the system offers. The cost of closing this continually widening gap between supply and demand is the greatest of any of the transport programs. The Taipei Mass Rapid Transit System, currently under construction, is the most expensive and one of the most controversial infrastructure projects in the history of Taiwan (China), largely, but not entirely, because of institutional problems (box 1–4).

Korea: Growing Demand for Telecommunications

The Korean government has actively supported telecommunications development. Until 1982 it accorded lower priority to telecommunications than to transportation, but when the Fifth Five-Year Economic Development Plan (1982–87) called for building up this sector, rapid development followed. In 1982 Korea had only 2.4 million telephone lines. By 1987 that number had increased to 10 million, and since then it has nearly doubled.

Box 1–4. The Taipei Department of Rapid Transit Systems (DORTS)

In the mid-1970s Taipei embarked on an ambitious program to build an 88-kilometer mass rapid transit system in the highly congested greater Taipei area. Construction began in 1990. The system, which is partly underground and partly elevated, was originally estimated to cost less than half of the more than US$17 billion now projected (nearly US$200 million a kilometer). This makes it the most expensive urban rapid mass transit system ever constructed. Delays have pushed the scheduled opening of the first line two-and-a-half years behind the original date, and completion of the entire system is not expected until at least 2001.

What went wrong? Identifying all the reasons behind the project's difficulties could take years, but it would be worthwhile for others embarking on major infrastructure projects to study what Taipei did wrong. Some of the most valuable lessons about what not to do relate to how DORTS handled its responsibilities. A summary assessment of some of the reasons behind the problems, as reported in the Asian Wall Street Journal (April 18, 1994), include the following:

- DORTS was originally staffed by "can-do" engineers who had supervised many of Taiwan's (China) large public works projects during the previous fifteen years, but who had no experience with urban mass rapid transit systems and were hamstrung by political decisionmaking.
- DORTS decided early on not to hire a primary contractor. Instead, it would supervise the work largely with recently graduated engineers. Consequently, experienced outside contractors found themselves with little or no authority to ensure that their technical inputs were adopted properly.
- DORTS hired a general consultant to act as an in-house adviser on technical matters, but the highly qualified and experienced group given this assignment has been given little authority or independence.
- Gross irregularities have occurred in the bidding procedures to ensure that contracts go to local and favored contractors, who in many cases are not qualified. Together with numerous unfair contract terms and conditions, this process has led many highly qualified international contractors to give up on this project.
- DORTS has been under pressure to ensure that contracts are spread widely among Taiwan's (China) construction industry. Work has been parceled out in relatively small contracts to firms that cannot perform the work and that then subcontract it out to other inexperienced firms.
- Widespread charges of corruption and extensive lawsuits and delays have further held up the program.

Although the project has a long way to go before completion, authorities and decisionmakers do not appear to have learned from their mistakes. DORTS is still keeping supervision to itself and refusing to enlist the help of experienced outsiders.

The 1982–87 plan called for promoting telecommunications development on at least two fronts: service and technology. On the service side, the first step was to separate policymaking and service provision functions. Accordingly, two public common carriers were established in 1982: the Korea Telecommunications Authority, later renamed Korea Telecom (KT), and the Data Communications Corporation (DACOM). KT's functions include establishing and operating telecommunications facilities, engaging in research and development, developing manpower for the sector, and performing other related tasks. Until recently KT was entirely government owned, but shares are now being sold to the public. DACOM was established to expedite the development of the information and communications sector and to lead the nation into the information and technology age by developing information and communications network businesses. DACOM is almost entirely publicly held (with 33 percent of the shares owned by KT). In 1991 KT's revenues, US$4 billion, were seventeen times DACOM's US$230 million.

A number of basic service providers also exist, for example, the Korea Mobile Telecommunications Company, the Korea Port Telephone Company, and the recently launched Shinsezye. The Korea Mobile Telecommunications Company was established as a subsidiary of KT in 1984. In 1989 it became a public corporation, but KT still owns 65 percent of the stock. The Korea Port Telephone Company was established in 1985 with investments from KT and the private sector to handle port communications. Shinsezye is privately owned.

In the area of technology development, Korea decided to produce its own switching system, TDX, based on Ericsson technology. Four private firms developed and manufactured Korea's system, which has been used in the extensive drive to upgrade telecommunications services and is also exported to other Asian economies. With the evolution of this technology and the related hardware and software, Korea expects to improve and expand its network without external assistance. The government has also strengthened the human capital necessary to support the industry by investing heavily in training and educating participants in the newly restructured sector. In addition, it recruited Koreans working in scientific fields overseas to bolster local capabilities.

Although the government has encouraged competition in principle, it has been limited in practice. DACOM and KT compete with each other in providing a variety of international services, including direct connection, collect calling, and credit card service. In other areas the greatest competition is among value-added service providers: about thirty private and government companies provide services over lines leased from government-owned companies. In the mobile telephone and pager service market, Korea has allowed a duopoly. The government has recently passed legislation to ensure greater competition in these and other services. Given that it recognizes the importance of competition in the sector for achieving international standards, it is likely to continue to move in that direction.

Taiwan (China): Attempts to Modernize the Telecommunications Sector

Taiwan's (China) telecommunications sector is less developed than it should be given its stage of economic development. However, the government recognizes that it needs to expand and modernize telecommunications services for the economy to sustain its growth and for Taiwan (China) to realize its goal of becoming a regional center for manufacturing and for the financial, trade, and transportation sectors. In the next few years the government will spend more than US$16 billion to promote research and development; strengthen training capabilities; improve local telephone lines; and upgrade long distance, international, and data communications.

Legislation for liberalizing and restructuring the sector was finally passed in 1995 and major changes are under way. Until the authorities opened wireless services to private competition in January 1997, the Ministry of Transportation and Communications provided all telecommunications services through the Directorate General of Telecommunications. The entity was corporatized in July 1996 and became Chung Hwa Telecommunications. Although Chung Hwa Telecommunications is relatively efficient—it has 36,000 employees for 8 million lines, a good ratio by international standards—and is reasonably profitable, services are not as extensive or as reliable as one would expect for an economy as developed as Taiwan (China).

The new legislation calls for the eventual privatization of Chung Hwa Telecommunications. Moreover, wire line services will be opened to private providers in a few years. Several value-added services are being opened up to private providers, but the extent to which foreign-invested service providers are allowed to participate in this market is still limited.

Korea: The Difficulties of Energy Development

The Korea Electric Power Corporation (KEPCO), which was established in 1961 and converted into a government-invested corporation in 1982, provides electric power in Korea. In 1989, 21 percent of the company's stock was sold to the public as the first step toward privatization. KEPCO is a world-class utility. In 1992 its return on investment was 10.6 percent, and in 1995 it recorded the highest profits of all companies listed on the Korean stock exchange. Fuel consumption for power generation has changed dramatically since the first oil crisis in 1973–74. From a heavy dependence on fossil fuels in the mid-1970s, by 1992, 36 percent (23,430 megawatts) of power came from nuclear sources. Dependence on fossil fuels was down to 52 percent and hydropower contributed the remainder.

The future will bring a number of challenges. For twenty years Korea's power generating capacity grew an average of 10 percent a year. In the last ten years, however, consumption has grown by 11.4 percent a year, bringing the reserve margin down to less than 10 percent, and in the summer to less than 5 percent. Recognizing that electricity generation has been a major contributor to pollution, the government is hoping to use more natural gas, nuclear power, and renewable energy sources. Another challenge is to find sites for new power plants. Public opposition to locating facilities in their neighborhoods is gaining strength as various special interest groups become more effective at challenging the utility's decisions.

An ambitious power plant construction and distribution program for the 1990s will generate capital requirements of more than US$70 billion, which will necessitate extensive new borrowing from both domestic and foreign markets. Because KEPCO is government controlled, it can borrow from the local market at a preferential rate; however, given the scale of borrowing required and the regulations that are imposed on its overseas borrowing, the cost of capital will be considerably higher than in the past.

The sector also faces deregulation challenges. Under the 1993–97 Five-Year Economic Development Plan, the government is giving top priority to deregulating the energy sector further and increasing competition. In an effort to stimulate industrial development, the utility currently fixes the price for electricity below its long-run marginal cost, but appears favorably disposed toward price liberalization. Also, the authorities are taking the first steps toward private sector participation by allowing independent power producers. The private sector will be allowed to produce electricity using coal, liquefied natural gas, and water power. Foreign investors will be allowed to hold up to half the equity in the new companies. In addition, KEPCO is being evaluated for further privatization. These endeavors will require significant changes in the legal framework, organizational structure, taxation and accounting rules, and other fundamental policies.

Taiwan (China): Public Providers Are and Will Remain the Main Source of Energy

Taipower is the sole electric power utility in Taiwan (China). It reports to the Ministry of Economic Affairs, but is run with a fair degree of autonomy. Although portions of the corporation's distribution operations will be privatized, a fully competitive market in this sector is highly unlikely.

Until recently the authorities always met the economy's energy requirements with suitable levels of investment and appropriate policies to make energy use efficient. Between 1954 and 1987 the economy grew by an average of 8.8 percent a year, while energy consumption grew by 9 percent a year. However, with rapid growth in demand, the reserve margin has dropped to less than 5 percent. The latest plan calls for an expansion program of US$33 billion. As in Korea, nuclear power has been an important source of energy in the past: Taiwan (China) built its first nuclear power plant in 1978, and it now derives 28 percent of its power from this source, but controversies about the construction of a fourth nuclear power plant have held up expansion of this energy source.

In an effort to circumvent the political and bureaucratic difficulties (including budget approvals and political haggling among interest groups) that keep public utilities from implementing expansion programs, the government is considering strategies for privatizing part of the energy sector, for example, encouraging cogeneration and independent power producers, as well as privatizing Taipower. However, these options are mired in controversy, and the outlook for meeting the plan's goals is not favorable.

Institutions, Pricing, and Financing: Similarities and Differences

Much of the impetus for investments intended to enhance productivity in Korea and Taiwan (China) came early on from strong political leaders who had considerable autonomy in formulating and implementing policy and who were backed by a complex planning process that set investment priorities. However, these institutional structures and decisionmaking processes appear less effective in dealing with current problems.

Korea: Traditional Planning Institutions Are Proving Inadequate

Korea's Economic Planning Bureau (EPB), which is headed by the deputy prime minister, is the most important agency in the infrastructure decisionmaking process. Its responsibilities include a wide range of activities in infrastructure development and operations, including coordinating ministerial plans, making policy recommendations, and allocating budgets (box 1–5). Several other ministries are also responsible for planning and managing infrastructure, namely: the Ministry of Transportation for rail and ports; the Ministry of Construction for highways, housing, dams, and water; the Ministry of Industry, Energy, and Resources for electricity and gas; the Ministry of Communications for telecommunications; and the Ministry of Environment. Local governments are responsible for local and urban transportation. Numerous government-funded research institutes study local and international developments, collect data, participate in conferences, follow trends, and participate in infrastructure development.[1] They are generally well funded. However, the president's office—the core of the government's power base—is where some of the most important decisions are made.

While this extensive set of institutions served Korea well in the past, today it appears to suffer from several significant weaknesses as follows:

Box 1–5. Controlling Infrastructure Development: Korea's Economic Planning Bureau

The deputy prime minister heads the EPB. Some of its more explicit responsibilities include the following:

- Coordination. Two divisions share the responsibility for coordinating infrastructure activities, one covering roads, the environment, water, gas, and electricity and the other covering everything else, primarily transportation. These divisions are responsible for coordinating the physical elements of projects, while another group coordinates budgets. The EPB focuses on the specifics of such large projects as the high-speed rail system and the new airport, rather than on comprehensive network analysis. In project analysis it relies on a Ten-Year Transport Plan prepared by a special task force and considers the impact of proposed projects on the long-term plan. It also considers the impact of new projects on the national and local economies. Projects that can be funded internally by government corporations, such as telecommunications, do not require approval and the EPB does not review them. Powerful agencies such as the Ministry of the Environment are also not subject to intensive coordination reviews.
- Performance evaluation. The Performance Evaluations Bureau evaluates the performance of government-owned corporations based on predetermined performance standards. Its responsibility will soon extend to performance reviews of corporations under contract to the government to manage infrastructure services, such as airports and parks. However, it has not yet developed standards for measuring performance in these activities.
- Economic policy. Coordination activities (physical, policy, and budgetary) depend on macroeconomic plans, which the Korean Development Institute generally prepares each year. The EPB provides inputs into these plans and furnishes the institute and other institutions with the economic and performance data that it collects.
- Budget approval. Another important function assigned to the EPB is budget approval and distribution. Whereas the Ministry of Finance collects money, the EPB determines how to use it. The EPB's Budget Office is the final authority for new projects and infrastructure budgets after extensive review and discussions with relevant ministries and the special task force on social overhead capital. Because telecommunications and power generation are self-sufficient, their budgets are not subject to EPB review.
- Regulatory activities. One of the EPB's most important activities is infrastructure pricing. The Welfare and Consumer Policy Bureau, which participates in all regulatory activities, handles this activity.

---

1. These include institutes associated with the Ministry of Transportation, for example, the Korea Transport Institute, the Korea Maritime and Ports Authority, and the Korea Maritime Institute; the Ministry of Construction, for example, the Research Institute for Human Settlements and the Korea Institute for Construction Technology; the Ministry of Telecommunications, for example, the Korea Information Society Development Institute; and the Ministry of Trade and Industry, for example, the Korea Energy Institute and the Korea Institute for Economics and Trade.

- No individual or group has assumed the strong leadership role that was so important during the early periods of infrastructure development.
- Planning is frequently too theoretical.
- Coordination among and within the institutions has been ineffective and is one reason for the insufficient attention devoted to development in some areas and the excessive attention being given to development in others.
- Performance evaluation is limited and data are generally spotty.
- Institutions have tended to avoid assigning priorities to activities.

Taiwan (China): Policymaking Institutions Effectively Coordinated, but Exhibit Weaknesses

The policymaking process for developing infrastructure and the economy in Taiwan (China) was also heavily influenced by strong and effective leadership, particularly during the 1950s through the mid-1980s. However, because of increased democratization, the leadership is now more diffuse and the process of setting policies, establishing priorities, mobilizing resources, and implementing projects is proving more difficult.

The organizational structure responsible for infrastructure policymaking differs somewhat from Korea's. The premier heads up the cabinet, which encompasses several ministries responsible for infrastructure: the Ministry of Transportation and Communications, which oversees railways, roads, ports, and telecommunications; the Ministry of Economic Affairs, responsible for power and industrial estates; the Ministry of the Interior, in charge of dams and irrigation;[2] and the Environmental Protection Administration, which looks after the environment. Local governments are responsible for urban transport and other utilities.

The Council for Economic Planning and Development is a high-level body within the executive branch of the government that is responsible for coordinating the plans of the various ministries and sectors, setting goals and targets for the national economy, monitoring the economy's performance, and resolving special problems (box 1–6). The council consists of ministers from each of the economy-related ministries. The chair holds ministerial rank and is highly influential. Three vice-chairs supervise and coordinate a dozen or so departments that conduct studies, prepare policy recommendations and

---

Box 1–6. Coordinating Plans and Removing Roadblocks: Taiwan's (China) Council for Economic Planning and Development

The government often calls on the Council for Economic Planning and Development (CEPD) to study and resolve economic planning, policy, and coordination issues. The need to revise the original Six-Year Development Plan (1991–96) was one example (see box 1-3). Another example was the CEPD's creation of the Asia Pacific Regional Operations Center, which promotes and coordinates activities and legislation aimed at making Taiwan (China) a regional center for six designated economic sectors.

The CEPD also led a task force to study the liberalization and privatization of Taiwan's (China) telecommunications sector. Opinions about what should be done to transform the sector and what needed to be done first varied widely. Consequently, little had been done to privatize the public provider or to liberalize the sector until the premier asked the CEPD to head a special task force—consisting of scholars, senior representatives from relevant government agencies, and private sector representatives—to study the issues and come up with a plan. The task force, together with the Asia Pacific Regional Operations Center, finally pushed through the legislation needed to proceed with liberalization.

---

2.   The management of Taiwan's (China) water resource infrastructure is an exception to the generally rational organization. The Ministry of Interior supervises water service to residential areas, the Ministry of Economic Affairs supervises water service to industry, and the Council of Agriculture supervises water used for irrigation. This division of responsibilities greatly reduces efficiency, particularly for finding solutions to such shared problems as water shortages.

monitor trends. Taiwan (China's) planning process incorporates greater coordination among ministries and sectors and between local and national plans than does Korea's planning process. Much of this is due to the effectiveness of the Council for Economic Planning and Development and the fact that national, provincial, and local government officials sit in on the meetings of the executive yuan (executive branch of government), where all projects are first reviewed and approved or rejected.

Despite their strengths, policymaking institutes in Taiwan (China) are also showing signs of weakness. Shortcomings in the infrastructure decisionmaking and policymaking processes include many of those referred to for Korea as well as two others. First, in the past decisions about infrastructure have largely been demand-driven, that is, they have responded to immediate needs. The principle that historically guided infrastructure investments was to keep them at the minimum level needed to meet demand. If a problem was identified, a request for a solution was generally approved quickly (first by the executive yuan, and then by the legislative yuan) and budgeted. Now that a new generation of infrastructure is required to attract new industries and investment, infrastructure projects need to be developed with the expectation of longer term demand. The review and approval process for these kinds of projects is more elaborate than the process used in the past, creating concerns about delays. However, greater prudence is also required when committing to more expensive projects, because errors in judgment can prove costly.

Second, as in Korea, the current institutional network structure is less effective at decisionmaking than in the past, largely because of the growing influence of the legislative branch in relation to the executive branch and because of the proliferation of special interest groups. Concerns about budget deficits are also weakening leaders' efforts to implement programs.

Korea: Prices for Public Services Are No Longer Over-Regulated

All the rates charged for public infrastructure services in Korea are regulated, regardless of whether the company is public or private. The EPB is the principal regulator of prices, and until early 1994 the primary determinant of how a price was regulated was its impact on the consumer price index. To apply for a price increase, the service provider sought a cost study from a government-approved institute, for example, the Korea Transport Institute. The relevant ministry studied the results, and if it approved the request, it was passed on to the EPB. Until early 1994 the EPB's decisions were based entirely on price indexing, with little or no consideration of return on investment, service improvement, or resource allocation efficiency.

Because the authorities have not allowed prices to increase sufficiently to recoup replacement costs, the supply of certain services—such as first-class railways and airlines—has not kept up with growing demand. Similarly, user charges for freeways have fallen far short of the cost of constructing new freeways, making the gap between toll revenue and construction costs nearly impossible to cover through the general budget. For example, between 1979 and 1990 toll revenues increased by a factor of thirty-two; however, construction and maintenance costs increased by a factor of sixty-three (Shon 1992).

Recognizing the limitations and inefficiencies of these price controls, the government has dramatically changed the system for regulating prices. Prices are now either deregulated entirely or regulated at the local, rather than at the national, level. National price index criteria are applied only to a few special commodities or services. With this move, most prices should reflect the service provider's financial requirements for expanding and improving its services.

Taiwan (China): Pricing Regulations Are Based on more Economically Valid Criteria

Pricing policies in Taiwan (China) generate fewer distortions than in Korea. In general, prices tend to move with changes in the cost of the service. For example, electricity rates are set on the basis of internationally accepted formulas and procedures. This approach is required because Taipower, even though it is a state-owned enterprise, borrows funds directly from international banks and is under pressure to operate efficiently. Railway passenger fares are an exception. Although they have been adjusted five times in the past ten years, the tariff structure does not cover operational expenses. As a result, service quality is poor. Nevertheless, passenger railway services are widely used because they are cheap and the expressways are congested. Rail freight traffic earns money for the railroad, however, because rates are determined according to market considerations and because services keep up with the competition.

Both public and private companies provide bus services, although the public companies tend to be less profitable than the private companies. A rate evaluation committee regulates the fares on city buses operated by public companies. The city assembly votes on proposed rate increases and usually rejects them. Given that city bus routes are generally divided between public and private companies, competition between the two types of providers is minimal. Where they do compete, private bus lines—which are not subject to price regulations—charge less because of a lower burden of regulation and, possibly, because of greater efficiency.

Korea and Taiwan (China): Enormous Investment Needs Will Require New Financing Sources

Current and projected financial needs for infrastructure in both Korea and Taiwan (China) are enormous. In Korea they are projected to be US$100 billion over the next three years, excluding telecommunications and some other programs outside the scope of the government's budget. In Taiwan (China) they are projected to be nearly US$300 billion over the next decade. Whatever the precise amounts, they far exceed what the government in either economy is able to fund: public budgets for infrastructure projects are between 50 and 75 percent of these projected amounts. Thus both governments must find new and innovative sources of financing, and the financing environment and institutions responsible for infrastructure services must change accordingly. Both Korea and Taiwan (China) have proposed creative strategies for generating financing for infrastructure, improving the performance of service delivery organizations, and attracting private funds, but none of these efforts will succeed unless the authorities implement appropriate reforms and restructuring initiatives.

In Korea the government has used a variety of public funding methods, but a shift to private finance is now occurring. The central government budget consists of two categories: the general account and special accounts. Special accounts are targeted for special projects and financial operations; the general account is the source for the government's overall fiscal activities.[3] Of the seventeen special accounts that existed at the end of 1990, several were applied directly to infrastructure development, including the railway special account, the communication service special account, and the highway special account (box 1–7).

The main sources of funding for Korea's infrastructure development include the following:
- Taxation. The primary source of funding will continue to be taxes and user fees, but a greater share of the funding is likely to come from special accounts rather than general funds.
- Designated funds. The government is introducing taxes earmarked for specific infrastructure sectors. For example, it imposed significant gasoline, diesel, and car excise taxes to fund major highway construction and railway projects. The taxes yielded revenues of US$4 billion in 1994 and are expected to grow each year. Special accounts such as these will continue to be a major source of funding for specific projects.
- Public pension funds. Several national pension funds are available for financing infrastructure. However, these funds are constrained in the choice of investments by government regulations.

---

3.   Another important component of Korea's central government consolidated budget consists of public funds. Similar to special accounts, public funds are used to carry out special functions, such as financing particular projects. Among the sixty-four funds are the National Pension Fund, the Petroleum Business Fund, the Government Pension Fund, and the National Housing Fund. For a more detailed discussion of public funds see Park (1992).

Box 1–7. Special Accounts Support Infrastructure Development in Korea

The following are some examples of special accounts in Korea.

Fiscal Investment and Financing Special Account

The Fiscal Investment and Financing Special Account was created in 1988 to strengthen the consolidated operations and management of fiscal resources and to respond to increasing demands for social development and social overhead capital. Its spending increased from 4.3 trillion won in 1988 to 5.8 trillion won in 1990 and it now claims more than half of the special account budget. It is one of the few special accounts that does not run a deficit.

Major funding sources include the sale of government stocks, postal savings transfers, and bond financing. The funds are used for various activities, including financing transportation, energy, housing, and sewerage projects. The account consists of three subaccounts: the Fiscal Investment Account, which invests in government institutions; the Financing Account, which makes loans to the government and the private sector; and the Foreign Loans Account, which makes loan redemptions and deposits on the Financing Account.

National Railroad Special Account

The National Railroad Special Account was established in 1964 to provide financial support for public railroad services. It is administered by the Korea National Railroad. During 1986–90 the account ran a budget surplus every year except 1988. Revenues come from operations (60 percent), transfers from the general account, and the Fiscal Investment and Financing Special Account. Massive borrowing from other accounts has contributed to the huge debt accumulation, which amounted to nearly 1.3 trillion won in 1990. This debt is an important issue in the strategy for privatizing the railroad.

Communication Service Special Account

The Communication Service Special Account is responsible for financing government projects related to postal services, postal banking, and telecommunications services. It was created in 1962 and is run by the Ministry of Communications. Revenue comes from operations, earnings from financial services (that is, postal savings), and subsidies from external sources. It has run a slight surplus over the years. More than half its spending goes for postal and financial services.

Road Sector Special Account

Established in 1989 and governed by the Ministry of Construction, the Road Sector Special Account serves a dual purpose: to encourage road construction and maintenance and to improve managerial efficiency. Its funding is derived from transfers from the general account, overseas loans, and transfers from the Fiscal Investment and Financing Special Account. The most significant portion of its revenue is generated by special excise taxes on gasoline, diesel, and passenger cars. In addition, foreign loans have come from the Asian Development Bank and the World Bank (although Korea is about to be reclassified as ineligible for loans from the World Bank). Revenues and expenditures have been about 1.3 trillion won a year.

Source: Park (1992).

- Private funds. Given that many of the proposed infrastructure projects are potentially profitable, private financing is a promising way to fund them. Good candidates for private funding include industrial estates, freight depots, wastewater and municipal waste treatment facilities, and local toll roads. Incentives for attracting private funding include allowing public agencies to acquire land, pairing marginal projects with profitable projects, arranging long-term financing from public funds, and allowing tax exemptions. The authorities are also considering alternative modes of private participation, including build-own-operate-transfer arrangements, joint ventures between the public and private sectors, and independent private ownership. Korea has also launched an ambitious effort to provide incentives for the private sector to invest in infrastructure projects (box 1–8).

Private financing is also assuming greater importance in Taiwan (China). A task force created to develop recommendations for financing Taiwan's (China) ambitious infrastructure program suggested establishing a public construction fund that would draw on the postal savings system, similar to what Japan and Singapore have done (box 1–9). This and other strategies for financing infrastructure projects are being discussed and implemented, for instance:

- User fees. In a survey, Tsia (1993a) found that people would be willing to pay higher fares if they received better service.
- Private investment. A variety of schemes have been proposed to attract private investors to utility and transport projects. These include purchasing power from independent power producers and opening up services and activities within a specific utility or transport mode to the private sector. Many of the proposals are similar to those being discussed in Korea and elsewhere. The government recognizes that private investment will occur only if legislation is enacted to provide greater incentives; to delineate investors' responsibilities, rights, and liabilities; and to liberalize the investment environment to allow investors to earn a fair return.
- Public enterprise privatization. The government is considering plans to privatize certain state-owned infrastructure services. Most of these privatizations will require substantial restructuring of the regulatory and business environments, as well as of the organizations themselves. Thus privatization is unlikely in the near future.
- Government bonds. The bond market is being tapped to finance a share of infrastructure development equivalent to 15 percent of GNP. Although this ratio is not large compared with levels in Japan, Singapore, the United States, and other economies, Taiwan (China) does not want this source to grow too quickly for fear of disturbing the rest of the financial market.

Box 1–8. Planning for Private Participation in Korean Infrastructure Projects

Seeking to raise funds to cover 75 percent of the estimated US$75 billion needed for infrastructure expansion between 1993 and 1997, the Korean National Assembly promulgated the Private Capital Mobilization Act. The act encourages the private sector to invest in infrastructure projects through such arrangements as build-operate-transfer, variations thereof, or various investor incentives or guarantees.

The act allows private builders of primary infrastructure, such as roads, railways, ports, and dams, to earn a profit until they have fully recouped their investment costs and have earned a fair return on their investment. Possession will ultimately return to the government.

Builders of secondary infrastructure, such as power plants and distribution complexes, will be permitted to operate and own them. Plans for electric power generation call for four private facilities: two 400-megawatt combined cycle plants using liquefied natural gas and two 500-megawatt plants using coal. Plans also call for a private water purification plant and other projects.

To encourage private investment in these projects, the act introduces measures for speeding up land acquisition and shortening approval procedures. It also attempts to ensure that private participants have managerial rights, such as permission to borrow from foreign banks and to issue corporate debentures. Operators will be allowed to determine prices without regulation, except when the service is for public use or the company has also been granted the right to engage in a profitable auxiliary business, such as site development, tourism, cargo terminals, and the like to offset an unprofitable project.

In addition, a fund to guarantee the credit of participants who borrow from funding sources abroad will be established. The fund will also help finance projects in niche areas by small and medium companies.

Finally, the act removes investment ceilings on the chaebols (large conglomerates) that have precluded them from engaging in such infrastructure projects in the past. The government is not only allowing these giant conglomerates to invest in such projects, but it is developing incentives that will encourage them to do so.

Box 1–9. Using the Postal Savings System to Fund Infrastructure Projects in Taiwan (China)

Although the government used Taiwan's (China) postal savings system to finance some small public projects during the 1970s, it did not use the system to generate funds for major construction and infrastructure projects until 1993. At that time the authorities created a special fund to receive all deposits above the current annual level of savings, which is NT$ 1,567 billion (about US$60 billion). That is, if total postal savings are more than this amount, the excess goes into the fund. With annual savings growing at about the same rate as the economy, the fund should receive about US$600 million a year. In addition, monies from the Postal Savings Life Insurance and certain pension funds are invested in the fund. Estimates indicate that the fund could raise NT$ 448 billion (US$17.2 billion) between mid-1994 and 1997. Funds will be used for such projects as the second north-south freeway, freeway extension, new industrial estates, energy and water resource development, and other self-sustaining and potentially income generating projects.

The postal system is a popular mechanism for savings because Taiwan (China) has more than 500 post offices where people can freely deposit and withdraw savings. The system is far simpler and more convenient than that in commercial banks; it pays dividends at a rate of 7.9 percent; and it provides additional services, such as allowing customers to pay their utility bills and life insurance installments from their deposits.

Conclusion

As Korea and Taiwan (China) look to the future, several emerging trends have important implications for infrastructure development and its role in their economies, namely:

Both economies are adopting more open and democratic systems of governance. With such changes, increased exposure of procedures associated with infrastructure development and the revelations of scandals have slowed down the pace of infrastructure development.

The World Trade Organization and other multinational bodies are increasingly pressuring both economies to open their doors to external providers of technology and services.

Rapidly developing technology, particularly information technology, is placing greater pressure on both governments to remove restrictions that impede innovation in infrastructure development.

Calls for liberalization and privatization are intensifying, together with a recognition that many infrastructure organizations require major re-engineering. Private interest in infrastructure investments is increasing.

In addressing these and other challenges, Korea and Taiwan (China) need to reorient their strategies. The private sector must play a major role in infrastructure development and operations, not just because of the need to share escalating investment expenditures, but also because the private sector can deliver some services more efficiently. Partial privatizations without more competition and autonomy in setting prices will be insufficient and will limit the growth of needed infrastructure. At the same time, provision of infrastructure services must be opened to all potential providers, not just domestic firms. Advanced developing economies such as Korea and Taiwan (China) require not only sophisticated technology, but also the management and operations experience of industrial economies. This experience will be particularly pivotal if they wish to create a globally competitive infrastructure. Failure to encourage international service providers to enter their markets will have increasingly unfavorable consequences as global industries focus less on labor costs and more on the availability of logistics-related services (see chapter 8).

Governments cannot, however, abandon their role as coordinators and facilitators of infrastructure development. Government coordination and support are important to ensure that infrastructure development is targeted at social and economic priorities. This objective may require restructuring the institutions that are now responsible for planning and coordination. They need to become more flexible and serve as information clearinghouses, with expert personnel who can assess projects' costs and benefits and design appropriate plans for government support. In evaluating major infrastructure projects, policymakers in Korea and Taiwan (China) must focus more on broader socioeconomic costs and benefits than on financial returns as they have tended to do. This has led to the delay or cancellation of economically or socially desirable projects that investors did not find attractive and has also prompted the governments to grant excessive incentives to attract investors.

References

Cha, Dong Deuck. 1993. "National Economic Growth and Transportation Investment." Korea Transport Institute, Seoul, Korea.

Chou, Gee. 1990. "A Survey and Assessment of Demand and Supply for Main Public Construction during the Next Decade in Taiwan." Chung Hua Institute for Economic Research, Taipei, Taiwan (China).

Council for Economic Planning and Development. 1993. Taiwan Statistical Data Book: 1993. Taipei, Taiwan (China).

Ho, Samuel P. S. 1978. Economic Development of Taiwan, 1860–1970. New Haven, Connecticut: Yale University Press.

National Statistical Office. 1993. Major Statistics of Korea: 1993. Seoul.

Park, Jong Koo. 1992. "Special Accounts and Public Funds." In Kwang Choi, Dong-Kun Kim, Taewon Kwak, and Kun-Young Yun, eds., Public Finance in Korea. Seoul, Korea: Seoul National University Press.

Ranis, Gustav. 1979. "Industrial Development." In Walter Galenson, ed., Economic Growth and Structural Change in Taiwan: The Postwar Experience of the Republic of China. Ithaca, New York: Cornell University Press.

Sakong, Il. 1993. Korea in the World Economy. Washington, D.C.: Institute for International Economics.

Shon, E. 1992. Comments made at the International Symposium on Transportation Infrastructure, September, Seoul, Korea.

Song, Bying Nak. 1990. The Rise of the Korean Economy. Hong Kong: Oxford University Press.

Tsai, Hung Hsiung. 1993a. "The Adjustment of Social Overhead Capital in the Maturing Taiwan Economy." Paper prepared for the Conference on the Evolution of Taiwan within a New World Economic Order, May, Chung Hua Institute for Economic Research, Taipei, Taiwan (China).

Tsai, Hsung Hsiung. 1993b. "Social Overhead Capital and Its Financing in the Maturing Taiwan Economy." Council for Economic Planning and Development, Taipei, Taiwan (China).

Yeh, W. A. 1979. "The Ten Major Development Projects and Taiwan's Economic Development." Industry of Free China (April): 8–23.

2

The Transition to Privatization: Malaysia

G. Naidu and Cassey Lee

The infrastructure that has emerged in Malaysia is robust. Its stock has grown rapidly and its overall quality is sound. This infrastructure has supported Malaysia's transformation into an industrial and manufacturing economy that has become integrated with world trade and investment flows. By increasing the geographic spread of services and operations, the government's infrastructure policy has also helped to alleviate poverty and redress regional disparities. Yet the infrastructure is not perfect: it is still hampered by a shortage of services in some sectors and by excess provision in others.

Much of the credit for the success of infrastructure development is due to the country's institutional bodies and to a seasoned development planning process. A dynamic central planning agency—the Economic Planning Unit—and a high-powered policymaking body—the National Development Planning Committee—have provided an effective administrative mechanism for implementing the government's economic and infrastructure policy. In addition, the government supports a policymaking process that relies on a combination of centralized and decentralized inputs to address the interests of the federal and state governments. Although this process is time-consuming, it has culminated in the country's five-year Malaysia plans and is an effective budgetary, operational, and development tool.

The government recognizes that its infrastructure policy has shortcomings and has demonstrated its willingness to adopt new service strategies, delivery mechanisms, and financing arrangements. Nowhere is the government's commitment to change more apparent than in its efforts—which started in the mid-1980s and continue today—to privatize many infrastructure services. Once the predominant provider and funder of infrastructure, the government is ceding this role to the private sector, although it still supports infrastructure with soft loans and preferential treatment. As a result, Malaysia's already sound service delivery system has improved, with favorable reactions from both providers and users. A feature of this progress is that privatization has proceeded in the absence of a complex regulatory framework for governing the sector.

Flexible Infrastructure Development

At independence in 1957 Malaysia already had a sound infrastructure base. According to a World Bank mission to Malaya in 1954, the country's telecommunications system was well developed, its railway system compared favorably with other systems throughout the world, its road system was one of the best in Asia, and its installed power capacity was high relative to peak loads. However, the government was not content merely to sustain this sturdy base. As it began transforming its economy into industrial and manufacturing activities in the late 1960s, it recognized the need to expand and modernize the infrastructure sector to support economic growth.

Support of Economic Growth and Poverty Alleviation

Two economic policies have driven infrastructure development in Malaysia since the early 1960s. First, the government has sought to enhance the country's competitiveness in world trade markets by strengthening its industrial base. Second, to strengthen its industrial base, the government has attempted to attract foreign direct investment. Both policies place a premium on the existence of a vibrant, modern infrastructure, and all evidence indicates that robust infrastructure development has facilitated Malaysia's high rate of economic growth.

Although the main thrust of infrastructure policy was to promote economic expansion, the government also felt compelled to use infrastructure to alleviate poverty and balance regional development throughout its federation of thirteen states. Thus the government gave high priority to expanding infrastructure to backward rural areas and helping the *bumiputra* (indigenous) communities become part of the larger economic landscape. The geographic spread of infrastructure is now more inclusive than at any time since independence. Thus while Malaysia's experience is similar to that of the Republic of Korea and Taiwan (China) in its focus on near-term infrastructure requirements, it differed significantly in terms of its focus on socioeconomic goals (see chapter 1).

Evidence of the importance of infrastructure development as both a catalyst to stimulate economic growth and a proactive mechanism for socioeconomic restructuring comes from the country's seven five-year plans, nearly all of which have allocated the largest share of development spending to infrastructure. The share of development spending allocated to infrastructure rose from about 33 percent in the Fourth Malaysia Plan (1981–85), to 46 percent in the Fifth Malaysia Plan (1986–90), and to more than 50 percent in the Sixth Malaysia Plan (1991–95). These shares were higher than those allocated to any other economic sector. The infrastructure sector is also treated preferentially in development budgeting, for instance, when fiscal constraints forced a 17.0 percent cutback in development spending in the Fifth Malaysia Plan, investment in infrastructure was pared by only 7.5 percent. The indications from the Seventh Malaysia Plan (the current plan) are that infrastructure expansion and modernization will continue to be a high priory throughout the l990s, even though the private sector is to undertake much of the investment.

Both Top-Down and Bottom-Up Planning Mechanisms Used

Several public institutions are involved in planning infrastructure development and implementing infrastructure projects, from government departments to ministries, state authorities, and local governments. National development planning comprises two processes. Top-down planning is formulated by the National Economic Council, a ministerial council chaired by the prime minister, and the National Development Planning Committee, which is staffed by top civil servants from various ministries. Bottom-up planning captures the policy needs and interests of ministries, statutory bodies, and state governments, which are required to submit programs for input into the five-year plans.

Both processes lead to the formulation of national development objectives and targets. The Economic Planning Unit, which is under the aegis of the prime minister's department, coordinates project proposals from the top and bottom. With responsibility for drafting the rationale for and logistics of medium- and long-term sectoral projects, the Economic Planning Unit is one of the most influential agencies in the development planning process. At the culmination of the two processes, the National Economic Council and the National Development Planning Committee produce the five-year Malaysia plans, seven of which have been crafted since 1966. The important role that the government plays in coordinating infrastructure development is a characteristic that Malaysia shares with Korea and Taiwan (China) (see chapter 1).

Effective Leadership and Planning Help Preclude Bottlenecks

Although government policies toward infrastructure have generally been successful, the system has its weaknesses. Infrastructure investment has sometimes lagged behind demand for services, thereby creating capacity constraints, particularly in the road and port sectors, and investments based solely on socioeconomic or political considerations have sometimes created excess capacity.

Nevertheless, these weaknesses do not appear to have seriously limited the availability or delivery of infrastructure services. Part of this success stems from the government's keen appreciation of how essential infrastructure is to economic development. The planning process has succeeded in creating a mutually beneficial relationship between enhanced trade and investment flows throughout the economy and improving the reliability and productivity of infrastructure facilities. In the process it has helped integrate Malaysia with world markets.

However, the most compelling factor linking strong economic growth to vigorous infrastructure development has been the government's flexibility in responding to the fiscal and operational constraints that emerged in the early 1980s, when the size and expense of the infrastructure sector became too large a burden on the public sector.

Effective Transition to Privatization

In the early 1980s the government recognized that some state-owned enterprises were performing poorly. As a result, since 1985 the government has pursued a privatization program to improve performance in the infrastructure sectors. By 1996 it had privatized more than ninety infrastructure projects, and all indications are that these projects are providing better, more responsive services than they did under government ownership (table 2–1).

Privatization has not meant that the government has completely withdrawn from the sector. It continues to finance the sector both directly and with soft loans to private infrastructure developers. In addition, public agencies that once provided services are now regulating the private providers. The regulatory system is still evolving and ultimately will be shaped and substantially modified by users' demands. However, Malaysia's regulatory experience is contrary to expectations in the industrial countries, suggesting that privatization and private involvement in infrastructure services, at least initially, need not wait for the creation of a comprehensive regulatory framework.

Rapid Action by the Government to Privatize

Until the early 1980s infrastructure services were delivered almost entirely by public suppliers, ranging from the federal government, to state governments and local authorities, to statutory bodies and state-owned enterprises. Each of these entities essentially operated as a local or national monopoly. The federal government was mainly responsible for funding infrastructure development at all levels of government by financing infrastructure projects directly and by providing grants and loans to state and local governments. The federal government also served as guarantor for statutory bodies that borrowed from domestic and foreign sources. During this period much of the funding came from government revenue, and the federal government also borrowed extensively from domestic sources (social security, provident, pension, and insurance funds) and from foreign development agencies. Unlike other East Asian economies such as Japan, Korea, and Taiwan (China), Malaysia has not resorted to earmarked taxes or special accounts to finance infrastructure development (see chapters 2 and 6).

As the 1980s unfolded, however, the government began facing fiscal pressures to reduce its public expenditures, and evidence was mounting that the performance of many service providers— particularly the state-owned enterprises—was dismal. The Ministry of Finance's 1987 *Economic Report*

Table 2–1. Major Infrastructure Privatizations, 1984–94

Sector	Method	Year
Roads		
North Klang Straits bypass	Build-operate-transfer	1984
Jln.Kuching/Kepong interchange	Build-operate-transfer	1985
Kuala Lumpur interchange	Build-operate-transfer	1987
North-South Toll Expressway	Build-operate-transfer	1988
Second link to Singapore	Build-operate-transfer	1993
Seremban-Port Dickson Highway	Build-operate-transfer	1994
Shah Alam Highway	Build-operate-transfer	1994
New Kuala Lumpur-Karak Highway	Build-operate-transfer	1994
Kulim-Butterworth Highway	Build-operate-transfer	1994
North-South Expressway Central Link	Build-operate-transfer	1994
New North Klang Straits bypass	Build-operate-transfer	1995
Cheras-Kajang Road	Build-operate-transfer	1995
Damansara-Puchong-Putrajaya Highway	Build-operate-transfer	1995
Ports		
Klang container terminal	Lease-sale	1986
Rest of Port Klang	Lease-sale	1992
Bintulu Port	Corporatization	1993
Penang Port	Corporatization	1994
West Port, Port Klang	Lease-sale	1994
Johor Port	Lease-sale	1995
Water supply		
Labuan water supply	Build-operate-transfer	1987
Ipoh water supply	Build-operate-transfer	1989
Larut Matang water supply	Build-operate-transfer	1989
Semenyih dam management	Contract	1987
Maintenance of tubewells, Labuan management	Contract	1988
Johor Water Authority	Corporatization	1994
Pulau Pinang Water Authority	Corporatization	1994
Electricity		
Tenaga Nasional Berhad	Sale of equity	1992
Sergari Energy Ventures	Build-operate-own	1993
YTL Power	Build-operate-own	1993
Genting Sayen Power	Build-operate-own	1993
Powertek	Build-operate-own	1993
Port Dickson Power	Build-operate-own	1993
Railways		
KTM Berhad	Corporatization	1992
LRT System 1, Phase I	Build-operate-own	1992
LRT System 1, Phase II	Build-operate-own	1995
LRT System 2	Build-operate-own	1995
Other		
Syarikat Telekom Malaysia Berhad	Sale of equity	1990
National sewerage system	Build-operate-transfer	1993

Source: Naidu (1992), updated by authors.

estimated that of the fifty-six nonfinancial public enterprises operating in the early 1980s, only four were turning a profit.

In 1983 the government announced its plan to allow private provision of some infrastructure services. It called its proposal "Malaysia, Inc.," a title that envisaged the private sector's expanded role in economic development. In 1985 the government issued the following guidelines on privatization that outlined its main objectives in allowing private entry into infrastructure provision:

- To relieve the financial and administrative burden on the government in undertaking and maintaining a vast and constantly expanding network of infrastructure services and investments
- To promote competition, improve efficiency, and increase the productivity of services
- To stimulate private entrepreneurship and investment to accelerate economic growth
- To reduce the size and presence of the public sector in the economy
- To achieve the objectives of the economic policy promulgated in the 1970s to induce a more equitable allocation of resources to the *bumiputra* communities.

In 1989 the government formulated a master plan for privatization that helped propel implementation of the privatization program by assigning priorities in two-year action plans. As noted, by 1996 it had privatized about ninety infrastructure projects. Although the private sector's performance has not yet been evaluated comprehensively, the extent and quality of services have grown significantly (particularly in roads, telecommunications, electricity, and ports) and privatized suppliers are more responsive to users' needs and preferences. Moreover, competition in some segments of infrastructure has become keener.

Effective Management of Privatized Infrastructure in the Absence of a Regulatory Framework

Infrastructure supply under private ownership requires appropriate arrangements for regulating the suppliers, not only to restrain them from exploiting their market positions, but also to give them sufficient incentives to perform efficiently. In Malaysia privatization of infrastructure has progressed rapidly, but the institutional structure that performs the regulatory functions has not evolved as quickly. Where infrastructure provision has been privatized, the government department or statutory body that previously supplied the services has assumed the regulatory role. This change in function has, in each case, necessitated new, empowering legislation, but the legislation has stopped short of creating independent regulatory agencies for each sector.

The government also mainstreams regulatory control by continuing to hold significant equity ownership in the privatized enterprises and by using the "golden share" mechanism, which gives the government veto power over major policy matters of the privatized firm. Thus the government ensures that the policies of privatized firms conform to its own policy objectives.

Regulation in Malaysia has meant control over market entry (through approval of operating licenses), supervision of tariffs, and maintenance of service standards. The scope of regulatory action is, however, fairly rudimentary. For instance, no clear link exists between the functions of the regulatory agencies and the creation of incentives to ensure that privatized suppliers provide infrastructure services efficiently, presumably because of the assumption that market forces would ensure efficient provision.

Considerable ambiguity also surrounds the independence of regulatory agencies from ministerial or political interference. The oversight ministries themselves still often make decisions. Moreover, a regulatory agency could bow to the inclinations of industry. Nevertheless, despite the regulatory mechanism's weaknesses, infrastructure delivery has continued to expand.

Since the mid-1980s avenues for financing infrastructure development have broadened considerably. Privatized infrastructure projects are being financed by the private sector through equity holdings and through borrowing from domestic and foreign financial institutions. Privatized providers have also broken new ground in financing their projects by borrowing from international capital markets.

Despite the increasing participation of the private sector in infrastructure financing, the federal government still plays a substantial role. It continues to provide soft loans to newly privatized entities and has served as guarantor to loans contracted by privatized providers. Moreover, the government is still a major investor in infrastructure development. This mix of public-private financing will probably continue in the future, but as financial markets deepen and as privatized projects prove to be viable undertakings, the private sector's role is bound to increase further.

Sector Priorities, Achievements, and Failures

Malaysia's infrastructure has generally expanded in line with the growing demands of the economy. In some instances, however, investment in infrastructure has lagged behind the growth in demand. Service shortages have cropped up, as has an excess provision of services, but in neither case have these weaknesses been glaring enough to undermine economic growth. Overall, the growth and performance of the key infrastructure sectors since the First Malaysia Plan have been impressive.

The Road Network: Significant Expansion Achieved

More than 90 percent of all cargo and passengers in Malaysia are carried by road transport. Between 1965 and 1995 the length of the road system quadrupled—from 15,000 kilometers to nearly 60,000 kilometers—with the most substantial expansion occurring during the Fourth and Fifth Malaysia plans (1981–90), when the road system doubled in length (table 2–2). Contributing to this expansion was the construction of rural roads under the rural roads development program, which brought the rural (mainly indigenous) population into the mainstream of the national economy.

At the start of the 1980s the existing road network showed acute signs of strain: the main federal roads had not been expanded for several years, and road conditions generally had deteriorated; a rapid increase in the number of vehicles along federal roads had significantly increased travel times; the roads in urban centers had been largely neglected; and bad investments and uneconomic projects plagued the sector.

As the government cannot provide the high level of investment required to upgrade and expand the country's road system, since the mid-1980s many road projects have been privatized, typically under build-operate-transfer (BOT) schemes. The private sector now holds a 2.5 percent share of the national road network, and its role will continue to grow as the more heavily trafficked portions of the road network are privatized.

STRATEGY. The government's strategy for the country's road network focused on development, feeder, and rural roads, along with trunk roads and the improvement of federal roads, as follows:
- *Development and feeder roads.* The government used a sizable portion of the funds allocated for road development to construct development and feeder roads to serve the internal transport needs of its land development schemes and to link them to urban and distribution centers. (These development schemes were part of the New Economic Policy, designed to balance regional development and eradicate poverty.) The construction of development and feeder roads was an important component of the road development programs during the first three Malaysia plans, capturing between 15 and 22 percent of total road expenditures.
- *Rural roads.* The government also built roads to improve the accessibility of rural population centers in an effort to promote economic and social activities and to facilitate the implementation of other sector programs. An important initiative in this area was the Rural Roads

Table 2-2. Infrastructure Growth, by Sector, Selected Years 1965–90

Sector	1965	1970	1975	1980	1985	1990	1995	Change, 1980-90 (percent)
Roads								
Length of roads (kilometers)	15,356.0	21,995.0	24,037.0	26,219.0	38,973.0	50,836.0	64,328.0	61.5.0
Paved	12,464.0	15,566.0	16,951.0	18,910.0	25,125.0	34,356.0	48,521.0	93.1.0
Unpaved	2,892.0	6,429.0	7,086.0	7,309.0	13,848.0	16,480.0	15,807.0	14.1.0
Federal	4,585.0	4,997.0	5,346.0	6,000.0	9,531.0	13,061.0	16,181.0	69.8.0
State	10,771.0	16,998.0	18,691.0	20,219.0	29,442.0	37,775.0	48,147.0	63.5.0
Vehicles per kilometer[a]	16.0	17.0	26.0	44.0	47.0	48.0	50.0	6.4
Railways								
Length of railway track (kilometers)	2,115.0	—	—	2,218.0	2,222.0	2,222.0	2,222.0	0.0
Number of passenger cars	394.0	368.0	314.0	367.0	357.0	263.0	341.0	-4.5
Number of freight wagons	5,676.0	7,501.0	7,638.0	7,005.0	7,155.0	7,371	7,876.0	10.0
Ports								
Number of major ports	2.0	2.0	2.0	6.0	9.0	9.0	9.0	0.0
Total handling capacity (millions of tons)	0.0	—	—	25.5	56.6	120.5	174.1	207.6
Number of container berths	—	—	—	4.0	6.0	10.0	15.0	150.0
Telecommunications								
Number of telephone subscribers	—	107,000.0	169,539.0	395,640.0	958,598.0	1,585,744.0	3,320,000.0	246.3
Number of telephones per 100 residents	—	1.0	1.4	2.9	6.1	10.316.6	172.1	
Number of ATUR subscribers[b]	n.a.	n.a.	n.a.	n.a.	4,630.0	78,000.0	700,000.0	951.2
Number of fax subscribers	n.a.	n.a.	n.a.	n.a.	559.0	35,002.0	58,090.0	903.9
Number of rural pay phones	—	11.6	—	23.0	250.0	7,500.0	21,00.0	7,444.4

(continued on next page)

33

Table 2-2. Infrastructure Growth, by Sector, Selected Years 1965–90 (continued)

Sector	1965	1970	1975	1980	1985	1990	1995	Change, 1980-90 (percent)
Electricity								
Electricity generating capacity (megawatts)	336.0c	836.0	1,022.0	2,385.0	4,197.0	5,030.0	11,427.0	172.3
Transmission lines (kilometers)	—	1,400.0	1,806.0	2,823.0	4,439.0	11,501.0	16,199.0	264.9
Distribution lines (kilometers)	—	2,085.0	4,402.0	11,513.0	17,840.0	32,120.0	52,687.0	195.3
Water supply								
Production capacity (millions of liters per day)	591.0c	1,118.0	1,672.0	2,642.0	4,162.0	6,103.0	9,442.0	126.9
Urban coverage (percent)	—	—	—	89.0	93.0	95.0	990	6.5
Rural coverage (percent)	—	—	—	43.0	57.0	66.0	77.0	35.1
Sewerage (percentage of residents)								
Centralized sewerage	—	—	—	4.0	5.0	—	—	n.a.
Septic/imhoff tank	—	20.6	—	22.0	31.0	42.0	—	n.a.
Pour-flush	—	—	—	30.0	39.0	45.0	—	n.a.
Bucket, pit, and hanging latrines	—	—	—	28.0	15.0	7.0	—	n.a.
Without any sewage disposal	—	—	—	16.0	10.0	6.0	—	n.a.

— Not available.
n.a. Not applicable.
Note: The figure for electricity generation capacity in 1985 was estimated based on the capacity in 1980 and that of projects undertaken during the Fourth Malaysia Plan as documented in the Fifth Plan. The figure for water production capacity in 1975 was estimated based on the capacity in 1970 and that of projects undertaken during the Second Plan as documented in the Third Plan.
a. Excludes motorcycles.
b. Automatic telephone using radio or cellular phone.
c. Malaya.
Source: Roads, railways, and number of major ports: Ministry of Transport, (various years); container berths, port authorities; telecommunications: Department of Statistics (various years) and Government of Malaysia (1991, 1996); electricity, water supply, and sewerage: five-year plans.

Program. First implemented during the Third Malaysia Plan, this program envisaged the construction of 1,243 kilometers of new rural roads and the upgrading of 1,369 kilometers of existing roads. The program increased the share of investment in rural roads in the Third, and especially the Fourth and Fifth, Malaysia plans. The policy priority for rural roads in the Sixth and Seventh plans is rehabilitation and upgrading, and the share of rural roads in total investment in roads has declined considerably.

- *Sabah and Sarawak roads.* Sabah and Sarawak had only rudimentary road systems when they joined the Federation of Malaya in 1965 to form Malaysia. (Malaysia comprises thirteen states, of which eleven are in Peninsular Malaysia, and Sabah and Sarawak are part of Borneo.) Since 1965 the thrust of road development policy in the two states has been to create a basic road network that provides interurban connections and improves access to ports. In Sarawak the first trunk road linking the major towns in the state was completed during the Sixth Malaysia Plan period, but Sabah still does not possess a good road network. Most roads in Sabah and Sarawak are unpaved, and even the main road systems are rudimentary and provide limited geographical coverage.
- *New trunk roads.* From 1971 to 1985 (coinciding with the Second to Fourth Malaysia plans) the government constructed several trunk roads, the main ones being the East-West Highway, the Kuantan-Segamat Highway, the Jerangau-Jabor-Tanjong Gelang road, and the Kuala Krai-Gua Musang road. The purpose of these roads was to open up new interurban links and to connect existing or potential production centers to ports, but because they were often located in the less developed regions of the country, their social function was at least as important as their economic function. One road—the East-West Highway—largely served security requirements.
- *Improved federal roads.* An important priority of the early five-year plans was to improve the three primary federal roads: routes I, II, and III. These roads, constructed before independence, connected major production areas to ports, markets, and sources of raw materials. However, improvements to these roads were not targeted at building capacity. Instead the plans focused on constructing bypasses and bridges or on widening, strengthening, and realigning the roads. In short, although the main road system was well maintained, routes I, II, and III essentially remained as two-lane roads.

THE ROAD NETWORK BECOMES STRAINED. In 1966 the road system had sixteen vehicles per kilometer; by 1985 it had forty-seven. This increase may not be incontrovertible proof of a general deterioration in traffic conditions on Malaysian roads, but as most of the growth in traffic occurred along the three federal routes—which were not expanded or supplemented until well into the 1980s, and in some cases not at all—the traffic conditions on these routes deteriorated quite seriously. This was particularly the case for Route I—then the economic lifeline of the Malaysian economy—where in the 1970s and 1980s journey times increased rapidly, accident rates rose alarmingly, and long detours (caused by floods) occurred frequently. Traffic conditions also worsened sharply along the Klang-Kuala Lumpur stretch of Route II. The inadequate capacity of the road links between Port Klang and Penang Port and their respective hinterlands seriously reduced the accessibility of these ports. Road congestion was the main reason the cost of moving freight between the ports and shippers' premises escalated in the 1980s.

Critical shortages along the main roads coexisted with significant excess capacity, for instance, in the new interurban highways. The road sector abounds with other examples of bad investments and uneconomic projects. The East-West Highway and the Kuantan-Segamat Highway could not have been justified by purely economic criteria. At the same time, critical shortages in capacity that had developed along the main roads on the west coast of Peninsular Malaysia were not addressed until the late 1980s.

Moreover, urban roads and transport infrastructure were not accorded the policy priority they deserved. As a result, traffic conditions in Malaysia's main urban centers, including Kuala Lumpur and George Town, suffered. Only recently has the government started to address urban transport problems by means of such projects as the privatized light rail transit projects and the double-tracking project of Keretapi Tanah Melayu (KTM) Berhad in the Klang Valley.

PRIVATIZATION CAN IMPROVE ROAD PROJECT PERFORMANCE. Different levels of government are involved in building and maintaining roads. State governments are involved in constructing and maintaining state roads using road maintenance grants from the federal government and also build rural roads. The Public Works Department of the Ministry of Works plans and implements development roads and land development schemes. Roads are financed extensively by the federal government either directly (federal roads) or indirectly (state and municipal roads through federal road grants.) The federal government plays the primary role in financing road investment because no direct user fees are charged for public roads, so state governments cannot recoup their expenditures on roads.

By the mid-1980s the government could no longer sustain the high level of investment required to expand and upgrade the country's road system and privatized many road projects. New legislation—the 1984 Federal Roads (Private Management) Act—was required before this could happen. The privatization method used in this sector has been BOT, where, under a concession agreement, a private company finances and constructs an infrastructure project; operates it for a designated period during which it collects user fees, such as tolls; and upon expiration of the concession, which is usually long enough to pay back the project's debt and equity investment, transfers the infrastructure to the government. The financing terms and concession conditions used in BOT agreements differ.

The most important road project to be privatized is the 869-kilometer North-South Expressway from Bukit Kayu Hitam on the Thai border to Johor Bahru at the southern tip of the peninsula (box 2–1). With the completion of the expressway in February 1994, Peninsular Malaysia now has a two- to three-lane dual carriageway along its developed west coast to complement Federal Route I.

Box 2–1. Completing the North-South Expressway—Privately

The North-South Expressway has become Malaysia's main thoroughfare, supplanting Federal Route I. The highway authority of Malaysia, Lembaga Lebuhraya Malaysia, started construction during the Fourth Malaysia Plan (1981–85). The authority, a public enterprise set up in 1980 to hasten the development of major road projects, was responsible for constructing, administering, and maintaining the new interurban expressways.

By the mid-1980s the government was facing severe budget constraints, and during the mid-term review of the Fifth Malaysia Plan (1986–90), the highway authority's budget was cut by 52 percent, from RM 4,428 million to RM 2,139 million. To prevent delays in the road program, in 1988 the government decided to complete the rest of the expressway by awarding a concession on a BOT basis to Projek Lebuhraya Utara-Selatan (PLUS). The terms of the agreement include an exclusive right to collect tolls from users of the expressway for thirty years. The government also provided a soft loan totaling RM 1.65 billion (US$660 million) over ten years. The government guaranteed to meet any shortfalls in forecasted traffic volume and any losses from adverse movements in the exchange rate or external loan interest rates for the first seventeen years (Hensley and Edward 1993). The project, estimated to have cost RM 3.2 billion (US$1.28 billion), was completed in February 1994, fifteen months ahead of schedule (Naidu 1992).

Observers have criticized the expressway for two reasons. First, they pointed to the lack of transparency in awarding the concession. Two companies submitted bids that were more competitive than the bid by PLUS, which was set up by United Engineers Berhad, a company with connections to the ruling political party (Gomez 1990). Second, they cited the inappropriate sequencing of construction: low-traffic segments in the north were constructed first, while the heavily trafficked Kuala-Lumpur-Ipoh stretch and Taiping-Butterworth segment were completed at the end of the project.

Other major road projects that have been privatized as BOT projects are the Jalan Kuching/ Jalan Kepong interchange and Jalan Kuching upgrade, the North Kelang Straits bypass, and the New Klang Valley Expressway (a component of the North-South Expressway). Nine other highway projects also have been privatized (see table 2-1). The Seventh Malaysia Plan identifies at least eight more road projects for development by the private sector.

The significance of private involvement in the roads sector goes beyond the 2.5 percent share of the national road network that privatized roads currently represent. Indeed, privatized roads constitute the most important portions of Malaysia's road system, and the role of the private sector in road provision will grow as the more heavily trafficked portions of Malaysia's road network are privatized. Thus it is possible that in the future the public sector will be confined to constructing development and rural roads. Interurban roads that have a significant volume of traffic, and whose costs could thus be recouped from tolls, will almost certainly be privatized. The potential for private participation is already evident in the roads program of the Seventh Malaysia Plan. Projections indicate that between 1996 and 2000 private investment in new roads will reach RM 17.5 billion (US$7.1 billion), compared with RM 9.8 billion (US$4.0 billion) by the public sector.

Railways: Modernization, Not Expansion, as the Goal

The overriding factor influencing government policy toward the railway sector has been the assumption that Malaysia's land transport needs could be met by the roads sector, and that the railway's market was confined to long distance freight and to passenger traffic. Despite occasional calls to strengthen the railway's role in the national transport system, the railway plays a supporting role to road transport. Until recently the main thrust of government policy toward the railway was one of rehabilitation and modernization, not expansion.

In line with government policy, the railway's track system has remained unchanged at slightly more than 2,000 kilometers (see table 2-2). The number of coaches for passenger transport has declined, and rolling stock for freight has increased only marginally. However, the haulage capacity of the railway has increased, because the government modernized its permanent way and signaling system and replaced obsolete rolling stock with more modern and larger freight wagons and passenger cars. The switch to diesel locomotives also increased the railway's capacity. Current proposals would significantly expand the rail network, and it would emerge as a regional commuter transport system.

IMPROVEMENT THROUGH INVESTMENT. An important component of government railway policy was the dieselization program, under which the government replaced the railway's mainline steam locomotives, which had become obsolete, with diesel locomotives. The switch to diesel locomotives during the Second and Third Malaysia plans increased train capacities and speeds.

Another priority area has been improving the railway's permanent way, or track network. Work on the permanent way has involved renewing track, mechanizing track maintenance, rehabilitating bridges, flattening sharp curves, and strengthening track formation. Investment has also been targeted at modernizing the signaling and telecommunications systems. In addition, the acquisition of new rolling stock has been an ongoing feature of the development and modernization of the railway, but these acquisitions mainly sought to replace old and obsolete freight wagons and passenger carriages, not to increase inventory.

The focus of the government's policy toward the Malayan Railway has been consistent with both established trends in the inland transport sector and the railway's long-term market potential. In this regard the priority accorded to improving the railway's rolling stock, rehabilitating its existing network, and improving its signaling system was appropriate. As a minor and declining transport sector with little scope for gaining a comparative advantage over road transport in the domestic transport market, the best approach was to consolidate the rail system with a view toward locating niche markets.

POLICY STANCE IS CHANGING. For many years the government ran the railway as a national monopoly. Despite the investments in the railway, the standard of service provided remains poor: train speeds are slow and delays and accidents are frequent. Calls for reorganizing the railway were first voiced in the 1970s, in part because of increasing losses, but it was not until the late 1980s that the government took the first steps toward commercialization and privatization. A reorganization of the railway commenced in 1988, when two separate marketing departments for its freight and passenger business were established, and decentralization was initiated with the appointment of six regional managers. These changes made the railway more commercially oriented.

An important initiative in the revitalization of the Malayan Railway was the decision to corporatize it in July 1989. In August 1992 KTM Berhad was incorporated and officially assumed responsibility for the operations of the former Malayan Railway. A sister company, the Railway Assets Corporation, was established to hold all landed assets of the railway in trust for KTM Berhad. The Ministry of Finance owns the equity of both companies. In 1996 the government selected a consortium of private companies to take over KTM Berhad. Actual privatization is expected to take place in 1997.

Expansion initiatives for the Malayan Railway began to appear in the Third Malaysia Plan. These included the acquisition of container flats to participate in the growing market for container haulage, the modernization of a workshop at Sentul, and the remodeling of the marshaling yard at Brickfields. Inland container depots were established to promote intermodalism and to improve services. Double-tracking was another new initiative. Initiated under the Fifth Malaysia Plan, KTM Berhad has completed construction of a new, double-track network. The program involved electrified double-tracking between Rawang-Kuala Lumpur-Seremban and Kuala Lumpur-Port Klang in an effort to ease traffic congestion in and around the Klang Valley. Completed in 1995, the railway is beginning to emerge as an important commuter transport operator in addition to its role as an intercity transport system. This shift is a significant departure from its traditional focus on interstate passenger traffic and long-distance freight transport.

The main aim of the rail proposals in the Seventh Malaysia Plan is to enhance the quality and efficiency of services to improve KTM Berhad's competitiveness as a transport mode for both passengers and freight. This goal is to be attained by doubling, strengthening, and electrifying tracks; modernizing signaling and communications systems; and investing in high-speed rolling stock. The construction of more inland container depots to expand the role of KTM Berhad in intermodal transport of containers is also planned. Freight transportation would be further enhanced with the construction of rail links to the North Butterworth Container Terminal at Penang Port, West Port of Port Klang, and Tanjung Pelepas Port in Johor. Completion of the Seventh Malaysia Plan projects will considerably expand the railway's role in the national transportation system. The government now appears to be convinced that traffic flows in the main transportation corridors are sufficiently large to support a high-density mode of transportation such as the rail system. Environmental concerns arising from an almost total dependence on road transportation may also be prompting the government to expand the railway's role in the country's transportation system.

Ports: Always a Priority

The port sector has expanded to meet the country's growing external trade. The physical capacity of ports has increased with the construction of new ports and the expansion of facilities at existing terminals. Physical expansion is apparent in the increase in combined handling capacity, from 25.5 million tons in 1980 to 120.5 million tons in 1990. The completion of the expansion programs of the Sixth Malaysia Plan increased the total capacity of Malaysian ports by another 44 percent, reaching 174 million tons in 1995 (see table 2–2). However, critics have noted that the port sector now suffers from overcapacity.

BLUEPRINTS FOR PORT DEVELOPMENT IN THE FIVE-YEAR PLANS. In 1970 Malaysia had only two substantive port facilities, Penang Port and Port Klang. The Second Malaysia Plan stipulated that two sizable facilities be built at Johor and Kuantan, not only to meet the growing demand for port facilities, but also to strengthen the regional development strategy of building large infrastructure projects as a catalyst for developing the backward states. Johor Port was completed in 1977, and Kuantan Port became fully operational in 1984. Two other ports were subsequently built, the Bintulu Port, completed in 1982, and the Kemaman petroleum supply base, finished in 1983. Starting from two major ports and several minor ports, some of which were in Sabah and Sarawak, Malaysia now has six federal ports and three other major ports, as well as eighteen minor ports. Under the Seventh Malaysia Plan a new privatized port, Tanjung Pelepas Port, will be developed in the state of Johor.

Starting with the First Malaysia Plan, the government embarked on major expansion programs at both Penang Port and Port Klang, and also undertook expansion at the ports in Sabah and Sarawak. During the 1970s these expansion programs substantially increased the handling capacities of the various ports. Major expansion work continued under the Fourth Malaysia Plan at Port Klang, Penang Port, and Johor Port. Under the Sixth Malaysia Plan the government undertook several large expansion projects, including the North Butterworth container terminal at Penang Port, the West Port project at Port Klang, phases three and four of Johor Port, and a second liquefied natural gas jetty at Bintulu Port. Under the Seventh Malaysia Plan port development will continue to focus on capacity expansion. Projects to be undertaken include constructing three additional berths at Port Klang's West Port and implementing phase two of the North Butterworth container terminal project.

Until the Fifth Malaysia Plan the main vehicles for developing the port sector were the construction of new ports and the expansion of existing ones. Improving ports' productivity was never a priority. Beginning with the Fifth Malaysia Plan, however, improving port efficiency has been a prominent strategy for coping with the rapid growth in trade. The plan focused on consolidating and strengthening existing port facilities, a strategy that continued in the Sixth Malaysia Plan. The government improved efficiency and productivity by strengthening road and rail connections to facilitate intermodalism, improving data and information technology, and adopting innovative managerial practices. The electronic data interchange system, introduced in Port Klang in April 1994, is another major initiative to improve the productivity of Malaysian ports. These efforts will be continued during the Seventh Malaysia Plan period. Measures to be taken to improve port efficiency and productivity include implementing berth appropriation schemes, introducing an advanced immigration clearance system and precustoms clearance of containers, and expanding the electronic data interchange system to cover all major ports. The most significant move toward enhancing port productivity, however, has been privatization.

PORT PRIVATIZATION HAS GAINED MOMENTUM. The guidelines on privatization issued in 1985 identified the provision of port services as an important area for private participation. Thus far, however, this strategy has been confined to federal ports. The first instance of privatization in the port sector was the privatization of the container terminal in Port Klang (box 2–2). The other facilities at Port Klang have also been privatized since that time, and other federal ports are being privatized. As a first step toward privatization, Johor Port and Bintulu Port were corporatized on January 1, 1993, and the Penang Port Commission was corporatized on January 1, 1994. Johor Port was privatized in 1995 and was listed on the Kuala Lumpur Stock Exchange in 1996. An interesting feature of the privatization of Johor Port is that the agreement requires the concession company to develop a new port at Tanjung Pelepas in Johor State. The only federal ports that have not yet been corporatized or

---

Box 2–2. Privatization of Port Klang

The container terminal in Port Klang—the major federal port in Malaysia—was the first instance of privatization in the port sector. Privatization was initiated with the formation of a company called the Kelang Container Terminal (KCT) by the Klang Port Authority. The majority shares of KCT (51 percent) were subsequently sold to a private company, Konnas Terminal Kelang Sdn Bhd. The method used was a sale-lease, in which the terminal's movable assets were sold to KCT and the immovable assets, including the berths and land, were leased to KCT. KCT operates the container terminal under a license granted by the Klang Port Authority. The license is valid for twenty-one years, which is the same time as the lease on the immovable assets. KCT has since been listed on the Kuala Lumpur Stock Exchange.

The rest of the facilities at Port Klang—twenty-two bulk, liquid, and general cargo berths—were privatized in 1992 to Klang Port Management, which has also developed a second container terminal in Port Klang that competes directly with KCT. The third component of Port Klang (known as West Port) was privatized on a sale-lease basis to Klang Multi-Terminal Sdn Bhd, a consortium of five private companies, when the first phase of the project was completed in 1994.

KCT's productivity grew by 13 percent a year during 1986–90, following the divestiture of the port facilities (Jones 1994). These improvements can be attributed to the changes in management and incentives under privatization. During 1993 Klang Port Management achieved productivity improvements of 38 percent (*Business Times*, January 1, 1994).

---

privatized are Kuantan Port and Kemaman Port, but both are expected to be privatized in 1997. Of Malaysia's nine major ports, Port Klang, Johor Port, Bintulu Port, and Penang Port account for about 73 percent of the total cargo shipped. Thus private sector involvement in the port sector is already substantial and will become even more significant once the corporatized ports are privatized.

EMPHASIS ON PORTS CREATED OVERCAPACITY. The total capacity of Malaysia's ports expanded substantially during the 1970s and 1980s. The National Ports Plan, completed in March 1988, did not identify any serious capacity constraints at the ports, although at Port Klang and Penang Port in particular, the authorities allowed traffic to build to near or beyond capacity before constructing new facilities to relieve the congestion. This was unusual, however, as overprovision characterizes Malaysia's ports, most notably at Kuantan Port. A major criticism of government policy toward ports is that the excessive number of ports has spread cargo too thinly among them. As a result, many shipping lines avoid making direct calls at Malaysian ports and prefer to feed Malaysian cargo through the terminals of Singapore Port. An estimated 40 percent of Malaysia's external trade is shipped through Singapore, and a much larger portion of Malaysia's container traffic is transshipped through Singapore Port. This has been a matter of concern to Malaysian officials, who intend to make Port Klang a load center port and a regional trans-shipment center. The government's plans for achieving this objective are outlined in the Seventh Malaysia Plan. However, the privatization of the facilities at Port Klang could complicate implementation of the government's efforts to transform the port into a national load center and a regional hub.

Telecommunications: Expanded, Modernized, and Privatized

The telecommunications sector has grown rapidly. For instance, the number of telephone subscribers increased from almost 400,000 in 1980 to close to 1.6 million in 1990 and to 3.3 million in 1995 (see table 2–2). Heavy investment in trunk and junction networks has kept the growth of telephone exchange line capacity commensurate with the increase in the number of telephone subscribers: between 1980 and 1990 the telephone exchange line capacity increased fourfold, from 660,500 to 2.7 million. Other significant features of the expanding telecommunications sector include the rapid proliferation of facsimile services, cellular telephones, and pay telephones in rural areas. Yet the telephone penetration rate in rural areas is still poor, and the quality of cellular services is questionable.

In response to complaints that the government monopoly—Jabatan Telekom Malaysia—was unable to meet the demand for terminal equipment by business users and for telecommunications services in general, the government corporatized the monopoly and divested its equity in the new company to the public. The government's role is now confined to regulating the sector.

INITIATIVES TO INCREASE CAPACITY. The government has undertaken a number of expansion and modernization programs in an attempt to address the inadequacy of telecommunications facilities and to meet the growing demand for telecommunications services. Advanced technology has allowed Malaysia to expand its telecommunications network, for example, the computer-controlled stored program control almost tripled the capacity of telephone links. Modernization also took the form of replacing manual exchanges with automatic ones. This technology required complementary investment in trunk and junction networks, which linked the various exchanges. New technology has also been instrumental in the proliferation of such new services as facsimile and videotext services and cellular telephones.

A major priority of the government's telecommunications development program has been improving telecommunications links between the two separate parts of the country. Telecommunications links between Peninsular Malaysia and Sabah and Sarawak were established during the First Malaysia Plan, upgraded during the Third Malaysia Plan with the installation of a submarine cable, and further modernized during the Fifth Malaysia Plan with the installation of a fiber-optic cable on the submarine cable.

In all the Malaysia plans the expansion of external services was an important component of the government's program to develop the telecommunications sector, because of the country's external trade orientation. Investment has been targeted at constructing regional cable links and two satellite earth stations. During the Sixth Malaysia Plan these facilities were upgraded. A third satellite earth station was completed at Labuan in 1995.

PENETRATION RATE OF TELEPHONE SERVICE IN RURAL AREAS STILL LOW. Telecommunications services have grown rapidly, particularly since the late 1980s. The number of telephones increased from 1 for every 100 people in 1970 to nearly 3, in 1980, to almost 17 in 1995. Achievements between 1970 and 1980 were disappointing, with the supply of telephone facilities lagging behind demand for them. As a result, the waiting list increased from 12 percent of total users in 1970 to about 23 percent in 1980. Between 1980 and 1990, and particularly between 1990 and 1995, large increases were achieved in the number of telephones. During the Sixth Malaysia Plan, for instance, the number of people waiting for telephones dropped by 46 percent, from 81,780 in 1990 to 44,383 in 1995.

Until the Sixth Malaysia Plan, when efforts to develop telecommunications in rural areas gained momentum, rural telecommunications capacity received little attention. In 1990, for example, the number of telephones in rural areas was 2.2 per 100 people, far below the national average of 10.3 per 100. In addition, Telekom Malaysia Berhad, the privatized telecommunications company, plans to target 26 percent of its development investment at extending telecommunications services in rural areas. The reduction in rental rates for rural telephones, regardless of their distance from exchange stations, will also enable more rural residents to afford private telephones.

The number of rural telephones has increased in the 1990s. In 1995 there were 5.5 telephones for every 100 rural residents which, while still low, was more than twice the 1990 level. The number of rural pay telephones has also increased rapidly, from 8,500 units in 1990 to 21,000 units in 1995.

Liberalization of the cellular telephone market has had a significant impact on the growth of mobile telephone services, particularly since the late 1980s. The number of cellular telephone subscribers rose from 4,630 in 1985, to 78,000 in 1990, to 700,000 in 1995. Despite such rapid growth, the quality of cellular telephone services remains questionable, and the Ministry of Energy, Telecommunications, and Post continues to receive complaints from customers about the services (*Business Times*, December 9, 1993).

TELEPHONE SERVICE PRIVATIZED, BUT STILL REGULATED. Until 1987 the government provided telecommunications services through its telecommunications department, Jabatan Telekom Malaysia (JTM), a monopoly. JTM was privatized in two stages in response to complaints that the company was unable to meet the demand for telecommunications services and for terminal equipment by business users. The company was corporatized on January 1, 1987, when Syarikat Telekom Malaysia Berhad (now Telekom Malaysia) was established to take over the provision of telecommunications services and networks from JTM. Telekom Malaysia operates under a twenty-year license granted by the Ministry of Energy, Telecommunications, and Post. The licensing was made possible by the 1985 Telecommunications Services Act, which allowed JTM's assets to be transferred to Telekom Malaysia.

The second stage in the privatization of the sector occurred in 1990, when part of the government's equity in JTM was divested through a public flotation; however, the government continues to hold a golden share through the Ministry of Finance, which means that important decisions affecting Telekom Malaysia must have government approval. In this way the government can make the actions of Telekom Malaysia consistent with government policies, but to date the government has not used this channel of influence.

The government's most important policy initiative in the telecommunications sector has been vertical and horizontal unbundling, which has led to the liberalization of entry into the various subsectors. The government's decision that the supply of terminal equipment was no longer to be a monopoly of JTM began the process of deregulating the sector and allowing private participation. Progressive liberalization has created a pluralistic market in all parts of the industry (box 2–3).

The government's current role in the sector is confined to regulating the industry. In this regard, the private sector has called for a more structured strategy for liberalizing the sector (*Business Times*,

---

Box 2–3. Fostering Competition in Telecommunications Services

The liberalization of the telecommunications sector began in 1982, five years before JTM was privatized into Telekom Malaysia. The government took steps were taken to liberalize the sector in response to complaints by business users about JTM's inability to meet demand for terminal equipment (Kennedy 1995). In June 1983 the Ministry of Energy, Telecommunications, and Post announced that users could obtain terminal equipment, such as telephones and teleprinters, from both JTM and the private sector. This move was followed by a government decision to liberalize the market for value-added network services. The first telecommunications service to benefit from this policy was radio paging in 1985. By 1992 the government had granted thirty-eight licenses to operate this type of service (Kennedy 1995). More recently, competition has increased to the point that competing paging companies have waged price wars (*Business Times*, November 1, 1993).

The ministry's licensing policy has brought greater competition to other segments of the telecommunications market. In the market for cellular mobile telephone services, Telekom Malaysia's ATUR450 service competes directly with Celcom's Art900 service; Mobikom's Mobifon 800; and since 1995 a fourth cellular operator, Binariang. Seven companies are now in the cellular mobile telephone services market. In the pay telephone market, Telekom Malaysia had a monopoly in the rural market and Uniphone Telecommunications Berhad (a subsidiary of Sapura Holdings, a private telecommunications equipment manufacturer) held one in the urban market. To increase competition, the ministry will allow both firms to enter one another's markets in the future. In addition, it has issued a license to operate a third private pay telephone network.

Another market segment that has become more competitive is domestic long distance, which has seen the entry of Time Engineering. The company is laying a fiber-optic fiber link along 869 kilometers of the North-South Expressway. (Telekom Malaysia already has a 1,140-kilometer fiber-optic network along other roads.) Time Engineering's fiber-optic network was initiated by PLUS, the operator of the North-South Expressway, for its internal use. As the contractor for the project, Time Engineering has exclusive rights to use the network's excess capacity for commercial purposes. The ministry has since issued four additional licenses, resulting in a total of six fixed line operators. Three of the services are already operational. As for international services, the ministry has licensed five companies to provide international gateway services.

August 13, 1993; *Malaysian Business*, May 15, 1993). The government has responded by formulating the National Telecommunications Policy, which outlines the industry's objectives and strategies through 2020. The policy seeks to ensure healthy and systematic competition. To complement the policy, the government will develop a telecommunications master plan during the Seventh Malaysia Plan period (1996–2000) to guide the orderly development of the sector. The plan will prescribe measures to rationalize the sector and provide guidelines for competition, interconnection charges, and tariff rates and a formula for sharing social costs and obligations. To meet the increasing challenges of a liberalized telecommunications regime, the government is also proposing to review the regulatory authority's role and functions.

Electricity: More People Have Access and Shortages Have Been Overcome

Considerable investment in electric power has created substantial generating capacity, which increased from 836 megawatts in 1970 to 5,030 megawatts by the end of the Fifth Malaysia Plan in 1990. During the next five years total installed capacity more than doubled, to 11,427 megawatts (see table 2–2). The transmission and distribution network has also been expanded in line with the increase in generating capacity. The rural electrification program, a key feature of government policy, increased coverage in rural areas from 345,600 households in 1970, to 790,000 in 1980, to 1.6 million in 1990. By the end of the Sixth Malaysia Plan in 1995, 92 percent of rural households were served with electricity, compared with 80 percent in 1990.

Yet system losses continue to be a problem in the sector, and supply constraints emerged in the early 1990s, particularly during peak hours. In 1987 the government corporatized the electric power monopoly, and in 1992 it divested 30 percent of its equity in the company to the public. However, critics have raised doubts about the company's ability to maintain a reliable supply of electric power. The government has sought to increase competition in the sector and promote investment by granting electricity generating licenses to independent power producers under build-operate-own agreements.

THE GOVERNMENT TRIES TO ENSURE AN ADEQUATE ELECTRICITY SUPPLY. Expansion of the electricity transmission and distribution networks has been a priority. The first phase in the integration of electricity transmission and distribution networks in Peninsular Malaysia was completed during the First Malaysia Plan, when the central network was connected to the northern zone. During the Second Malaysia Plan the national grid network was connected to the east coast in Kuantan, making electricity from the national grid cheaper for rural areas and fulfilling policy objectives.

Investment in expanding and upgrading the transmission and distribution networks was also driven by the need to distribute hydropower more evenly. As much as 70 percent of the country's hydropower resources, or 29,000 megawatts, are located in Sarawak. The uneven distribution of hydropower has prompted the government to construct inter-regional transmission facilities.

The Sixth Malaysia Plan called for expanding and upgrading the transmission and distribution networks in an effort not only to widen the coverage of the grids, but also to reduce system losses and improve reliability and efficiency. This effort is being continued in the Seventh Malaysia Plan, when about 57 percent of investment in the electricity sector will be used to expand and improve transmission and distribution systems.

Diversifying energy sources for electricity generation has been an important objective in the electricity sector since the Fourth Malaysia Plan. The oil price shocks of the 1970s raised the costs of electricity from oil-based thermal stations. In response the government decided to reduce the country's dependence on petroleum for electricity generation and developed its so-called four-fuel (oil, gas, hydropower, and coal) diversification policy. The policy's objectives are to cut down on oil consumption, reduce overdependence on any one source of energy in the generation of power, and promote the use of nonoil indigenous resources. As a result, by 1995 the share of gas-based electricity generation had reached 68 percent, up from 26 percent in 1990. In contrast, oil-based electric generation declined from 42 percent in 1990 to 11 percent in 1995. Projections indicate that by the end of the Seventh Malaysia Plan coal-fired plants will increase their share in the power supply. For the country's less developed regions (the east coast of Peninsular Malaysia, Sabah, and Sarawak) the government has emphasized diesel-based generating stations, solar installations, and minihydropower stations.

Rural electrification has been an important component of electricity sector development since the Second Malaysia Plan. The rural electrification program not only provided better living conditions for rural residents, it also helped balance regional development. (Taiwan [China] used a similar strategy; see chapter 1.) By providing rural areas with access to electricity the government also expected some measure of industrial dispersal, particularly among industries based on agriculture. By the end of the Seventh Malaysia Plan (in 2000) all rural residents in Peninsular Malaysia will have full access to electricity. Coverage will be 75 percent of residents in Sabah and 80 percent in Sarawak.

THE EMERGENCE OF POWER SHORTAGES. System losses continue to be a serious problem for the electricity sector. Between 15 and 17 percent of transmitted power is lost (National Electricity Board various years). As recently as 1990, system losses ranged from 21 percent in Sarawak to 16 percent in Peninsular Malaysia. This problem has been attributed to low-quality transformers, electricity theft, and under-registration. Manufacturers have also voiced complaints about fluctuating voltages, which damage machinery and equipment (*Business Times*, March 15, 1994).

In the early 1990s electricity generating capacity grew at a slower rate than the growth in demand. As a result, supply constraints emerged, particularly during peak hours. The reserve margin of electricity supply declined from 33 percent in 1990 to 18 percent in 1993. (A reserve margin is the excess power supply that is available to meet unexpected surges in demand. A safe reserve margin for the Malaysian power sector is about 30 percent.) The shortage created uncertainty about the security and reliability of the power supply system. On September 29, 1992, a nationwide blackout caused losses of RM 218 million (US$87 million) to the manufacturing sector alone. In response to this crisis Tenaga Nasional Berhad (the privatized electricity utility) is auditing the transmission network's protection facilities.

LICENSES GRANTED TO INDEPENDENT POWER PRODUCERS. The National Electricity Board was formed in 1949 as a statutory body for the generation and distribution of electricity. The board operated as a nationwide monopoly under the jurisdiction of the Ministry of Energy, Telecommunications and Post.

In 1987 the board was privatized. In 1990 the government passed the Electricity Supply Act to allow the board's assets to be transferred to the newly corporatized Tenaga Nasional Berhad (TNB) on September 1, 1990. The act also defined the regulatory duties of the Ministry of Energy, Telecommunications, and Post in the electricity sector. The ministry is now responsible for determining performance standards and ensuring optimal supply at reasonable prices through its control over tariffs and over the issuance of licenses to generate electricity. On May 28, 1992, the government divested 30 percent of its share in TNB through a public flotation.

The nationwide power failure in September 1992, which occurred just after privatization, was a significant event in the electricity sector. Although the breakdown was attributed to a freak accident, it raised doubts about TNB's ability to maintain an adequate and reliable electricity supply. The energy shortages prompted massive investment in the sector to build up electricity generating capacity. To promote investment, the government issued generating licenses to the private sector. The entry of independent power producers into the sector was also motivated by the government's desire to increase competition. Electricity generated by the independent producers is sold to TNB for distribution by TNB. The terms of the power purchase agreements between the producers and

TNB were arrived at through negotiations, including the contract term (twenty-one years), the tariff structure (a two-part tariff structure for capacity charge and energy charge), and a cost and performance guarantee (Ani 1994; Tan and Rahim Noh 1994). The government has granted licenses to operate power stations to five producers with a total generating capacity of 4,115 megawatts when fully operational.

Critics have charged that using independent producers to solve the power shortage problem is too expensive. For instance, the average cost of electricity from the independent producers ranges from sen 15.8 to sen 17.8 (US$0.07 to US$0.08) per kilowatt-hour, while TNB's generation cost is estimated at sen 9.0 per kilowatt-hour. The Malaysian government ignored the economies of scale in power generation that TNB enjoys over independent producers (see chapter 6 on Japan for a contrasting approach). That the independent power producer plants were built on a fast track explains only some of the difference between the independent power producers' and TNB's power supply costs. The higher returns assured to the independent power producers is also responsible for the higher cost of power to TNB and, ultimately, to consumers.

Water Supply: More Reliable, but Full Privatization Required

Since 1970 water supply production has increased by about 50 percent during each of the five-year plan periods (see table 2–2). Between 1970 and 1980 the government completed several major water supply projects that increased the capacity of treatment plant production. It maintained this momentum during 1981–95 with the expansion of major water treatment facilities. In addition, it commissioned several new water projects in the 1980s, particularly during the Fifth Malaysia Plan period. Figures for rural water programs indicate that substantial progress was made from the mid-1970s to 1995.

Despite the increases in productive capacity, several states still suffer from water shortages. In response, the government has developed a program for the interstate transfer of water and has begun to privatize water supply services on a piecemeal basis. The Ministry of Works has noted, however, that none of the private companies has renovated the aging water distribution systems. The ministry has called for a comprehensive privatization program that encompasses all components of water supply services.

POLICIES ATTEMPT TO ENSURE AN ADEQUATE WATER SUPPLY. The growth of industry and rapid urbanization have been the primary reasons for investment in urban water supply systems. The share of resources devoted to expanding and upgrading these systems has fluctuated from one-third to more than 80 percent of the total annual allocation for developing water resources.

The development of rural water supply schemes has been a priority only in the more recent Malaysia plans. Besides improving the quality of life for rural residents, the government hopes to encourage industries to locate in selected areas. The share allocated to developing rural water supply in the total water resource allocation has ranged from 11 to 62 percent per year. Investment in rural water systems accelerated under the Fifth and Sixth Malaysia plans, and the policy to increase accessibility to safe water in rural areas is being continued in the Seventh Malaysia Plan. During 1996–2000 the government will implement about 3,600 projects, located mostly in isolated rural areas and benefiting about 262,400 households.

Water losses are a major problem. A 1989 study found that water losses averaged 43 percent of total production. Losses are mainly caused by meter under-registration, leakages, and so on. Making the water supply more efficient is now a high priority. Beginning with the Sixth Malaysia Plan, the authorities instituted measures to improve the efficiency of water supply by reducing the rate of nonrevenue water. The program replaces water meters and pipelines and refurbishes treatment plants. As a result of these efforts, the national nonrevenue water rate decreased to 38 percent in

1995. The upgrading and rehabilitation program will be extended during the Seventh Malaysia Plan, and by the end of the plan (in 2000) the nonrevenue water level is targeted to be 28 percent. Rehabilitating and upgrading water treatment plants and distribution systems to reduce water losses will remain major priorities in the water sector.

Water supply development is one component of a broader development program that encompasses the entire range of water resources. The program emphasizes multipurpose water schemes, such as storage dams that can mitigate floods and alleviate pollution. Nevertheless, several states have reported water shortages. In response the government has developed a system for the interstate transfer of water supply. The Sixth Malaysia Plan called for developing interstate and interbasin water transfers to rectify the uneven distribution of water resources. These measures should also prevent the emergence of water-stress states. Under the Seventh Malaysia Plan the government plans to establish a national water council to resolve legal, institutional, and financial issues and to improve river basin development and management to ensure long-term sustainability of the water supply.

WATER SUPPLY BELOW EXPECTATION IN RURAL AREAS. Water production capacity has grown sufficiently to meet demand, and urban areas receive satisfactory water supply coverage. In 1995, 99 percent of the urban population had access to piped, treated water. Coverage in rural areas is below that of urban areas. Nevertheless, 77 percent of the rural population had access to potable water in 1995, compared with 67 percent in 1990.

In addition to rehabilitating the water supply infrastructure to reduce system losses, the administrative structure for managing water supply must be improved in some states. Modernization of the administrative systems of the various water authorities, including accounting systems, began only in the Fourth Malaysia Plan. To overcome management problems, the government is expected to privatize some of the state water authorities.

PIECEMEAL PRIVATIZATION INSUFFICIENT. Water supply has long been the responsibility of state and local governments, each of which acts as a monopoly. Water supply services have been privatized on a piecemeal basis, mainly water treatment plants with BOT agreements. Under most of these agreements the privatized treatment plants sell water to the local water authorities. The government has also privatized water supply by contracting out the management of state-owned water treatment plants.

The Ministry of Works has expressed its dissatisfaction with the privatization of the water supply, mainly because the aging distribution systems have not been improved under the partial privatization initiatives. The ministry has expressed its desire for a comprehensive privatization program that encompasses all components of water supply: construction, production, distribution, and maintenance. As a first step toward full privatization, the ministry corporatized the Johor and Pulau Pinang water authority in 1994, to be followed by the corporatization of the Melaka, Pahang, Perlis, and Selangor water authorities.

Sewerage Development: A Late Start

In 1970 just 21 percent of Malaysia's population had flush systems that discharged to communal or municipal sewers or to individual disposal units. The rest of the population was served by bucket collection or used pit latrines or open drains. By 1990, however, 87 percent of the population had access to acceptable sewerage facilities, defined as centralized sewerage, a septic/imhoff tank, or pour-flush facilities (see table 2–2). Nevertheless, progress in developing sewerage systems has been slow, and the hope is that privatization will increase sewerage coverage to 100 percent.

In the past sewerage development programs were undertaken mainly in the major urban centers in Peninsular Malaysia. In the first four Malaysia plans, for example, allocations for sewerage development focused on expanding and upgrading the sewerage systems in the major urban centers of Kuala Lumpur, George Town, and Ipoh. In the Fourth Malaysia Plan the government announced its intention to provide centralized sewerage systems for state capitals and major towns, but the financial and human resource constraints local authorities faced made progress in this area extremely slow. By 1985 only six urban centers had centralized sewerage facilities. Only in the Sixth Malaysia Plan did sewerage development become a priority, largely because the government adopted a comprehensive and integrated approach to water resources planning that recognized the effect inadequate sewerage systems have on water pollution.

The sewerage system is one of the last infrastructure facilities to be privatized. In December 1993 the government and the Indah Water consortium signed a RM 6.2 billion (US$2.5 billion) concession agreement to privatize the national sewerage system on a BOT basis with a twenty-eight-year concession period. Efforts began in March 1994 in Langkawi, which was chosen because of its importance as a tourist resort, and will be followed by projects in Kuala Lumpur, Penang, Port Dickson, Labuan, and other urban and tourist centers. By late 1995 management of the sewerage system had been handed over to the Indah Water consortium in 82 of 143 local authorities.

The consortium is focusing on constructing works (such as multipoint sewerage systems) and on modernizing and refurbishing existing systems, which will help centralize the country's sewerage system. Once it has completed these efforts, expected to take eighteen years, nationwide sewerage coverage should reach 100 percent. To centralize the provision of sewerage services, the government enacted a new sewerage services bill and amended four other ordinances. The amendments transfer the responsibility for providing sewerage services from local governments to the federal government.

Privatized Infrastructure: The New Challenges

Ten years ago, the public sector dominated infrastructure development. Since then, however, the situation has changed dramatically. The private sector's role is expanding in every infrastructure sector, and privatized firms are now the sole suppliers of some infrastructure services. In other sectors the private sector's role is increasing as the public sector's role diminishes.

The planned allocations for infrastructure development under the Seventh Malaysia Plan reflect these changes. The private sector is set to spearhead infrastructure development into the next century, with an expected RM 68.3 billion (US$27.5 billion) in investment, more than three times the RM 19.2 billion (US$7.7 billion) that the public sector plans to spend on infrastructure during this period (Naidu 1996a). Thus private financing will account for 78 percent of infrastructure investment during the five years of the plan.

Privatization Procedures Lack Transparency

Despite the success in attracting private participation in infrastructure, some observers have questioned the effectiveness of the government's privatization policy. The main criticism is that privatization procedures lack transparency (Naidu 1995, 1996b). Because the private sector is free to identify projects for privatization, the government used a first-come, first-served rule when awarding unsolicited projects. Moreover, even privatization projects the government initiates have not been awarded in an open tender system. To the contrary, infrastructure projects have often been awarded without a transparent selection process. This is true of the divestiture of ports, the privatized road projects, the independent power producer projects, and the sewerage and light rail transit projects.

Regulatory Frameworks Are Still Evolving

One aspect of privatization that has not received sufficient attention in Malaysia is the role of the government in the postprivatization era. Privatization on the scale that has occurred requires regulatory institutions to perform supervisory functions, not only to serve as a buffer between private suppliers and users, but also to effect government policies. Yet even though privatization of infrastructure began more than a decade ago, the country's regulatory system is ad hoc and still evolving.

In all the cases where the government has privatized infrastructure, the government department or statutory body that previously supplied the services has assumed the regulatory role. These agencies have neither the personnel nor the independence to regulate the private operators of infrastructure facilities. Moreover, the scope of regulatory action is fairly rudimentary, for example, no clear link exists between the functions of the regulatory agencies and the development of incentives to encourage privatized suppliers to be efficient. Another problem is that the ministers who supervise infrastructure sectors appear to have retained considerable influence over the policies of the privatized suppliers. Rate revisions in telecommunications, power, and toll roads are not determined by the regulatory agencies and appear to almost always require ministerial, or even cabinet, approval.

The difficulties encountered in coming up with a tariff adjustment formula in the power sector and in resolving interconnection and equal access issues in the telecommunications sector suggest that the absence of an effective regulatory system is causing problems. Similarly, the difficulties encountered in the sewerage sector, including the question of user fees and quality standards, indicate that the regulatory framework is inadequate for coping with private provision of infrastructure. If unresolved, the absence of a comprehensive and effective regulatory framework could undermine the infrastructure reform program. A tenable regulatory framework is essential, both because of the extent of privatization, and because, in its absence, privatized service providers will be more likely to exploit their market power.

Conclusion

Malaysia's experience with infrastructure development, though at times problematic, has achieved impressive results. Infrastructure has generally kept pace with rapid economic development. Road development, in particular, also helped reduce regional inequalities and achieve social objectives (even though in some cases facilities were underused). Strong planning mechanisms guided shifting priorities.

Throughout, the government has been the dominant source of funds and principal operator, with government utilities granted national or local monopolies, but the use of private resources is on the rise. Nevertheless, government financial support continues through soft loans and guarantees, its management role persists through retention of equity in privatized enterprises, and its policy role is effected through golden shares. Privatization has been gradual, but promising, although regulation remains rudimentary.

References

Ani, Arope. 1994. "Progress in Tenaga Nasional after Privatization." Paper presented at the Private Power in the Pacific Forum of the Tenth Meeting of the Pacific Economic Cooperation Council, March 23, Kuala Lumpur, Malaysia.

Department of Statistics. Various years. *Yearbook of Statistics*. Kuala Lumpur, Malaysia.

Gomez, E. T. 1990. "Politics in Business: UMNO's Corporate Investments." Kuala Lumpur Forum, Kuala Lumpur, Malaysia.

Government of Malaysia. 1991. *Sixth Malaysia Plan 1991–95*. Kuala Lumpur: Government Printer.

———. 1996. *Seventh Malaysia Plan*. Kuala Lumpur: Percetakan Nasional Malaysia Berhad.

Hensley, M. L., and P. W. Edward. 1993. "The Privatization Experience in Malaysia." *Columbia Journal of World Business* 28(1):70–82.

Jones, Leroy. 1994. "Malaysia." In Ahmed Galal and Mary Shirley, eds., *Does Privatization Deliver?* Washington, D.C.: World Bank.

Kennedy, Laurel. 1995. "Telecommunications." In K. S. Jomo, ed., *Privatizing Malaysia: Rents, Rhetoric, and Realities*. Boulder, Colorado: Westview Press.

Ministry of Transport. Various years. *Transport Statistics*. Kuala Lumpur, Malaysia.

Naidu, G. 1992. "Private Provision of Physical Infrastructure: The Malaysian Experience." Economic Development Institute of the World Bank, Washington, D.C.

———. 1995. "Infrastructure." In K. S. Jomo, ed., *Privatizing Malaysia: Rents, Rhetoric, and Realities*. Boulder, Colorado: Westview Press.

———. 1996a. "Mobilizing Private Sector Financial Resources for Infrastructure Development in Indo-China: Lessons from the Experience of Malaysia." Paper presented at the Seminar on the Mobilization of Private Sector Financial Resources for Infrastructure Development in Indo-China, Economic and Social Commission for Asia and the Pacific, June 24–26, Bangkok, Thailand.

———. 1996b. "Power Sector Reform in Malaysia: Privatization and Regulation." Paper presented at the Pacific Trade and Development Conference on Business, Markets, and Governments in Asia Pacific, Taiwan Institute of Economic Research, December 9–11, Taipei, Taiwan (China).

National Electricity Board. Various years. *Statistical Bulletin*. Kuala Lumpur, Malaysia.

Tan Ah Kow, Philip, and A. Rahim Noh. 1994. "Negotiating for Private Power Generation." Paper presented at the Private Power in the Pacific Forum of the Tenth Meeting of the Pacific Economic Cooperation Council, March 23, Kuala Lumpur, Malaysia.

3

Private Participation with Strong Government Control: Hong Kong

Kwong Kai-Sun

Government thinking about Hong Kong's infrastructure is shaped by one over-riding concern: meeting consumers' service, quality, and price demands in the face of scarce natural resources, a small geographic area, and a densely concentrated population that continues to expand rapidly. To balance these competing realities, the government has long relied on an array of operational mechanisms and ownership structures: the government itself, public corporations, and private provision. The outcome is an infrastructure whose performance is mixed: service delivery is effective in most sectors, but does not respond adequately to consumers in a few critical sectors. Many of the positive aspects of delivery come from private initiative, which the government recognizes, but the government also believes that it has a responsibility to protect consumers, which compels it to regulate profit margins. Thus far, competition in delivery has also been limited. An interesting denouement will soon come in the telecommunications sector, where the imminent expiration of government monopoly franchises is evoking strong support for the entry of competitors.

The Government Controls Service Provision to Varying Degrees

Infrastructure services are provided by entities that are under varying degrees of government control, ranging from complete government ownership and operation, to intermediate degrees of government control, to no control (figure 3–1). Government policy toward infrastructure is continually shifting toward privatization and market competition.

Figure 3–1. The Spectrum of Government Control

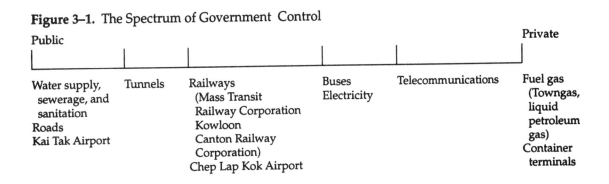

Public					Private
Water supply, sewerage, and sanitation Roads Kai Tak Airport	Tunnels	Railways (Mass Transit Railway Corporation Kowloon Canton Railway Corporation) Chep Lap Kok Airport	Buses Electricity	Telecommunications	Fuel gas (Towngas, liquid petroleum gas) Container terminals

Complete Government Control: Water Supply, the Road Network, and the Airport

Water supply has always been the responsibility of the government, which plans, builds, and operates reservoirs, pumping stations, and pipelines. The Water Services Department is one of the largest government departments. The government also provides sewerage and sanitation facilities. Under an overall environmental protection plan, the government plans to invest heavily in sewerage, drainage, and waste disposal facilities and will use a polluters pay scheme to finance it.

With the exception of three private tunnels, the government built and operates the entire road network, along with Kai Tak Airport, which the Civil Aviation Department operates. Franchised private enterprises provide ancillary facilities, such as the cargo terminal, aircraft maintenance, inflight catering, passenger baggage handling, and retail operations at the terminal.

Weaker Control: Most Infrastructure Services

Under slightly weaker government control are the only private portions in the road network, the three tunnels constructed under build-operate-transfer schemes. The private enterprises are bound by stringent contracts that govern construction and operations parameters; completion dates; pricing mechanisms; and operational periods, which range from twenty-five to thirty years. A fourth tunnel is currently under construction.

Under still weaker government control are the two public corporations: the Mass Transit Railway Corporation and the Kowloon Canton Railway Corporation. Another public corporation, the Airport Authority, will soon be established, with responsibility for constructing and operating the new Chek Lap Kok Airport. While the government owns public corporations, because they are established by statutes as independent enterprises operating according to commercial principles, the government does not have full control over management policies and their boards and a management team manage them. They plan, build, and operate facilities.

Under even less control are the bus and the electricity companies. These investor-owned companies have monopoly power. The government grants route monopolies to the bus companies to protect them from competition. The scale of the networks of the electric companies effectively protects them from competition, but their pricing, rates of return, environmental impact, and service quality and quantity are regulated heavily by the government.

Weaker regulation is found in telecommunications, where only local telephony is regulated. Investor-owned companies provide both local and international services under franchise.

No Control: Fuel Gas and Container Terminals

Unregulated private enterprises provide several important infrastructure services. Commercial enterprises provide fuel gas in the form of a manufactured gas (Towngas) or liquid petroleum gas. Private enterprises also build and operate container terminals, a key infrastructure in Hong Kong, on land acquired from the government. The government has little control over the pricing and business operations of these enterprises.

Government Controls Respond to Sectoral Needs

The organizational structures of infrastructure providers are defined by the mechanisms that are used to operate and control them. These mechanisms have not been static. The government has applied them surgically in some instances and has modified them in others in response to consumers' demands.

Franchises Granted to Some Monopolies to Protect Them from Competition

In some cases the government grants franchises to protect monopolies from the entry of competitors and from the expansion of other monopolies into certain service areas. Franchises are granted for specific lengths of time, commonly for twenty-five to thirty years, and for specialized services, such as airport baggage and cargo handling and aircraft maintenance. The government monitors these franchises assiduously to ensure that they maintain delivery and production standards. For instance, as already noted, it grants bus franchises guaranteed routes that are free from competition, but on one occasion it altered a franchise to ensure that it did not abuse this privilege.

Control Schemes in Place to Limit Profits and Protect Consumers

Where the government grants a franchise to protect providers from competition, it has put control schemes in place to protect consumers from any attempts by the franchises to maximize profits. The government negotiates with franchises and other monopolies to set a rate of return that is tied to fixed assets. Profit beyond a certain threshold goes into a development fund, which also tops up profits if they are below the agreed threshold. Price revisions are also subject to government approval.

These schemes of control are not static. The government has adapted them to balance consumers' demands and service providers' needs. For example, the government approved bus fare increases when the Mass Transit Railway began eating into the franchises' profits. Conversely, when electricity consumers complained that the money they were paying for services was allowing the monopolies to increase their profits by selling energy to China, the government mandated a substantial rebate to customers.

Private Sector Provision Where the Government Believes Delivery Will Be More Efficient

While the government contracts service provision out to private providers where it believes the private sector can provides specific services more efficiently, the process for selecting private providers is not necessarily transparent. For recurrent services, such as road maintenance, the government usually selects contractors from a pool of private sources it has used in the past and been satisfied with. For nonrecurrent services, such as consultation or research and development, the government solicits proposals from the private sector, narrows the list down, and submits the final list to an internal committee for selection. However, the government is not required to inform the public about who the applicants are or by what criteria they are judged. This arrangement allows the government to make selections without the burdensome process of public debate. At the same time, the government has implemented a system of checks and balances that mitigate rent seeking and corruption. These include an independent judiciary system, an independent commission on corruption, an auditing department, and committee decisionmaking.

The Government Treats Each Sector Differently

As already noted, the level of government control varies from sector to sector; however, the types of control mechanisms it uses are sometimes not suited to meet consumers' demands and providers' needs.

Transportation: The Range of Modes Creates Problems

The transportation system comprises an intricate road network and more than ten transport modes. Because of traffic congestion, the government has been forced to control and regulate the operations of each transportation mode. It controls the number of vehicles in each mode either by licensing (for public modes) or by taxation (private vehicles). Moreover, it uses franchises to control the fares, routes, and levels of service of the bus companies, the most important transport mode. Government-owned corporations operate the railways, and the government controls the number of taxis and their fares. Nevertheless, the government refrains from actually operating any of the modes itself and they are run primarily by private enterprises and entrepreneurs, or in some cases by public corporations.

The government faces numerous challenges in its attempts to create a sound transportation infrastructure. Despite two decades of government effort (box 3–1), inefficiencies continue to plague the transportation system. Congestion is a persistent problem, buses are underutilized, and the costs of transportation increase much faster than inflation. These problems stem from three factors: the unintended negative impacts of government efforts to alleviate traffic congestion, an inadequate response by the government to address those negative impacts, and public opposition to government attempts to introduce pricing mechanisms.

Focus on road use priorities and bus and railway services. Traffic congestion developed in the late 1960s. In the early 1970s the government tried to address the problem by formulating three strategies that remain in effect: priorities should be in effect for road use, public bus service should be improved, and railways should be improved and expanded.

The government wanted to induce commuters to shift from private cars to public buses and railways, that is, from low capacity modes to high capacity modes. To discourage the use of private cars the government had to improve public bus and railway service and restructure bus routes to make them accessible to railway stops. Smoother traffic patterns enabled buses to run faster, which attracted more commuters and helped reduce congestion even more. The government spared goods vehicles as a target for restraint because they had no substitute available, and because they were necessary for economic growth. As concerned taxis, however, the government faced a dilemma: although they were inefficient in terms of road space, the public demanded them because they provided route flexibility in an otherwise rigid system.

The government has implemented these strategies gradually during the past two decades. In road use management it gave priority to large buses by introducing bus only lanes in 1973 and 1974 and expanding the zones in which only large buses were permitted. The government also vastly expanded the bus fleet and replaced single deckers with double deckers. In addition, it introduced measures to restrain the use of private cars by imposing a registration tax, license fees, and a fuel tax. In off-road modes the government invested heavily in the construction of the massive underground Mass Transit Railway, the electrification of the British section of the Kowloon Canton Railway, and the construction of the Light Rail Transit.

Box 3–1. Government Activities in the Transportation Sector

1969	Passenger vans legalized, referred to as public light buses
1972	Comprehensive transportation principles established by the government
	Private tunnel connecting Hong Kong Island to Kowloon completed
	First container terminal opened
1973	Bus only lanes introduced
1975	Franchise of bus companies changed from area monopoly to route monopoly
1980	First line of Mass Transit Railway completed
	Bus fares of the Kowloon Motor Bus company increased by 60 percent, route coordination started
1981	Kowloon Motor Bus company fares increased by another 30 percent
1982	Kowloon Canton Railway privatized from a government department to a public corporation
	First registration tax on private cars doubled
1988	Light rail transit, owned and operated by the public railway corporation, begins operation
1992	Twenty-six monopoly routes taken from China Motor Bus and awarded to Citybus through public tender

Concurrently, the government strengthened its transport administration by establishing a policy branch within the secretariat and expanding the Transport Department. The transport secretary, who reported directly to the chief secretary, was responsible for such broad policy matters as the implementation of the road use principles. While the Transport Department continued to engage in such tasks as collecting license fees, it became increasingly involved in coordinating bus routes, regulating franchised bus companies, and monitoring the traffic flows and service levels of all public transportation modes.

The government sought the assistance of outside consultants in undertaking transport planning, design, and feasibility studies. The consultants, who were contracted out on a project basis, had experience in tackling similar problems in other cities. They helped in the transfer of technology and greatly improved the level of knowledge in engineering, construction, and planning.

The government also sought the advice of special committees on planning and management, of which the most important was the Transport Advisory Committee, which regulates and coordinates all public transport modes except railways. The committees consisted of government officials, academics, legislators, professionals, and business people. Although it has no statutory power, it has a strong influence on the government. After hearing all sides of the issues at hand, for example, fare increases or improper behavior by taxi drivers, the committee submits a recommendation to the government. Perhaps the most important function of this committee is its presentation of the frequently opposing views of operators and consumers to neutral members of the public, thereby softening the confrontational stance among regulators, regulated operators, and the public.

PROLIFERATION OF TAXIS. The strategy to reduce congestion by restraining private cars and expanding and modernizing the railways and buses did not work out quite as planned. Public corporations that were entirely owned by the government ran the railways, but they had complete operational and financial autonomy. This organizational structure did not provide their management with sufficient incentives to minimize costs, and high construction costs exacerbated the problem. If the railways were to break even, they had to keep fares high. To ensure high patronage despite the elevated fares, the government had to minimize competition from large buses. It attempted to do so by preventing large buses from competing directly with the railway lines and by allowing the franchised bus companies to increase their fares.

An unforeseen consequence of this chain of events was that taxi fares, which the government also regulated, were not increasing as fast as bus fares. As a result, excess demand for taxis developed in urban areas as many commuters used them for feeder services and for short journeys. The consequence was that taxis created more congestion in urban areas. At the same time, because of the shortage of taxis rate gouging by taxi drivers became common as the regulated fare fell below what drivers could charge as the market fare.

ATTEMPTS TO LIMIT PRIVATE CAR OWNERSHIP. Given the high costs of public transport and the excess demand for taxis, car owners were reluctant to give up their cars, thereby exacerbating congestion. In response the government imposed fiscal measures to restrain the growth of private cars (although restraints on car use would have been more appropriate). In 1982 the government doubled the first registration tax for new private cars, which ranged from 80 to 100 percent of the import price. It increased annual license fees for private cars three times and raised the fuel tax significantly in 1982 and 1983. Also in 1983, the management of government multistory car parks was contracted out to private companies by open tender. Parking fees increased rapidly in subsequent years in accordance with the market situation. These increases, coupled with the generally depressed economy, helped reduce the number of licensed private cars for a brief period. The number of private cars increased until 1982, fell through 1986, but then increased from 1987, while the number of goods vehicles and taxis kept increasing.

ELECTRONIC ROAD PRICING SYSTEM TESTED. Given its failure to reduce urban congestion, the government proposed, and then tested, a road pricing scheme that employed advanced electronic sensors (box 3–2). However, the public opposed its implementation for a variety of reasons, including invasion of privacy grounds and a lack of reliability. Although the scheme was a step in the right direction, it was mishandled politically and had to be withdrawn.

MIX OF PUBLIC AND PRIVATE FUNDING FOR ROADS. Until 1967 the road networks of Hong Kong Island, Kowloon, and the New Territories were not connected. Hong Kong Island was separated from the mainland by Victoria Harbor, and commuters and motor vehicles traveling between Hong Kong Island and Kowloon had to rely on ferries. Kowloon and the New Territories were separated by high ridges, and the main connection between the two regions was a single-lane road. The population was concentrated in Hong Kong Island and Kowloon. The New Territories were sparsely populated and agricultural activities predominated.

In 1967 the government completed Lion Rock Tunnel, thereby offering an additional connection for motorists traveling between Kowloon and the New Territories. The tunnel supported the development of new towns in the New Territories, in line with the government's intention to move the population away from urban areas. Ten years later, a second tube was constructed alongside the first.

In 1972 the Cross-Harbor Tunnel, which consisted of two dual-lane tubes under Victoria Harbor, was opened. In effect, the tunnel connected the two hitherto separate road networks on Hong Kong Island and Kowloon into a single network. For the first time, a private company built and operated a section of the road network and charged a toll. The tunnel was the first in Hong Kong constructed under a build-operate-transfer scheme and had a contract period of twenty-five years. The tunnel opened the way for bus companies to carry cross-harbor traffic, previously the domain of ferries. The opening of the tunnel also led in 1974 to the merger of Hong Kong taxis and Kowloon taxis, which thereafter operated on the same fare scale.

With the exception of the two cross-harbor tunnels and the Tate's Cairn Tunnel, built in 1991 between Kowloon and the New Territories, the entire road network—lane expansions, new highways, other tunnels—was constructed with public money. While the private tunnels receive toll charges from motorists, four government tunnels are also toll tunnels. Whether a tunnel is financed privately or publicly depends primarily on the volume of projected traffic. For the first harbor tunnel, the potential demand was clearly huge, because the ferries were the only mode available

---

Box 3–2. The Electronic Road Pricing Scheme: Innovative but Unacceptable

In 1983 the government experimented with an innovative road pricing scheme. Known as electronic road pricing, the system called for private motorists to pay a toll each time their vehicle passed through a certain checkpoint. The toll was expected to discourage motorists and thus reduce the use of private cars in congested areas. Each motor vehicle that was subject to the toll had to be fitted with an electronic license plate that identified the vehicle. A sensor installed at the checkpoint would then electronically sense the vehicle. A central computer recorded the signal and a bill was issued to the vehicle owner. The system could easily be fine-tuned to charge different rates at different times of day and at different points in the road network. The advantage of this system was that motorists were not taxed for owning a vehicle, as they were under the prevailing private vehicle restraint measures, but were charged for using the road network and for contributing to congestion.

The system was tested satisfactorily in 1983–84, but the public opposed it. The government also failed to assure car owners that road pricing would reduce their license fees. In the final round of the controversy, the government approached each district board for its endorsement of local implementation. To the government's disappointment, none of the district boards supported the scheme, perhaps for fear that their endorsement would set their district up as a pioneering area for road tolls, to the disadvantage of local residents and businesses. In 1985 the government reluctantly shelved the scheme.

for crossing the harbor. The second harbor tunnel was planned only after congestion at the first tunnel had become a serious problem. The Tate's Cairn Tunnel was planned only after the limited capacity of the Lion Rock Tunnel caused miles of traffic backups at its entrances. In this connection, the government faces a financing dilemma: building roads, tunnels, and bridges ahead of demand requires government financing; building them after the demand is evident may attract private financing, but that may occur only after congestion is already high.

Although the government has spent billions on road construction, it has actually received more from the transportation system than it has put in. The first registration tax, license fees, taxi concession fees, and fuel tax generate enormous revenues. In particular, the 1983 fuel tax increase sharply accelerated revenue, and increases in new car registrations after 1987 boosted the revenue from the first registration tax. As a result, total revenue has increased much more rapidly than expenditures, and the surplus has increased since 1983 (figure 3–2).

PREVALENCE OF OVERCHARGING BY TAXI DRIVERS. The taxi is an affordable and personalized mode of public transport. The government controls taxi fares by means of meters. The government also controls the quantity of taxis by restricting the number of taxi licenses, which are issued to operators through public auction. License holders may operate taxis themselves, hire employees, or simply rent taxis to drivers. The license has no specified expiration date; it is renewed each year on payment of a small fee. The market price of a license reflects the profitability of taxi operation.

The government has had difficulty in deciding on the number of new licenses to issue. In a system where the government controls the routes of most public modes and discourages private car use, the demand for taxis is high. However, the presence of too many taxis could exacerbate congestion. In the 1980s, when the number of taxis was insufficient, opportunistic drivers demanded fares that were higher than the official fare. This and other kinds of unprofessional behavior by taxi drivers became the most common source of complaints about the transportation system. The government responded by allowing a moderate increase in fares, while stepping up police enforcement of official fares.

Figure 3–2. Government Surplus in the Transportation Sector, 1972–90 (millions of Hong Kong dollars)

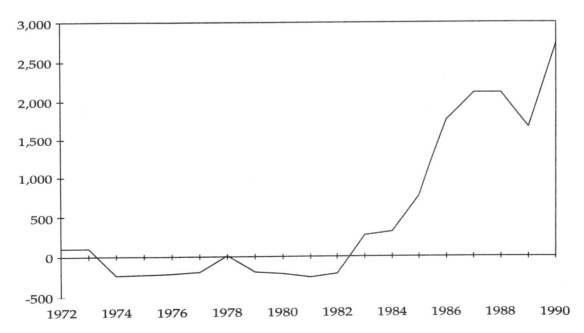

RAILWAYS: A PROFITABLE SUBSTITUTE FOR BUS SERVICE. Three separate railway systems serve Hong Kong: the Mass Transit Railway (MTR), which runs throughout most urban areas; the Kowloon Canton Railway (KCR), which provides service in the new towns in the New Territories; and the Light Rail Transit, which runs throughout the northwestern part of the New Territories. The service areas of the three railways are almost entirely separate, and they do not compete with each other.

The MTR was planned in the mid-1970s as a substitute for large buses, with the main aim being to ease road congestion. The first phase of the railway was completed in 1980. A public corporation, the Mass Transit Railway Corporation (MTRC), which is owned by the government, planned, constructed, and operates the MTR (box 3–3). The system comprises three linked lines: the Kwun Tong line, opened in 1980; the Tsuen Wan extension, opened in 1982; and the Island Line, opened in 1985. The three lines run along major corridors, connecting all major district centers. Thus the railway has had a widespread and far-reaching impact on the entire transportation sector. Because it was designed to serve the major traffic corridors, its speed and air-conditioned comfort quickly absorbed a large share of bus passengers. Rather than competing directly, the franchised bus companies were forced to open new routes, such as feeder routes to the MTR stations and routes to serve towns the railways did not serve.

Box 3–3. MTRC: An Effective Public Corporation

The MTRC is the largest public corporation in Hong Kong. Not only does it operate the Mass Transit Railway, it has also entered into real estate development at sites along railway lines.

A board and seven executive directors appointed by the board govern the corporation. The nine-member board, appointed by the governor, consists of government officials, executive counselors, and financiers. The executive directors are responsible for special projects, operations, property, personnel, finance, marketing and planning, and legal matters. Apart from the operation of railway, MTRC has also developed residential and commercial properties, solely and jointly with private enterprises, and derived substantial profits from these ventures. In 1992 about 85 percent of the MTRC's recurrent revenue was from fares, with the balance derived from advertising and concessions for commercial operations at the stations, property rental, and property management.

The MTRC has a high degree of financial autonomy and has raised a substantial amount of funds from external sources. At the end of 1992 its debt was 3.4 times its equity and its accumulated losses (after interest charges) stood at HK$ 3,068 million. Of the debt, 33 percent consisted of capital instruments, such as bearer participation certificates, Hong Kong dollar and yen bonds, medium-term notes, and commercial paper denominated in dollars and European currencies; 55 percent consisted of bank loans and overdrafts provided mostly by international banks; 9 percent was attributable to financial leases; and 3 percent was accounted for by a variety of other loans.

The MTRC also has commercial autonomy in negotiating, executing, and enforcing contracts with outside private enterprises and has arranged many contracts in railway construction, in supply of rolling stock and equipment, and in real estate development. Much like a commercial enterprise, the MTRC has its own set of accounts, has its accounts audited annually, and has profits that are subject to tax. The MTRC also has the authority to set fare levels to ensure adequate long-term rates of return. It does not require government permission to raise fares, although public pressure has limited fare hikes.

The MTRC probably has a long payback period. The company has made a continuous stream of operating and real estate development profits. When the railway was constructed, the government chose a financing method involving small equity, but large external debts that it guaranteed. The high interest charges led to net losses every year of the first decade after operation. This required the government to inject further shareholder equity to reduce external debts. Continuous net losses suggest that the private rate of return to government investment is not high. Of course, a much higher private rate of return can be achieved by fare increases, to the detriment of consumers. Short of raising fares, the MTRC has difficulty increasing its revenues, and hence its profits.

There is little doubt, however, that the MTRC is playing a vital role in the local transport system, and passengers do not appear to be dissatisfied with the service. Judging by performance figures such as safety and reliability, service quality is internationally comparable. During peak hours a train runs every 2 to 2.25 minutes. Of 528 passenger journeys, an average of 1 is delayed by more than 5 minutes.

The KCR has a long history. It started as a railway that offered fixed-track diesel train service to supplement the public bus service in the New Territories. It began at the southern tip of the Kowloon Peninsula and ended at Lo Wu, near the border with China. In the early days, passengers going to China had to alight at Lo Wu, walk across the border to reach the Chinese section of the railway, and board another train for their onward journeys. It was only in 1979, when China was liberalized, that through-train service between Hong Kong and China became available.

In the late 1970s the government was planning to expand several new towns in the New Territories. Transport planning for these new towns was crucial. The prevailing idea was that a fixed-track railway, together with feeder bus service, should be developed to ease the traffic burden. To this end it modernized the KCR, with full electrification completed in 1982, and dramatically improved both travel speed and service frequency. Another public corporation, the Kowloon Canton Railway Corporation (KCRC), undertook operation and development of the modern railway. As with the MTR, the government directed the Kowloon Motor Bus company to run feeder routes to KCRC stations and routes that KCR did not cover.

Two exogenous factors helped KCRC. First, it inherited the railway from the government, so its debt burden and interest costs were much lower than those of the MTRC. Second, the rapid growth of south China in the 1980s and the development of the new towns quickly increased the number of passengers. KCRC began to generate steady profits immediately.

In light of the KCRC's success, the government planned a new light rail in the mid-1980s. The Light Rail Transit, completed in 1988 and also operated by the KCRC, serves the Tuen Mun and Yuen Long region in the northwest New Territories. Large buses were not allowed to run competing routes after Light Rail Transit came into operation.

Bus services: franchises and controls. Two bus companies, China Motor Bus (CMB) and Kowloon Motor Bus (KMB), operate large public buses on franchises granted by the government. A third franchised bus company, New Lantau Bus, operates on a small scale and only on Lantau island and is not discussed here. Citybus, a new entrant into the market, began by operating large, private buses, but was recently granted several routes on Hong Kong Island.

Until 1975 the CMB had exclusive rights to operate large, public buses on Hong Kong Island, and the KMB had exclusive rights in Kowloon and the New Territories. They were thus area monopolies and did not compete with each other.

In 1975, when the existing franchises expired, the government changed the form of franchises granted to the two bus companies so that it conferred route as opposed to area monopolies. This change was necessitated by the opening of the Cross-Harbor Tunnel in 1972, after which both companies ran the same cross-harbor routes and each company crossed over into the other's territory. The new franchises also allowed the Transport Department to specify the routes, timetables, fares, journey distances, journey times, vehicle allocation, and vehicle capacity of both bus companies. In exact terms, the route monopoly means that no other operator can run a regular, fare paying, large bus service along the same routes. (The only exceptions are the cross-harbor routes. Both KMB and CMB have buses that run on these routes and share the revenue from them.) However, the franchised bus companies are not protected from regular, fare paying, small bus service or from regular, nonfare paying, large bus service. Aside from the shared cross-harbor routes, the KMB still has all the routes in Kowloon and the New Territories, and the CMB still has all the routes on Hong Kong Island.

The government must approve any fare increases. The rate of return of 15 or 16 percent under the control scheme has always been well above the prime bank rate. The government regards this rate of return as fair and reasonable; however, critics contend that the government has been too lenient in allowing price increases. Many argue that the scheme is outdated, and that it was appropriate only in the early years, when the bus companies required a safe return to motivate investment. Yet the government's dilemma is clear. After the MTR began operation, the bus companies' ridership, and therefore profits, fell drastically. As the government protected the railway, it took the profitable routes away from the bus companies and gave them to the railway. To compensate the bus companies, higher fares were necessary. In 1981 the government even paid HK$ 40 million in compensation to the KMB. In later years, as the government directed the bus companies to expand their fleets, additional fare increases became necessary.

In 1991 the government again changed its franchised bus policy. It granted monopoly rights over an urban route on Hong Kong Island to Citybus. This was the first time that two companies had operated in the same area, although they ran buses on different routes. The government was apparently dissatisfied with how CMB maintained its vehicles and handled staff matters. In 1992 the government took the unprecedented step of taking twenty-six routes away from the CMB and putting them up for open tender. As a result, the routes were granted to Citybus. At the same time, the government abolished control through regulation of the rate of return. In its place it introduced a new system to limit price increases. The full effect of these changes on pricing and service is as yet unknown.

LIMITED SERVICE BY PUBLIC LIGHT BUSES. In 1967 a series of urban riots—the most serious in Hong Kong's history—broke out. Buses, ferries, and trams suspended their services for several weeks. Because demand for transportation in the urban area still existed, dual-purpose goods and passenger vans came from the rural area of the New Territories to fill the need. Although they were illegal, the government did little to stop them. After the government had restored order, buses, ferries, and trams slowly resumed their services, but the illegal vans continued to operate. The government legalized them in 1969. These new types of licensed vans—known as public light buses—were allowed to operate on any route, except in some congested areas, and at any fare.

Although the light buses are now legal, the government has never favored this mode of public transportation, believing that they create traffic chaos. Indeed, when the government decided to expand the scope of the restricted zones for these buses, their drivers strongly opposed the move and for a few days waged a general strike, but traffic improved significantly, and the large buses moved faster, confirming the government's theory. In addition, the franchise bus companies argued that their route monopoly was being eroded in effect, if not in law. A revelation also surfaced later that public light bus terminals were controlled by underground societies that received bribes from drivers for the "right" to park. For these reasons the government was adamantly opposed to expanding this mode.

To exert greater control over the light buses, the government began to phase in a fixed-route variety of light buses, known as green buses. The green buses have operated on nontrunk routes at fares specified by the government along routes allocated by public tender. In recent years the government has managed to persuade a greater number of light bus operators to travel these fixed routes.

Water Supply: Reliability Has Been a Struggle

The government assumes sole responsibility for providing all fresh water and controls all services. Through the Water Services Department, it plans and constructs reservoirs, treatment plants, and pump stations and operates the distribution network. It has always set water charges below average costs and subsidizes consumers heavily.

WATER SUPPLY HAS ALWAYS BEEN A PROBLEM. Throughout Hong Kong's history, water shortages have been a persistent problem that have depressed the economy's overall economic well-being.

Hong Kong, including its outlying islands, occupies a land area of just 398 square miles. This small area does not contain either a river or a lake of sufficient size to supply water. The amount of exploitable underground water is also insignificant. Thus the only source of fresh water is rainfall, yet three-quarters of the annual rainfall comes during the wet season from May to September and must be collected and stored for the following dry season. If an insufficient amount of water is in store by the end of the wet season, water rationing is required until the following wet season. Moreover, the demand for water has increased rapidly with Hong Kong's explosive population growth, exacerbated by its rapid urbanization and industrialization.

RESERVOIRS AND CATCHMENT AREAS. In the past, the government's main solution for the water shortage problem was to construct reservoirs to save enough water for the dry season. From the first reservoir that was built in 1863 in Pok Fu Lam on Hong Kong Island, to another thirteen reservoirs built on Hong Kong Island, in Kowloon, and in the New Territories, Hong Kong had a reservoir capacity that could support full demand for about four months by 1940. But the distribution system fell into disrepair during World War II, and the government lacked funds to renovate existing reservoirs or to build more until 1957. Even after it had built the Tai Lam Chung reservoir, with a capacity of 4,500 million gallons, that year, the government recognized that the rapidly growing population required an even greater number of reservoirs. It built the Shek Pik reservoir during 1958–63 at a cost of HK\$ 200 million. Its benefit was felt in 1965, the first postwar year in which no shortage occurred. However, the government realized that storage capacity would not be sufficient by the end of the decade and had to consider more remote sites. Thus in 1962 it began building the largest reservoir ever planned in Hong Kong, Plover Cove. The construction of Plover Cove took almost eight years, at a cost of HK\$ 520 million. Just as Plover Cove came into operation, another reservoir of similar size, High Island, was being planned. The High Island reservoir was built between 1969 and 1979.

The construction of these reservoirs required cutting-edge technology. Given the urgency involved, the government frequently had to experiment with unproven technologies. For example, the dam at Shek Pik was constructed with a pioneering technology called grouting. The construction of the Plover Cove and High Island reservoirs was even more demanding technologically. To construct the two reservoirs, engineers built dams across narrow natural inlets along the coast. When the dams were in place, the sea water inside was impounded to make a giant hollow for the storage of rain water. Moreover, to construct the reservoirs the government had to resettle villagers who had inhabited the sites. The government typically compensated the villagers for lost land at market price and offered them relatively modern housing to start a new living.

To increase the intake of rainwater, engineers built large catchment systems around the reservoirs that in most cases were several times the size of the reservoirs. Rainwater was also collected with miles of concrete-lined catchment channels. Tunnels had to be built to pass through intervening hills and extensive forestation was undertaken in the catchment areas to maximize rain penetration.

Yet another way to maximize water collection was to tap the water from natural streams, which became valuable water sources after heavy rains. To tap this source, engineers built shafts of several hundred feet along the courses of the streams. The stream water was then collected, first by small subsidiary tunnels, and then by main tunnels that led directly to the treatment plants. In addition, the government installed a wide urban network of salt water for domestic flushing purposes and for fire fighting. Individual household metering was gradually introduced in new premises to encourage residents to ration their water consumption.

DESALINATION. Desalinating sea water to provide fresh water had been an option under consideration since the end of World War II. At that time the technology was still unproven and the cost was too high. Thus it was not until the early 1970s that the government studied desalination seriously.

In 1969 it let tenders for the supply of equipment for an experimental desalinization plant. The design phase began the following year. The plant was completed in 1974 at a cost of HK\$ 200 million. A contract of HK\$ 337 million was then awarded to a Japanese company for installing the world's largest desalinization plant at Lok On Pai, supposedly the most suitable site for a large permanent plant. The plant, which was expected to be fully operational in 1975, was to produce 40 million gallons of raw water daily. In 1976 the government obtained a loan of US$21.5 million from the Asian Development Bank, repayable in ten years.

The Lok On Pai project encountered many obstacles: the recruitment of qualified personnel was difficult, especially at senior levels; the supply of equipment was delayed when the oil crisis led to a worldwide recession; and the need to provide protection against corrosion by sea water led to many engineering problems. As a result the plant did not become fully operational until 1977. After a brief operational period between 1977 and 1978, the government decided to close it, as abundant rainfall in 1979 and 1980 and the completion of the High Island reservoir made it difficult to justify the high cost of running the desalter. In the meantime, Hong Kong grew increasingly dependent on Kwangtung (formerly Canton) for its water supply, and the commitment of the Kwangtung government to sustain and increase the supply in the next decade greatly mitigated fears of a water shortage. In 1991 the desalter was dismantled and removed, leaving the site to be used for the construction of the new airport.

AGREEMENT WITH KWANGTUNG. Beyond the boundaries of Hong Kong, Kwangtung represents the most abundant nearby source of water. Nevertheless, the absence of diplomatic ties between China and the United Kingdom after 1949 prevented Hong Kong from relying extensively on this source. It was not until China was liberalized in 1979 that Kwangtung represented a long-term solution to Hong Kong's water shortage problem.

The first agreement with the Kwangtung government for a regular supply of water was signed in 1960. Under this agreement, 5,000 million gallons of water, mostly in the dry season, would be transported annually by pipeline from the Shum Chun reservoir to Hong Kong. This volume represented about 15 percent of normal consumption. Regular supply was maintained until 1963, when the entire region was affected by a drought. During that year only 1,400 million gallons were supplied to Hong Kong. The situation was so desperate that the government chartered a fleet of tankers to make 603 round trips in 1963 and 768 in 1964 up the Pearl River to have their tanks filled with water.

In 1964 another agreement was signed. The Kwangtung government guaranteed a supply of 15,000 million gallons a year at a price of HK$ 1.06 per 1,000 gallons. Supply would be maintained throughout the year from the East River. The new agreement forced the Hong Kong government to increase its water charge from US$1 to US$2 per 1,000 gallons. The new arrangement was maintained for two years; however, in 1967 China was unable to supply water during the summer months, which necessitated water rationing. Full supply resumed in 1968. From 1972 to 1980 new agreements for increased supply were reached every year. Finally, in 1980 a landmark agreement was reached whereby China agreed to increase its supply continuously each year until 1994. The Chinese source accounted for 60 percent of total demand by 1994, and the government is confident that China will meet all future increases in water demand.

Electric Power: Closely Regulated

Hong Kong's economic development depends on the availability of sufficient electricity. Since 1972 total electricity output increased more than fivefold, reflecting growing consumption needs by both domestic consumers and businesses. Higher incomes have allowed households to purchase more electrical appliances, and business activity has gradually shifted to the services sector.

Private, but regulated, monopolies handle all electricity production and distribution. Although the companies do not hold franchises, their rates of return are regulated under the government's control schemes. The companies have not been subsidized by the government in the past three decades, and the public has accepted their prices.

ELECTRIC POWER COMPANIES INVESTOR OWNED, BUT OPERATE UNDER CONTROL SCHEMES. Two electricity companies provide all the electricity consumed in Hong Kong. The Hong Kong Electric Company (HEC) supplies output to Hong Kong Island and two outlying islands, while China Light and Power (CLP) supplies electricity to Kowloon and the New Territories, including some of the outlying islands, and also exports electricity to southern China. Because the service areas of the two suppliers do not overlap, consumers cannot choose one supplier over the other, but because the distribution networks of the two companies are interconnected by submarine cables, the companies do share facilities, which lowers their operating costs and provides backup in case one of the networks fails.

Neither company operates under a government franchise. Both are entirely investor owned, and the government does not hold any shares in the companies. Shares in the companies are traded on the Hong Kong Stock Exchange. HEC is part of a multidisciplinary group of companies that comprises real estate, retail, and telecommunications businesses. Despite this apparent autonomy, the government closely monitors the financing plans of the two companies. Their rates of return to internally financed net fixed assets are controlled under schemes agreed to by the government and the companies (box 3–4).

The HEC owns its distribution network and its generation facilities. Because it is part of a group with a substantial interest in real estate, the company's planning strategy is integrated with that of the group. For example, in 1989 the company began relocating power stations from Ap Lei Chau Island to Lamma Island. The site on Ap Lei Chau was later developed into a large, middle-class residential estate.

Box 3–4. Control Schemes Help Ensure Equitable and Consistent Electric Supply

The importance of electricity to a modern economy such as Hong Kong is beyond question, yet the government has not played an active role in supplying it. Electricity generation and transmission are entirely in the hands of private investors, subject to a voluntary scheme of financial control.

The history of this control scheme dates to the late 1950s. At that time the government was concerned that the configuration of the two electricity companies, CLP and the HEC, might not be the best arrangement for consumers and for long-term economic growth. Economies of scale were not exploited, and monopoly pricing was suspected. A 1959 report by an independent electricity supply commission suggested that the two suppliers be merged and taken over by the government as a public corporation. In 1962, after three years of negotiations between the government and the boards of the two suppliers, a provisional agreement was reached whereby the two companies would be merged and their dividend increases linked with a reduction in charges. CLP's shareholders did not go along with this agreement, however, and by the end of the year a voluntary merger was clearly not feasible.

Thus in 1964 the government and the two suppliers agreed to a control scheme that tied permitted profits to net fixed assets. Both suppliers were allowed an annual profit equal to 13.5 percent of the average net fixed assets, plus 1.5 percent on any average net fixed assets financed by shareholders' investment. Profits were derived from the profit after taxation plus interest payable on long-term financing. If actual profits exceeded permitted profits, the excess was transferred to a development fund. If profits fell short of permitted profits, the development fund was drawn down. The profit that was available to shareholders for the year was the permitted profit less an amount reserved for consumer rebates and any interest payable on long-term financing. The amount reserved for consumer rebates was equal to 8 percent of the average balance of the development fund, which represented idle funds not used for physical expansion. The interest payable on long-term financing could not exceed 8 percent annually.

To allow the suppliers to earn enough revenue to meet the allowed rate of return, the government has to approve regular revisions in tariff charges. While both suppliers are financially sound, their profitability has not been identical. During 1983–92 CLP and its associated generating companies consistently made a profit that exceeded the permitted profit. Consequently, the size of its development fund grew. According to annual reports, the permitted return in recent years turned out to be about 16 percent of net fixed and current assets and 28 percent of shareholder funds. By September 1993 CLP's development fund had a balance of HK\$ 3.2 billion, raising questions about whether tariff revisions were still necessary. For the HEC, money had to be transferred from its development fund in four of the ten years. According to annual reports, the permitted return was 13 percent of net fixed and current assets and 24 percent of shareholder funds. By the end of 1992 the HEC's development fund had a balance of HK\$ 0.4 billion.

CLP owns its transmission and distribution network, including several thousand primary and secondary substations. It buys its electricity entirely from Castle Peak Power Company, which is 60 percent owned by Exxon and 40 percent owned by CLP. In the future, power generated by facilities in China that are partly owned by CLP may be fed into its distribution network in Hong Kong. The control scheme requires that Castle Peak sell electricity exclusively to CLP.

PARTNERSHIPS WITH CHINA INTENSIFY. In 1964 CLP obtained help from the Esso Corporation in setting up a new power station. The government approved this plan, and a new company, Peninsula Electric Power, was formed to own the new station. While Esso held 60 percent of the new power company and CLP only 40 percent, CLP was responsible for constructing and operating the power station and for distributing the output. Esso supplied fuel oil at market price.

In 1979 economic growth prompted the formation of another company, Kowloon Electric Supply, using the same joint venture formula that had been used to form Peninsula Electric Power. CLP was again responsible for constructing and operating the company and for distributing its output. During that summer a power failure led to a widespread half-day blackout in Kowloon and the New Territories. The incident prompted CLP to lay a submarine cable under the harbor to connect its networks with those of the HEC, thereby providing emergency backup resources.

After China was liberalized in 1979, CLP was quick to establish connections with enterprises there. Modernization and industrialization in southern Guangdong required a large volume of extra electricity, and in 1979 CLP began exporting electricity to Guangdong during off-peak periods. The volume of exports increased gradually throughout the 1980s. In 1983 CLP established a wholly-owned subsidiary, Hong Kong Nuclear Investment, to embark on electricity generation using nuclear power and entered into a joint venture with Guangdong Nuclear Power Investment to construct and operate a nuclear power station at Daya Bay in Guangdong. The station is 25 percent owned by CLP and 75 percent by Guangdong Nuclear Power Investment. In 1986 CLP signed another contract to supply electricity to Shekou, a rapidly developing industrial area in Guangdong. It was also revealed that CLP would buy 70 percent of the output from Daya Bay to meet the demand from its Hong Kong network. In 1992 the company announced plans to set up a new station in Hong Kong, fired on natural gas piped from Hainan Island in China. The three separate power generators—Peninsula Electric, Kowloon Electric, and Castle Peak Power—were consolidated under the Castle Peak name, with the same ownership structure.

As the connection with China grew stronger, concerns emerged about the increasing tendency of CLP and its associated generation companies to trade with China using facilities in Hong Kong. Consumers argued that production capacity in Hong Kong had been made possible with guaranteed profits earned locally, and thus that they had a claim on the profits of electricity exports to China. The government responded to the public's concern by revising the control scheme, which, as of October 1, 1993, mandates that 80 percent of the profits from exports be rebated to local consumers.

However, CLP may soon be buying electricity from the new Daya Bay generator in China. This new generator, which became operational in February 1994, is partly owned by CLP, but does not fall under the purview of the control scheme. CLP could conceivably pay a high price for imports from this generator and ask for a price increase locally. Even if the government refuses to grant a price increase, any profit shortfall can be compensated for by drawing down the development fund. The current control scheme deals with this problem by mandating that the price of electricity bought from Daya Bay must not exceed the cost of electricity generated by CLP's coal-fired plants.

Telecommunications Services: Private and Profitable

Telecommunications services are almost completely in the hands of Hong Kong Telecom, a private company that holds two franchises, one for local telephone services and the other for international services. The local telephone network, which used to operate under profit regulation, is now governed by a price-cap formula. Nevertheless, the price charged for local telephone service is relatively low, and the network does not generate much profit. Most of Hong Kong Telecom's profits come from international services, whose profit and price are not controlled. Greater competition was evident in the local network after the local franchise expired in 1995. Hong Kong Telecom is responding to potential competition by stepping up its marketing activities; keeping its prices low; exploiting its economies of scale; and diversifying into new products, such as video on demand. These activities may deter entry by competitors. For international services, no competition will appear until at least 2006, when the international franchise expires.

FRANCHISES GRANTED WITH AND WITHOUT CONTROL SCHEMES. Hong Kong Telecom, the dominant telecommunications company, is a private, investor-owned monopoly whose shares are traded on the Hong Kong Stock Exchange. Hong Kong Telecom has two main wholly-owned subsidiaries: Hong Kong Telephone and Hong Kong Telecom International. Hong Kong Telephone held an exclusive government franchise to provide local fixed-line telephone services until 1995. Hong Kong Telecom International holds an exclusive government franchise to provide international services (including telephone, facsimile, telex, telegram, and leased circuits for data transfer) until 2006. The government receives a royalty for the franchises, which in 1991 and 1992 amounted to about 2 percent of turnover.

The local telephone franchise was granted under a control scheme that allowed a rate of return of no more than 16 percent of shareholder funds. A development fund was set up to smooth out excesses and shortfalls over the years. In April 1993 this profit provision was replaced by a price cap that limits tariff increases to 4 percent below the prevailing rate of inflation. This condition has not significantly affected profit levels, however, because most of the group's profit is derived from international services.

The franchise for international services was not granted under a control scheme. Thus as the government has had little control over Hong Kong Telecom International's rate of profit, it has earned huge profits in recent years. For example, in 1992 the company yielded a shareholder profit of HK$ 5.6 billion on a shareholder fund of HK$ 12.2 billion, a return of 47 percent. International services account for 60 percent of Hong Kong Telecom's total turnover, compared with 15 percent for its local services. In addition, the volume of international services has been growing much more rapidly than the volume of local services, primarily because of the liberalization of China in 1979 and because of the many emigrants who have left, but who still maintain ties with Hong Kong.

LIMITED COMPETITION. By the mid-1970s it was apparent that Hong Kong Telephone had grown too rapidly and was burdened by heavy debt. In 1975 the government had to approve a 30 percent increase in charges for local services to increase profits, a move that prompted the government to appoint an independent commission to investigate Hong Kong Telephone's financial situation, expansion plans, and service quality. In 1981 the government restructured the group. That year it granted a locally registered company, Cable and Wireless, a twenty-five-year franchise (without a control scheme) to provide international services. The government held 20 percent of the share capital of the new company. In the following years, the government gradually reduced the amount of shares held. Later, the whole group was restructured, and Hong Kong Telecom International was established to replace Cable and Wireless.

Toward the end of the 1980s the government was under public pressure to introduce competition into the telecommunications sector. It thus granted suppliers nonexclusive licenses to provide radio pager and mobile radiophone services. The demand for these services grew rapidly immediately after their introduction. In 1988 the government announced a landmark decision inviting tenders for the installation of a second fixed-line network. This network was allowed to provide both cable television and local nontelephone communication services, in competition with some of the services offered by Hong Kong Telephone. In 1993 the government decided to license three new entrants into the local telephone service market after 1995, when the local franchise expired. Using the second network, the cable television company will be allowed to offer a competing local telephone service. Part of this second network is now in place, but at present only cable television service is offered. Besides the cable television company, the other two licensees are well-established providers of paging services and mobile radiophone services.

The control scheme that applies to Hong Kong Telecom's local, but not its international, services is controversial, particularly because it derives most of its profit from the international services. By the end of 1992 the development fund was depleted and the profit fell below the permitted level, raising issues about whether international users were unfairly subsidizing local users. In response to public debate about the regulatory mechanism, the government announced that it would revise the control scheme to replace profit regulation with price regulation. However, such regulation not only institutionalizes cross-subsidization between the services, it will probably also help Hong Kong Telecom deter entry by competitors after its franchise expires. The price of local service has always been low. Introducing the price cap sends out a strong signal that the incumbent can sustain low prices in the future and forces future entrants to provide multiple products to cross-subsidize the local telephone service. The extent of these cross-subsidies could be quite large in the beginning, given the high cost of matching the incumbent's extensive network.

Meanwhile, Hong Kong Telecom has announced that it will offer multimedia services through its present network and has applied for a cable television license. This move comes at a small cost, because the existing network is almost entirely digital and is thus technologically ready to launch such new services. Research on introducing video on demand is also well under way. Clearly Hong Kong Telecom is positioning itself to enter new markets and, in doing so, to protect its local telephone business.

In view of the industry's increasing complexity and the rapid advances in technology, the government established a regulatory body, the Office of the Telecommunications Authority, to monitor developments. Although Hong Kong Telecom has agreed to give other licensees access to its network, access charges and such technical details as number portability have been under negotiation for more than a year without nearing resolution.

Gas Services: Private, but Noncompetitive

Gas services are completely private. Commercial, industrial, and domestic customers use three types of fuels: Towngas, liquid petroleum gas, and kerosene. An unregulated monopoly that is not protected by a franchise provides Towngas (gas manufactured from naphtha), however, its high capital cost is a deterrent to entry by competitors. Liquid petroleum gas is a mixture of butane and propane, a by-product of the petroleum distillation process. Private oil companies supply it in two forms: in portable cylinders for individual customers and from installed pipes connected to central storage for small communities. Only a small number of industrial users use kerosene.

SINGLE COMPANY SUPPLIES TOWNGAS, BUT MANY SUPPLIERS OF LIQUID PETROLEUM GAS. Hong Kong and China Gas manufactures Towngas at two stations, an older and smaller one in Kowloon, and a newer and larger one in Tai Po in the New Territories. Hong Kong and China Gas is a completely private company; its shares are traded on the Hong Kong Stock Exchange. The company does not operate under a government franchise or control scheme. In 1992 the company had 910,000 industrial, commercial, and domestic customers and supplied 63 percent of all gas consumed locally. The distribution network consists of underground, submarine pipes that cross the harbor to serve Hong Kong Island.

Hong Kong and China Gas has grown rapidly in the past two decades, particularly during the mid-1970s to the mid-1980s. During this period the government was rapidly building new towns in the New Territories. Hong Kong and China Gas took advantage of this opportunity to extend its distribution network to the new towns and quickly increased its customer base. In 1975 total output was a mere 1.6 million gigajoules, but by 1985 it had increased to 8.0 million gigajoules, with increases primarily in the domestic and commercial sectors. The number of customers increased sevenfold during the same period.

All the major oil companies import liquid petroleum gas. It is supplied in two forms. The most popular form is 15-kilogram pressurized, portable cylinders, and dozens of dealers supply it in this form. Customers living in older buildings and in areas with a low population density rely on this form of supply. The other form of supply, which is less hazardous, comes from pipes connected to a central storage facility that serves small communities. This form is used in the large residential estates that are not covered by the Towngas network. Given the fire hazard of cylinder liquid petroleum gas, the government has encouraged real estate developers to install central liquid petroleum gas storage when they build new residential blocks. In 1983, 90 percent of liquid petroleum gas consumed was supplied in cylinders, but by 1992, only 63 percent of liquid petroleum gas was supplied in this form.

DIFFERENT MARKET NICHES FOR TOWNGAS AND LIQUID PETROLEUM GAS. The demand for Towngas depends largely on the extent of its network. Real estate developers can choose the type and form of fuel to be used. In urban areas, including new towns, Towngas is typically the choice, given the existence of underground Towngas pipes. The growth of new towns has boosted Towngas consumption, but many suburban areas are not covered by the Towngas network. If a development project is large, the installation of a central storage facility can be incorporated into the overall estate design. If a project is small, cylinder liquid petroleum gas may be the only feasible alternative. Thus, from the user's point of view, the different types of fuel do not compete directly with one another. Of course, if Towngas is much more expensive than cylinder liquid petroleum gas, some users might switch. New housing that uses Towngas will then be viewed unfavorably. At this level, one could argue that some competition exists between Towngas and liquid petroleum gas, but to the extent that competition is not direct, obvious questions arise about the possibility of collusion and anticompetitive pricing. Nevertheless, because fuel accounts for a small percentage of household expenditures, the public has not paid much attention to these issues.

Conclusion

The government has adopted a range of approaches to the organizational arrangements for providing Hong Kong's key infrastructure services. Rather than imposing a single approach to the development and administration of these services, it has allowed them to develop as best suits the economy's needs and resources. Whether services are nearly private (gas, telecommunications), under government supervision (buses, railways), or very much a government responsibility (water, roads) depends on what the government perceives as serving the economy's best interests. While this approach has not always been successful, the government recognizes the benefits of privatization and is gradually opening some sectors to more competition.

In recent years several important developments have occurred in Hong Kong's infrastructure sectors. In 1995, for example, local telephony was deregulated. Although the government licensed three new companies, generating considerable excitement, the three companies have not yet committed to providing local services. Instead, they are offering long distance services in direct competition with Hong Kong Telecom, which holds a legal franchise on long distance services. The services the new entrants offer are identical to those Hong Kong Telecom offers, but their rates are much lower for most calls. The government has not found these services to violate its agreement with Hong Kong Telecom, and there is talk of terminating the company's franchise early. Should that occur, the government might have to pay compensation to Hong Kong Telecom.

Hong Kong Telecom faces other threats as well. Although it has experimented with video on demand and understands the system's technological requirements, it has put the service on hold because it cannot offer it at a competitive price. Renting a movie at a video store costs about HK$ 25, and users are unwilling to pay much more for video on demand movies. In addition, as the delivery of a movie ties up users' telephone lines for about ninety minutes, the system could generate considerable congestion. The potential demise of voice mail is another threat. As the number of Internet users continues to grow exponentially, users may start using the Internet to transmit calls.

As concerns gas provision, some are worried that Hong Kong and China Gas, the producer of Towngas, is becoming an overwhelming monopoly. The company holds a monopoly on the market for manufactured gas and almost controls the market for piped gas because of falling demand for liquid petroleum gas. However, if electricity is considered to be a substitute, the company controls less than half of the market. As a result the government has ignored calls to regulate Hong Kong and China Gas.

In electricity provision, the public is increasingly dissatisfied with CLP's routine applications for price hikes. Another issue is that although the company has clearly overextended its capacity, it continues to move ahead with massive expansion plans. The recent slowdown in demand is not temporary, however. It stems from the relocation of manufacturing out of Hong Kong, reduced demand from China, and general market saturation. Yet because of rate of return control, which amounts to a rate of return guarantee, capacity expansion is directly translated into price increases.

4

Infrastructure Geared to International Economic Activity: Singapore

Lee Tsao Yuan

The key lesson that emerges from Singapore's successful history of infrastructure development is the importance of government vision, leadership, and commitment. To address the economy's problems—a low standard of living and a dearth of employment opportunities for a rapidly growing population—Singapore's government articulated a broad national policy of economic expansion and then forged the institutional forces, financial resources, and public consensus needed to implement it effectively. This policy was based on government recognition of three economic facts as follows:

- That the entrepot trade, the traditional mainstay of economic activity, would not be enough to stimulate economic growth and new employment. The government thus pursued an outward-oriented policy of industrialization and export activity and let the private sector lead the effort.
- That industrialization would require foreign investment. To attract investment, the government created a robust economic infrastructure (the port and airport) and durable industrial infrastructure (industrial estates). These investments made Singapore a hub for trade and business activity, as well as an export competitor in world markets.
- That prudent budgetary policies were required to finance the infrastructure. Rather than create and maintain infrastructure with deficit financing, the government wanted most projects to be self-funding and to generate budgetary surpluses.

In many ways, the government acted like an entrepreneur. It assessed opportunities and assumed the risks of inherent in infrastructure projects. These projects required a large commitment of public funds, and success was not guaranteed. Fortunately for Singapore, the investment in infrastructure development paid off handsomely.

This vision and strategy enabled Singapore to build a physical infrastructure that now has a solid reputation worldwide. The port and airport are consistently ranked among the best in the world, and Singapore is beginning to export its expertise in developing and managing industrial estates to other developing economies. Telecommunications were also was an integral element of the infrastructure strategy and achievements were impressive; however, this chapter does not cover the telecommunications sector.

Development Fostered by Strategic Planning, Implementation, and Financing

The government used two strategic planning documents as blueprints for the economic expansion. The Winsemius Report recommended that Singapore pursue industrialization; the State

The author is grateful to Bhanoji Rao and Augusto Santos for comments on an earlier draft and to Gwee Wee-Chen for research assistance.

of Singapore Development Plan, 1961–64, acknowledged that infrastructure development was the key to industrialization. In addition, the government introduced prudent financing mechanisms and granted financial autonomy for service-generating statutory boards. To promote its views, the government

- Set up statutory boards in relevant ministries, giving them financial and policymaking autonomy for developing and managing infrastructure projects
- Established a public sector agency—the Economic Development Board (EDB)—to spearhead industrialization and attract foreign investment
- Created several industrial estates, the most prominent of which is in Jurong
- Mandated that the statutory boards charge for services rendered, thereby enabling them to generate operating surpluses to fund their development expenditures
- Mandated compulsory savings by employers and employees, a percentage of which the government initially used to fund housing and other infrastructure projects
- Maintained high domestic capital formation by separating public and private investment activity, devoting public investment to service provision and private investment to profit making activities.

The Push toward Industrialization

The Winsemius Report was named after the leader of a United Nations team that visited Singapore in 1960 and 1961 to assess its economic planning. At that time the main problem facing the economy was the low level of manufacturing, which accounted for just 14 percent of gross domestic product. Of 471,000 economically active people, only 61,000 were engaged in manufacturing. The report supported the government's conclusion that rapid industrialization was critical for creating employment opportunities.

The report also determined that Singapore would need to provide 214,000 new jobs between 1960 and 1970, of which 78,000 would be primary jobs, largely in export industries. The report advocated a ten-year industrial program and incorporated recommendations about the role of market expansion, trade policies, industrial relations, and capital investment; the development of domestic manufacturing capabilities; the promotion of foreign cooperation; and the parts labor, entrepreneurs, and the government should play in the program. The report also supported two crucial elements of Singapore's industrialization planning: the establishment of the EDB as the lead agency for industrialization, and the establishment of industrial estates, especially in Jurong. These industrial estates—with their prepared factory sites, transportation and communication networks, and utilities—have been central to Singapore's economic success.

The Pursuit of Domestically Financed, Self-Funded Infrastructure

The State of Singapore Development Plan, 1961–64, recommended that the government accelerate industrialization by significantly improving and expanding the country's infrastructure. Even though one of the government's main objectives was to improve social services, the plan merely called for not allowing services to deteriorate. The plan allocated more than half of the stipulated development expenditures to economic development, with most going to establishing the EDB, developing the industrial estates, and upgrading public utilities.

The plan also identified four sources of infrastructure financing: loans, revenue surpluses, foreign grants (a small amount), and transfers from government accounts to a development fund. The significant point about these provisions was that the plan called for raising almost half of all loans domestically, and several infrastructure sectors—electricity, water, gas, and certain telecommunications and port projects—were to be self-funding. This provision for domestic financing and self-funding was an important element in Singapore's economic development, eventually accounting for more than half of all development expenditures.

The plan recognized that economic prosperity would not result if the government had to rely on external financing for extended periods. The government's policy has been to finance infrastructure with domestic funds—both revenue and loans—and to avoid subsidizing industrial infrastructure (with the exception of social infrastructure such as housing, education, health, and public transport, which it has subsidized heavily). Two factors have enabled Singapore to implement extensive infrastructure with domestic financing. The first is the government's strict policy of budgetary controls and prudence. This policy has filtered down to the agencies and statutory boards, many of which are mandated by the government to charge for services rendered. The government's fiscal policy also mandated compulsory savings by employers and employees, who are required to contribute a percentage of their savings to the Central Providence Fund.

The Role of Strong Leaders and Institutions

Singapore's industrialization and economic development benefited from capable leadership: a visionary prime minister, strong finance ministers, and dedicated civil servants. Together the leadership established a public sector ethos based on efficiency, meritocracy, and intolerance of corruption. Some of the best minds in Singapore were recruited into the public sector by, for example, awarding scholarships to prestigious overseas universities in exchange for a promise to serve in the government. If not for the efficiency of the public administration, infrastructure in Singapore would not have developed so well.

Strong government institutions also facilitated implementation of infrastructure projects. One important move was giving the responsibility for developing and managing infrastructure to quasi-government agencies—the statutory boards—under the overall supervision of their respective ministries. The government granted these boards significant autonomy in establishing financial policies, recruiting personnel, and allocating line items in their budgets. Along with this autonomy came responsibility for the bottom line. Their drive for efficiency enabled the boards to turn in operating surpluses and to use these surpluses to finance capital expenditures.

The government's most important organizational move was to establish public sector agencies, first the EDB and later the Jurong Town Corporation (JTC), to guide industrialization. Both agencies were one-stop centers for creating the engine behind industrialization: the industrial estate of Jurong. They quickly proved to be effective coordinators of infrastructure projects, both in providing public support during the planning phases and in obtaining private support during construction. The EDB is also responsible for attracting foreign investment.

Focus on Sectors with Global Potential

Three infrastructure components have been central to Singapore's economic success: the industrial estates, the port, and the airport. The government developed the industrial estates as an engine for attracting foreign investment. It created the EDB (and later the JTC) to develop the estates, and chose Jurong as the centerpiece industrial estate.

Singapore is also ideally located for exports, a fact its ports have exploited. Key to developing the Port of Singapore into a full service port was the establishment of the Port of Singapore Authority. The port authority improved the port's efficiency by constructing a container complex, computerizing shipping and cargo handling schedules, providing training for port administrators and labor, and generating operational surpluses to finance its development projects.

Finally, the government built an international airport to serve business travelers and tourists.

Industrial Estates: The Engine of Industrialization

The Winsemius Report and the development plan supported the government's view that vibrant industrial infrastructure was necessary to attract private capital, particularly foreign capital, into Singapore's manufacturing sector. The key industrial facility was the industrial estate. Industrial estates are groups of industries that are located according to their infrastructure and resource needs. The government encouraged industrialists to locate their businesses in industrial estates by providing ready-made factories, transportation and communication links, and utility hookups.

The most prominent industrial estate is in Jurong. The EDB quickly got Jurong up and running by acquiring land and resettling residents, by contracting construction to private companies, and by providing an array of social amenities that encouraged employees' families to settle in the local town. Jurong immediately had an excellent takeup rate, prompting the board to devolve its management and operational authority over the industrial estate to the JTC. The corporation has consistently generated a net operating surplus, which it is using to upgrade existing complexes and to build new ones to sustain Singapore's competitive edge. It has also begun exporting its expertise to neighboring countries and has recently entered into joint ventures to build industrial estates overseas.

Industrial estates are located in several regions throughout Singapore. Concentrating them geographically has several advantages. First, they can share services and facilities, such as telecommunications; waste disposal facilities; electric, gas, and water supplies; and sea, road, and rail transport. Second, industries can be zoned according to environmental considerations, with land-intensive and heavily polluting factories (such as sawmills) located away from densely populated areas and close to ports, and labor-intensive, nonpolluting factories (such as garment manufacturing facilities) close to urban centers and pools of workers. Third, prepared land sites with ready connections to utility supplies and a transportation network in place, or even ready-built factories, significantly reduce the time required to begin production, an important incentive for industrialists to locate in Singapore.

Jurong: A Testament to the Government's Flexibility and Entrepreneurship

Several factors made Jurong the ideal choice as Singapore's major industrial site. First, it has plentiful, reasonably flat land, along with deepwater access and a well-protected harbor. Thus the water supply is adequate for industries that require water and it is the best location for polluting industries, especially those that need a waterfront location. Second, Jurong is only thirteen miles from the main commercial port installations. Road connections could thus be provided at reasonable cost. Third, adequate land meant that Jurong could be developed as a town, complete with housing, social, and recreational amenities. Finally, as the government already owned most of the land, acquiring land and resettling residents would not pose an insurmountable problem.

Jurong was the only waterfront area in Singapore that "possessed all the necessary conditions for development as an integrated town with the economic base centered around an industrial estate of considerable magnitude" (UN 1963, p. 34). The Winsemius Report recommended establishing an integrated township that would consist of about 16,000 acres, significantly larger than the 9,000 acres a team of Japanese experts had proposed earlier.

The lead industrialization agency, the EDB, had three strategic considerations in mind during the early phases of the Jurong project: location, land acquisition, and ownership. To achieve logistical efficiency and reduce transportation, distribution, and production costs, the EDB gave great weight to surveying, planning, and zoning. For example, it integrated related industries, such as grain silos, feed mills, vegetable oil plants, and sugar refineries, into one unit and located them near the wharf. Another group consisted of industries that produced such chemicals as caustic soda, chlorine, pulp and paper, calcium carbide, and PVC and were located near the canal. A third group comprised all plywood and timber industries, which were situated near the river to permit efficient log transport and handling. The EDP also grouped together parts and components manufacturing and engineering industries and placed steel mills, iron ore loading and unloading terminals, and shipbuilding and shipbreaking enterprises next to each other. In addition, the EDB provided for the expansion of various industrial complexes and the entry of new industries into each integrated group.

Another issue facing the EDB was land acquisition and squatter clearance. Even though the land was rural and primarily state owned, some land still had to be acquired and some residents resettled. Although resettlement was expedited by the development of resettlement villages, for example, at Lim Chu Kang, land development could proceed only as fast as squatter resettlement, which often posed problems.

The third consideration was institutional arrangements for developing an industrial township from swampland and marshes at a speed that could cater to the urgent need to create jobs. As stated in the EDB's 1964 annual report (EDB 1964, p. 28): "One of the most urgent and complex challenges posed by industrial development at Jurong was the necessity to provide social amenities for Residential Neighborhood I." At that time, the Housing and Development Board was responsible for building the apartments in Jurong. Work on building more than 200 apartments began in 1963, and by 1964 these had been completed and offered for rent. But the takeup rate was slow given the absence of such social amenities as schools, health clinics, and markets. In October 1964 the government decided to transfer ownership and management of the housing units to the EDB. This meant that the board had overall responsibility for Jurong New Town, including the industrial estate. The EDB launched a program was launched in the latter half of 1964 to provide basic social amenities as quickly as possible, and by year's end a post office, health clinics, a primary school, a police station, a bank, and residential telephone services were in place in Residential Neighborhood I. The EDB's staff increased from 80 at the end of 1961 to 685 by the end of 1967, in line with the extra work involved in promoting and facilitating investment.

Two aspects of the implementation of the Jurong project illustrate why Singapore's industrialization was so successful. First, the EDB did not carry out the actual construction work, but awarded contracts to the private sector. The most important priority in 1961 was access, and the EDB awarded a contract for constructing a new access road in October. The project also required construction of a causeway across the Jurong River, which had the added benefit of turning the river's upper reaches into a reservoir and a potential source of water for industry. Earthworks were required to level a hill to provide a site for the steel rolling mill, and shoreline land had to be reclaimed for shipbreaking yards. The reclamation of large areas of prawn ponds was also required to facilitate access and to develop the proposed harbor works. By contracting to private companies, the EDB avoided construction bottlenecks and could go with the companies that offered that most competitive prices.

Another notable aspect of the implementation process was the government's institutional flexibility during industrialization. By 1968 it realized that the industrialization drive needed stimulating and had to be more vigorous, and that this effort would unduly burden the EDB's administrative capacity. Thus the government set up the JTC in June 1968. The JTC was responsible for providing facilities to the industrial estates and sites and for promoting the well-being of the people working in them and living in the area. The JTC strove to make Jurong fully self-contained as a working and residential area (box 4–1) and assumed the management of other, smaller industrial estates. One of the offshoots of this decision was the spectacular influx of foreign investment into Singapore in 1969, especially in oil rig fabricating and electronics industries. The demand for waterfront land for shipbuilding and repair and for timber industries also increased sharply.

The change in institutional authority was beneficial in other ways. When the JTC took over from the EDB, about 3,400 acres of land had been developed in Jurong since 1961. By the end of 1969 another 1,195 acres had been developed, bringing the total to 4,595 acres, an increase of 35 percent. The accelerated pace of land development continued, and by 1971, 6,578 acres had been developed. In December

---

Box 4–1. The JTC Made Jurong Town Livable and Prosperous

Until the JTC's creation in June 1968, amenities in Jurong were meager, and recreational and social activities were such that "life in Jurong cannot be other than spartan" (*JTC Annual Report* 1968/69, JTC 1969, p. 2). The JTC strove to improve living conditions, and by the end of 1968 all the apartments and nearly all the shops were occupied. A waiting list even developed. The JTC then began enlarging the town and building executive apartments. By 1972 Jurong was a fully self-contained town with a population of 32,000. Amenities included an olympic size swimming pool, tennis courts, a children's center, an air conditioned movie theater, and Singapore's first drive-in movie theater. Other amenities included tourist attractions, such as the Jurong Bird Park; Jurong Hill Park; and the 700-acre Jurong Park, with a golf course and Japanese garden, plus a sports stadium and Chinese garden under construction.

Thus by the early 1970s Jurong was a self-contained, industrial, satellite town, with the largest industrial estate in Singapore, its own deepwater port, and a sizable residential complex. The JTC moved into its own premises, Jurong Town Hall, which was completed in 1974. One could now say that the first phase of building Singapore's industrial infrastructure was complete.

1968 a waiting list for land appeared for the first time. From a total of 170 factories, including 116 in production at the time of the takeover, the number of factories had more than doubled by 1970 to 380, including 271 in production (table 4-1). By this time the JTC was spending considerable time and effort looking for new sites for industrial development, because Jurong was already reaching its limits.

Land development, the construction of new industrial estates, and the enlargement of existing ones continued throughout the 1970s. The JTC also improved and enlarged Jurong Port and Jurong Marine Base.[1] During the 1974 oil crisis and subsequent world recession, foreign investment inflow into Singapore dropped significantly, but work on industrial development was able to continue, thus supply was adequate to cope with the higher than expected demand of the 1978 boom.

Table 4–1. Number and Operational Status of Factories in Jurong, 1968–78 (cumulative as of end of year)

Year	Factories in production	Factories being planned or constructed	Total
1968[a]	116	54	170
1968	153	77	230
1969	202	120	322
1970	271	109	380
1971	337	95	432
1972	430	77	507
1973	504	143	647
1974	543	225	768
1975	613	205	818
1976	675	203	878
1977	818	187	1,005
1978	902	220	1,122

a. As of May 31, 1968.
Source: JTC (various years).

---

1.   The first berth of Jurong Port was completed in 1965. When the JTC was formed, Jurong Port had five deepwater berths, three of which were equipped with fully integrated bulk-handling equipment, and adequate warehousing facilities. Two-thirds of the cargo imported through the port was in the form of bulk cargo. The port handled more than 800,000 tons in 1968 and by 1970 had surpassed 1 million tons. A smaller port, Jurong Marine Base, was constructed specifically as a forward supply base for the offshore oil exploration industry, which boomed in Southeast Asia in the late 1960s and 1970s.

The success of Singapore's industrialization is most evident in the context of land use. The JTC works within the framework of the country master plan, which was the responsibility of another statutory board, the Urban Redevelopment Authority. Work on the first master plan started in 1965. It is by working within this plan, with active interagency cooperation, that land development in Singapore is orderly and complementary.

As noted earlier, the Singapore government used sound fiscal policies to finance industrialization. The financing of development expenditures at the level of the statutory board is best illustrated by the JTC. Most funding came from government loans. Total government loans outstanding at the end of 1969 were S\$ 190.7 million, including a loan of S\$ 33.4 million made during that year. In addition to government loans, loans came from external agencies, such as the Commonwealth Development Corporation and the Asian Development Bank, which provided funding in 1971 for the expansion of Jurong Port.

A second, smaller source of funding was operating surpluses. The JTC achieved a net operating surplus from the beginning from its revenues from factory tenancies, land leases, apartment rentals, wharf tariffs, and the premium payable on leased lands. The net surplus from June to December 1968 was US\$2.7 million, which had increased to US\$26.7 million by 1974. In 1975 the level of net operating surplus, while still positive, declined for the first time, and in 1976 the JTC had an operating deficit of US\$11 million. The main reason for the deficit was the adverse global economy, which slowed the allocation of new land and factory space and reduced income from port tariffs. With the recovery in the world economy, the demand for industrial land picked up, as did the volume of cargo the port handled. The JTC has been able to achieve operating surpluses in most years since that time.

The JTC has also been profitable because it has avoided the problems of empty factories and vacant sites by maintaining a good takeup rate. Working closely with the EDB and the Trade Development Board, the JTC has planned its facilities in line with anticipated demand. During recessions it has given industrialists rebates and reduced rents, and it has also implemented policies to keep out speculators. Unlike private developers, however, profit is not the JTC's sole objective. For example, the JTC holds about 10 percent of the stock of ready industrial land and 7 to 8 percent of ready-built factories for potential investors, which is a heavy financial commitment. The advantage of this is that the JTC can meet investors' demand for available factory space, a point in Singapore's favor when investors are scouting for locations for their enterprises.

Singapore Stays Ahead by Building and Upgrading Industrial Estates and Exporting Expertise

At the same time that the JTC was establishing itself as a major industrial force, work continued on developing smaller industrial estates at other locations (box 4–2). Some of these are more specialized than Jurong. For example, the Kallang Park Industrial Estate, situated on the Kallang River, is used for marine industries such as shipbuilding and ship repair; the Kranji/Sungei Kadut Industrial Estate was developed to accommodate such industries as sawmilling and woodworking; and the Singapore Science Park is the flagship industrial infrastructure project for high-tech and research and development industries. Established in 1981, Singapore Science Park currently caters to ninety-five companies in information technology, microelectronics, electronics systems, materials technology, manufacturing technology, biotechnology, medical sciences, and food and agrotechnology. It is located within the Technology Corridor, where a high concentration of high-tech companies and support industries are situated.

The beginning of the 1990s saw new trends in industrial estates. The rapid development and industrialization of the countries around Singapore has prompted the JTC to improve its products and services to remain competitive. As a result it is rejuvenating old factories and building higher quality ready-built facilities, facilities targeted at specific industries, and customized facilities. One such project is the International Business Park, a 40-hectare, integrated commercial, office, and industrial complex

---

Box 4-2. The Ten-Year Master Plan Offered New Directions for Industrial Development

By 1980 the JTC was managing nineteen industrial estates covering 7,225 hectares. More than 2,000 companies were operating in these estates, which employed 71 percent of Singapore's manufacturing work force. The government recognized that in accordance with its overall macroeconomic thrust of upgrading technology and value added, it had to make changes in the design and quality of industrial infrastructure and support services. The JTC formulated a ten-year master plan for 1980–90 that contained new directions for development, including the following:

- Decentralizing industrial estates. The JTC built smaller, more aesthetically pleasing industrial parks to house modern multistory factories near population centers and housing estates. This configuration not only reduced transportation requirements, but also encouraged maximum labor participation in industry, particularly among women.
- Improving commercial services and social amenities in major industrial estates. To increase the percentage of the labor force living near their place of work, which already ranged from 34 to 56 percent, the JTC developed more commercial services and social amenities.
- Applying physical and town planning techniques for the location and layout of industrial estates. To ensure optimal use of limited land resources, the JTC implemented sophisticated town planning techniques, including providing more open, green areas and implementing energy saving measures in existing and new industrial buildings.
- Providing facilities for special industries. The JTC emphasized the development of industrial facilities for skill- and technology-oriented industries, including an international petrochemical manufacturing and distribution complex at the Southern Islands and a Science and Technology Park adjacent to the National University of Singapore for research and development companies.
- Setting up estates for resettled and small, modern industries. These estates catered to small industries affected by urban redevelopment and resettlement programs and supported the development of small, modern industries.
- Providing training facilities. While other agencies in Singapore were responsible for establishing and managing such training institutes as the German-Singapore Training Institute, the French-Singapore Training Institute, the Japan-Singapore Training Institute, and other joint government-industry training institutes, the JTC provided land and buildings to upgrade the technical skills of industrial workers.

---

that will enable tenants to conduct all research and development, design, production, marketing, and distribution functions in one building. Located at Jurong East, the park will be a well-developed town with social and recreational amenities linked to the city and the airport by expressways and the subway.

A second new direction is the establishment of industrial estates overseas. During the past twenty-five years the JTC has acquired ample expertise in planning, constructing, and managing industrial estates and integrated townships and is making this expertise available to other countries as they develop industrial estates. A subsidiary of the JTC, Jurong Environmental Engineering (JEE), was established in 1980 to provide consultant services. At first these services were limited to pollution prevention, energy conservation, engineering, water treatment, and landscape architecture, but they have recently been expanded to include planning, developing, and managing industrial estates.

One of the JEE's better known overseas projects is the Batam Industrial Park on Batam Island in Indonesia. The JTC planned the park as a self-contained estate with its own infrastructure, commercial center, dormitories, and social and recreational facilities. The development of the first phase of 110 hectares began in early 1990 and the first factories were operating by 1991. By early 1997 eighty-five companies owned by investors from various countries were operating, employing about 54,000 workers. The second phase, which covers 100 hectares, is currently being developed.

The overseas projects in which the JTC is involved follow a specific pattern. First, the JEE holds an equity stake in the company that develops the industrial estate. Because the JEE is a private company, it has flexibility that JTC, as a statutory board, does not. Second, a local joint venture partner, such as the Salim Group in the Batam industrial estate, is involved. Third, Singapore companies have adopted a consortium approach to projects that involve large capital expenditures and long gestation periods.

A Vital Port: Still Growing

One of the most important factors in Singapore's economic success is its location. It was this locale at the southern tip of the Straits of Malacca, a strategic position at the center of the maritime trade routes between Europe and Asia, that led the United Kingdom to found Singapore and to its prosperity as a port of call under British rule. As entrepot trade in rubber, tin, sugar, spices, and other natural resources from Southeast Asia flourished in exchange for industrial products from the West, Singapore developed as a major seaport. An efficient seaport infrastructure became vital to the national value chain. Eventually it became central to Singapore's economic life as the means of importing raw materials, other inputs, and consumer products for industry and exporting manufactured products. The port's role has evolved from being a major distribution hub and cargo port for the trans-shipment business to a total service port that uses sophisticated information technology to offer fast turnaround times at competitive rates. The Port of Singapore Authority (PSA), another example of the government's advanced thinking in infrastructure development, is responsible for this success.

INNOVATION AND PLANNING CENTRAL TO THE PSA'S SUCCESS. The PSA was established as a statutory board in 1964 to replace the Singapore Harbor Board at a time when Singapore's industrialization efforts were moving into high gear. The PSA has continually upgraded its port facilities, which because of the long lead times involved have often been ahead of anticipated demand. To improve port efficiency and economic competitiveness, the PSA initiated four port development strategies: containerization, computerization, skills development, and self-financing. The PSA is sustaining its competitive edge by planning investments in new port services, including freight futures, ship management, and ship brokering.

In 1966 the PSA made a landmark decision to construct a container complex. At the time the technique of handling cargo with containers and container ships was still relatively new, and few ports had such facilities. Japan was the only country in Asia to have container ports. The container terminal at East Lagoon was developed for an estimated S$70 million. It required such preparatory work as land reclamation, dredging, and wharf construction and the provision of such ancillary services as freight stations, transit sheds, a control tower, container servicing and repair facilities, a container marshaling yard, and hardstanding for open storage cargo.

Containerization proved to be a worthwhile risk. From 14,000 twenty-foot equivalent units in 1972, when the first three container berths were opened at the Tanjong Pagar Terminal, the volume of container traffic had passed the 1 million mark by 1982. The newest container terminal, Brani Terminal, began operating in December 1991 and is linked to the main port area by a four-lane causeway across the Keppel Channel. In 1996 the eighteen main berths and twelve feeder berths handled 13 million twenty-foot equivalent units of cargo.

In land- and labor-scarce Singapore, technology and automation have been regarded as critical for increasing operational efficiency and reducing costs. Computerization was introduced in 1967, when the PSA established a data processing department using a leased mainframe computer. The next phase was a logical extension of containerization. The first online information system for handling containers became operational in 1973. This sped up the process of locating containers and reduced the time port users had to wait to take delivery of their goods. Real-time computer applications also helped shipping companies and freight forwarders remain competitive by planning their tight schedules and monitoring their cargo movements.

The PSA has continuously introduced further computerization measures. For example, PORTNET is an electronics communications system that streamlines the flow of information among the maritime and trading communities and the relevant government agencies, for example, by enabling port users to submit declarations, plans, and manifests electronically. From 319 subscribers in 1989, PORTNET now has more than 1,500. A terminal operations system integrates, plans, and manages all container terminal operations through a central computer. An equivalent system is being developed for noncontainer gateways. Another computer system tracks and manages vessel movements in the Singapore Strait and within port waters and plans for the deployment of pilots, tugs, and launches to match job requirements with time, duration, difficulty, and priority. In the past five years the PSA has invested more than S$ 150 million in computer technology.

In line with increased automation and computerization is an ongoing effort to upgrade skills. The PSA's commemorative volume (PSA 1990, p. 92) contains a description:

Back in the 1950s, the very first machines to be introduced were simple mechanical aids such as forklifts. And even then, the introduction of these labor-saving devices met with some resistance from the dock workers who feared that the machines would rob them of their livelihood. It was a simple but important lesson which the PSA learned well. Educating the staff to accept change is as important as explaining the mechanics of how the technology works. Its training department now shoots its own videos so that potential users can be informed well in advance of the new technology to be implemented.

In 1990 the PSA's training department was upgraded to become the Singapore Port Institute, with an annual budget of S$ 6 million. The PSA has also taken such measures as introducing quality circles and a productivity suggestion scheme to improve productivity.

Computerization, automation, and skills development have reduced staffing needs despite the continuous increase in the volume of cargo handled. From the establishment of the PSA in 1964 to 1996, total cargo increased more than fifteenfold, from about 19 million tons to 314 million tons. During this time the number of staff increased from 11,316 in 1964 to a peak of 12,563 in 1965, but then fell systematically to reach 7,110 by 1996.

The PSA's ability to generate surpluses has contributed to its capacity to self-finance its development projects. With the exception of one World Bank loan of US$15 million and one Asian Development Bank loan of US$8.1 million, the PSA's capital expenditures have been almost entirely self-financed. As a result of its pricing strategy, the authority has consistently had an operating surplus that increased from S$ 1 million in 1964 to S$ 896 million in 1996. The PSA ensures that its tariff remains competitive so that its customers find using the port to be cost-effective. The PSA also strives to maintain a high level of service, and Singapore has established itself as one of the world's most efficient and productive container ports. Not only does computerization vastly improve efficiency, but the intensity of equipment used in Singapore's container terminals increases productivity. The main container berths are equipped with four quay cranes, whereas the norm is two cranes. This configuration creates fast turnaround and lower port charges.

The PSA continues to modernize and expand facilities. The PSA's current objective is to convert the port into a total service port in line with Singapore's economic and social development goals for the 1990s. It is continuing to invest in port facilities, such as the new nine-berth Brani Terminal, and is building a megacontainer terminal at Pasir Panjang. This latter project will involve four phases over thirty years and, when completed, will have about fifty container berths and an annual cargo handling capacity of up to 36 million twenty-foot equivalent units. Phase one, which involves reclaiming 129 hectares of land, began in 1994. In addition, the Keppel Distripark, a highly automated container freight station of 120,000 square meters, was completed in 1994. The recently opened Singapore Cruise Center is designed for luxury cruise liners and is part of the PSA-owned World Trade Center complex, which has shops, restaurants, exhibition halls, and other leisure-related activities. Other new developments introduced to enhance Singapore's role as a premier maritime center include freight futures, ship management, and ship brokering services.

The environment is also a priority item for the PSA. To ensure that port waters are as free of pollution as possible, PSA maintains a twenty-four-hour sea patrol on all anchorages and fairways in the port. An oil skimmer and a fleet of flotsam retrievers, debris collection boats, and garbage collection craft are deployed daily. The PSA has developed a model to predict the flow and spread of oil in the event of an oil spill. Finally, the authority has undertaking extensive landscaping and tree planting to create a greener, more pleasant port environment.

Airports: Developed to Meet Demand

The development of Singapore's airports has been dictated by supply and demand considerations: technological improvements in the size and capacity of airplanes on the supply side and the increasing requirements for air transport on the demand side. Singapore opened it first airport at Kallang in 1937. Despite runway extension and strengthening, by the early 1950s it was unable to handle the newer, four-engine airplanes. A new airport was built at Paya Lebar and opened in 1955. Throughout the 1960s the government made continual improvements to the Paya Lebar Airport, including extending the runway, constructing parking aprons for jet aircraft, and building a permanent passenger terminal to handle increased passenger movement. By the early 1970s, however, signs of strain were evident. One factor contributing to the rapid increase in passengers was the introduction of jumbo aircraft such as the Boeing 747 and the McDonnell Douglas DC-10. The terminal building had a capacity of 1 million passengers a year, but by 1972 arriving passengers alone surpassed that number. In 1975 the Paya Lebar Airport handled 4 million passenger movements.

A committee on airport development was formed in 1975. Its studies showed that the Paya Lebar Airport was not well suited to expansion because it would have required large-scale resettlement. Issues such as noise, safety, and land use were also primary concerns, and because Paya Lebar was near the city center, this would necessitate placing limits on the construction of tall buildings under flight paths, which would be an uneconomical use of land. Thus the site eventually selected for the second runway straddled a river and a decade-old public refuse dump. However, transforming it to withstand the weight of jumbo jets would not only present engineering problems, it would also take too long.

Therefore the committee recommended that Singapore build a new international airport. The location chosen was Changi, situated at the eastern tip of Singapore and about 20 kilometers from the city center. Building a new airport at Changi had several advantages. To begin with, Changi already had an airport that the Japanese had built during their occupation of Singapore in 1943–44 and that the British Royal Air Force had taken over and developed as its main base east of the Suez until the early 1970s. Thus land acquisition was not a problem, fewer families needed to be resettled, and the flight path would be over the sea, thereby reducing noise pollution. In addition, technological advances in soil treatment, consolidation, engineering, and mechanical construction meant that about half the total area of the new airport could be reclaimed from the sea.

Building Changi Airport was a monumental effort: more than sixteen organizations were involved in the first phase alone, including the Public Works Department, the PSA, the Department of Civil Aviation, and the Ministry of Communications. In addition to financial monitoring, project evaluation review was used to ensure efficient coordination of about 4,000 activities. Completing this phase in six years was no small feat, even by international standards.

When the airport opened in 1981, S$ 1.5 billion had been spent, of which S$ 1 billion was government expenditures and S$ 500 million came from private companies such as the Singapore Airlines group and Changi International Airport Services for the construction of their own facilities.

Increasing passenger and cargo traffic would have been difficult had Changi Airport not been built. From annual passenger movements of 4 million in 1975, Singapore's airports handled 23 million passengers in 1995. Air freight tonnage increased more than sixteenfold between 1975 and 1995.

The current plan for Changi Airport has been designed for projected capacity until 2012. By then two runways, three terminals, and supporting facilities will be able to accommodate 64 million passengers, 340,000 aircraft movements, and 4.28 million tons of cargo a year. The three-phase construction of the airport will allow the airport to grow gradually with the traffic. The second terminal opened in 1990. Expansion of both terminals is currently under way to maximize their capacity before construction begins on the third terminal, along with land reclamation to accommodate another runway and a fourth terminal building.

Conclusion

In many ways, the smooth course of Singapore's infrastructure development was the product of a confluence of unique factors: Singapore is a small city state with no rural economy; it had a relatively high per capita income at the beginning of industrialization; and it had developed a tradition of international commerce, as well as sound public administration and legal systems. In addition, political and social objectives after independence provided the necessary impetus for the belt-tightening measures required during the initial phase of industrialization.

Nevertheless, Singapore's experience does offer some universal lessons. The most useful one is the importance of good governance. Infrastructure development requires political leaders who are committed to achieving rapid economic progress. In addition, the public sector's ability to plan and implement infrastructure projects rests on careful attention to organization and staffing, so that efficiency, sound financial management, and intolerance of corruption become the cornerstones of infrastructure development, whether the public sector is directly or indirectly involved.

References

EDB (Economic Development Board). 1964. *Annual Report.* Singapore.

JTC (Jurong Town Corporation). 1969 and various years. *Annual Report.* Singapore.

PSA (Port of Singapore Authority). 1990. *A Port's Story, A Nation's Success.* Singapore.

UN (United Nations). 1963. "Industrial Report: Industrial Sites and Estates." New York.

Part II
Topics in Finance, Regulation, and Organization

5

Financing Japan's Infrastructure: A Blend of Gradualism and Diversity in Financial Instruments

Morio Kuninori

The national government, local governments, or public corporations have, directly or indirectly, financed most infrastructure in Japan. Government policy and financial incentives have guided private investment. The diversified configuration of financing allowed the Japanese government to play a pivotal role in sustaining infrastructure development, and hence Japan's high rates of economic growth from the 1950s through the 1980s.

To alleviate the burden on general tax revenues, the Japanese government undertook several measures. It created public corporations that charged user fees and issued corporate bonds to borrow from public and private financial institutions. It also established several special accounts for major infrastructure projects that were financed with user fees and earmarked taxes. The government adopted a restrictive policy toward issuing public bonds until the early 1970s. However, bond issuance for public works has since become an important financing instrument, especially during periods of general economic downturn.

The Fiscal Investment and Loan Program (FILP) has been a major device for financing Japanese infrastructure. The program takes funds from postal savings and social security pensions and funnels them to public corporations and private sector investment as interest bearing loans. The program has enabled the government to stimulate investment in infrastructure without directly increasing taxes and to provide capital to expand private investment through government financial institutions. The program was intended to ensure accountability. Because public corporations have to repay the loans with interest, they are forced to pursue profitability, and because government institutions channel funds to the private sector, the public sector has a vehicle for monitoring the direction and efficiency of investment in infrastructure. In reality, however, some public corporations have often failed to meet this accountability criterion, because certain types of infrastructure, which should have been paid for from general tax revenues, are simply unprofitable. Also, a recent surge of funds from the FILP has sparked debate about the appropriate size and organization of the program's institutions and of the program itself. As a result, the system has been undergoing administrative reforms, although a final framework has yet to be implemented.

The most pressing current policy issue is whether strong government control over infrastructure financing is still needed to ensure achievement of the country's economic policy goals. The recent growth in private financing of construction and operation of certain types of infrastructure

The author is grateful for research assistance from Hideaki Tomita and Kimiko Hanabusa. The author is also indebted to Iwan Azis, Kenjiro Kobayashi, Ashoka Mody, Prathap Ramanajuan, Tatsuo Takahashi, and Hirofumi Uzawa for their helpful comments. The opinions expressed are solely those of the author and do not express the views of the Japan Development Bank.

shows that Japan is reaching a more pragmatic stage in the configuration of financing. The ongoing administrative reforms at the various levels of the policymaking processes stress the importance of introducing market-based criteria in the construction of infrastructure without sacrificing the quality and coverage of infrastructure services.

This chapter first identifies the various funding sources for Japanese infrastructure, discussing both their strengths and limitations, and then describes the use of these sources in different infrastructure sectors.

The Diversity of Funding Sources

The notion of public works or infrastructure only became well established in Japan after World War II (Miyazaki 1962). In 1946 public works appeared for the first time as a unified general account in the national budget. Since then their supply-side effects as social overhead capital and their demand-side effects as an economic stimulant have played an important role in Japanese economic policy debates. Spending for national public works grew markedly during reconstruction to fill the gap between insufficient social overhead capital and private productive capital.

The bulk of infrastructure financing in Japan comes from the national government and from municipalities through the national government. The government must strike a balance between fiscal and social policies objectives as it pursues infrastructure development. While taking into account social objectives such as the environmental ramifications of project construction and operations, an important concern has been taxpayers' opposition to assuming an excessive financial burden for infrastructure financing. A configuration of various sources of financing—public corporations, special accounts, public borrowing through bond issues, and the FILP—has enabled the government to pursue its policy objectives, while at the same time limiting demands on general revenues (see box 5–1).

Financial liberalization in the private sector since the mid-1980s has affected how infrastructure projects will be funded in the future. Several concerns have been raised about the sustainability of some financing components and the need for others. These concerns include

- Whether the system of special accounts funded through user fees and earmarked taxes should be retained
- Whether bond issuance has crowded out the private sector
- Whether the FILP can compete with other sources of funding as interest rate differentials narrow.

Box 5–1. Sources of Public Financing of Japan's Infrastructure

Entity	*Source*
National government	General account
	Special accounts (user fees and earmarked taxes, transfers from several accounts)
	National bonds (construction and deficit financing)
	FILP
	Other (public stock sales)
Local government and private financial institutions	National government
	Local bonds (FILP)
	Local taxes (general account and earmarked)
Public corporations	General account
	Corporate bonds
	FILP
	Bonds and loans from private financial institutions

Charging for Infrastructure: Public Corporations and Special Accounts

To ease the budget constraints facing the national and local governments, Japan established public corporations to assume some of the burden for financing and constructing infrastructure, as well as several special accounts to finance major projects with user fees and earmarked taxes. The public corporations included the Aichi Irrigation Public Corporation, established in 1955; the Forest Development Corporation and the Japan Highway Public Corporation, both set up in 1956; the Tokyo Expressway Public Corporation, established in 1959; and the Agricultural Land Development Public Corporation, established in 1974. Public corporations could issue their own bonds and borrow from the private sector.

The special accounts include ones for specific land improvements (1957), road improvement (1958), flood control (1960), and harbor improvement (1961).[1] These special accounts effectively enabled the government to target fees and taxes at major projects; however, critics have noted that special accounts may limit the government's fiscal flexibility. The major sources of revenue earmarked for infrastructure expenditures include a gasoline tax for road improvement and three-quarters of an automobile weight tax for road construction (these two categories make up 90 percent of the national budget for the road sector). An aviation fuel tax is targeted at airport improvement, and a tax is imposed on consumers to increase the generation capacity of electric power plants to contribute to the construction of public works in surrounding areas.

User fees go toward the construction and maintenance of certain infrastructure facilities and are, for the most part, not imposed on consumers as a means of deterring overuse. Fees are directed to the special accounts for major infrastructure projects. User fees provide the only avenue for cost recovery in some sectors, such as water supply, and are used to supplement funding in other sectors, for instance, roads and airports. Fees to prevent excessive use are clearly required. Electricity charges for industrial use are adjusted to deter use during peak periods, but this is an exception.

Earmarking taxes has both merits and shortcomings. On the one hand, beneficiaries are willing to pay a tax if they perceive that it will go toward the infrastructure construction for which it is intended. On the other hand, once earmarked, the tax is targeted at that specific purpose and diverting it to other purposes is difficult, even if doing so would mitigate the overuse of the original infrastructure. One of the underlying reasons for this type of inflexibility might be the absence of a comprehensive plan for coordinating the different types of infrastructure. At the same time, fierce rivalry exists among ministries for funding from the general account (for a discussion of bureaucratic rivalry see Aoki 1988).

Public Bonds: Another Source of Financing

Fiscal discipline is expressed in the Public Finance Law, which limits the issuance of national government bonds to guard against hyperinflation and the accumulation of national debt, as had occurred in the past. For a decade after the start of economic expansion in 1955 the government was able to avoid issuing deficit financing bonds, largely because the progressive income tax system provided sufficient revenue for supporting rapid growth and also because the large number of young workers did not drain social security funds. However, Article IV of the Public Finance Law allows the government to issue construction bonds or borrow money to finance public works. After a decade in which the only bonds the public sector issued were government guaranteed bonds by public corporations and local governments, the government was forced to use this article to raise resources for infrastructure projects. In 1965 a severe economic slump led to a shortage of tax revenue, and the government decided to issue national bonds amounting to ¥ 200 billion.

---

1.   Japan's national budget currently includes eight special accounts for infrastructure development. The accounts for road, airport, and harbor improvement are the largest. Railways are a notable exception to the special account approach.

This interpretation of the Public Finance Law became the standard method for bond financing whenever the economy faced a slowdown or recession. For example, in 1971 the economy faced a slump caused by what is referred to as the "Nixon shock." The central government adopted an expansionary policy to stimulate the economy and issued about ¥ 2,000 billion of bonds a year during 1972–74. In 1973 the first oil crisis hit Japan, causing a severe economic recession and a large, unexpected shortage in tax revenues. In addition, social security spending was rising as a result of changes made to the social security system in the early 1970s. In 1975 the central government issued construction bonds worth ¥ 318 billion, but it also issued deficit financing bonds worth ¥ 2,090 billion. The enactment of an Exceptional Law on Bond Issue each year it became necessary permitted the issuance of deficit financing bonds. Although the law was meant to be temporary, financing by this method became routine in the late 1970s, and the amount of construction and deficit financing bonds issued reached ¥ 14,170 billion a year by 1980.

Since the late 1980s the government has pursued a more restrictive fiscal policy in an attempt to limit the use of deficit financing bonds. Although the government was able to halt deficit financing bond issues in 1990, in the early 1990s it started once again to issue a massive volume of both types of bonds to cope with the economic slump caused by the collapse of the so-called bubble economy. The government will likely continue to issue construction bonds for infrastructure spending for the foreseeable future.

The issuance of public bonds has not caused serious economic problems because of the high level of savings in the household sector (Noguchi 1993). It may, however, have put pressure on the balance sheets of private financial institutions, who were "allotted" national bonds before the 1980s, when interest rates were regulated (Yaginuma, Kuninori, and Tokui 1987). Until 1975, national bonds allocated to private financial institutions were subsequently purchased by the central bank within specified limits, but the increase in national bonds after 1975 was beyond the central bank's buying limits.

Thus the issuance of national bonds accelerated the liberalization of Japan's financial markets in the 1980s. As the stock of bonds issued and outstanding grew, private institutional investors and individuals acquired them. Also, a secondary bond market developed, where the sale and purchase of existing bonds and transactions are based on market-determined interest rates.

The FILP: Funnels Money to Public Corporations and the Private Sector

The main story of infrastructure financing in postwar Japan concerns the FILP. The FILP is a unique, comprehensive policy instrument that serves as a financial intermediation mechanism for investment and loan activity that takes money from private savings, the general account, and bond issues and filters it into a financial pool known as the Trust Fund Bureau. The bureau then provides interest bearing loans to public corporations for construction purposes or funds to government financial institutions, such as the Japan Development Bank, for on-lending, including to the private sector. FILP funds are not grants or subsidies: users of FILP funds are required to pay back the principal to the lending organization with interest. Yet by supporting public corporations and government-backed financial institutions, the FILP ensures that the infrastructure needed to achieve policy objectives is built.

The FILP is often thought of as the second national budget. However, FILP funds are passive, in the sense that they are not collected through a compulsory system, and they differ from national bonds, because the government does not predetermine the amount of funds collected (Tachi 1993). In addition, when the economy has been in recession or the general budget has been severely constrained, FILP expenditures on infrastructure have increased, which indicates that the program is used as a tool to stabilize the macroeconomy.

Although analyzing the macroeconomic or monetary implications of the FILP is beyond the scope of this chapter, the system clearly enables the government to accumulate a massive, diverse infrastructure. Supporters of the program argue that it has simultaneously attained two objectives: national policy and project efficiency (Noguchi 1989). Had financing been left solely to the private sector, projects with a long payback period would most likely have not been built, or the government would have had to fund them through the general account. And had the infrastructure been built with general account revenue, political pressures would have led to inefficient public expenditures. However, as the FILP has become larger and more complex, some parts of its operations and institutions are often susceptible to administrative inefficiency.

Figure 5–1 shows the flow of funds through the FILP. Table 5–1 shows the shares of funds collected by the various components of the FILP from 1955 to 1996. While the FILP's purchases of national bonds are increasing, the main source of funds is the Trust Fund Bureau, which accounted for almost 80 percent of FILP funds in 1996. The bureau, an authority within the Ministry of Finance, allocates private savings to various public corporations and to government institutions for their own use and for government-directed policy lending.

Figure 5–1. The Flow of Funds through the Fiscal Investment and Loan Program, Proposed Figures for Fiscal 1996
(billions of yen)

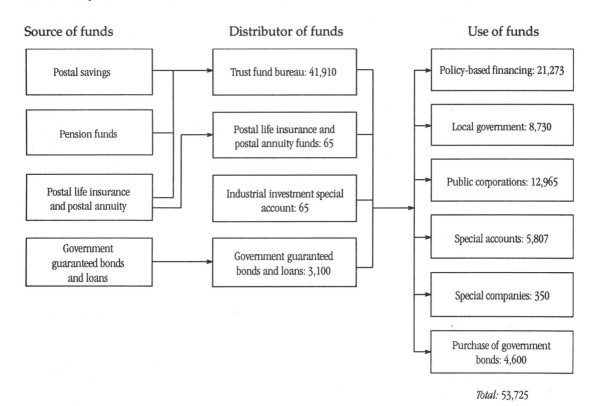

Source: Ministry of Finance (1996).

The largest contributor of funds to the bureau is the postal savings system (see chapter 2 for the use of postal savings in Korea and Taiwan (China). This system has been in place for more than 100 years, and more than 24,600 branches are currently located throughout Japan, collecting savings and deposits from households. Through mobilizing small deposits, the postal savings system had accumulated more than ¥ 213 trillion in outstanding balances by the end of fiscal 1995, which represented about 20 percent of private household savings in Japan. The system is by far the largest

Table 5-1. Funds Collected by the Fiscal Investment and Loan Program, Selected Years 1955–96

Source	1955 Amount (billions of yen)	1955 Share of total (percent)	1965 Amount (billions of yen)	1965 Share of total (percent)	1975 Amount (billions of yen)	1975 Share of total (percent)	1985 Amount (billions of yen)	1985 Share of total (percent)	1996 Amount (billions of yen)	1996 Share of total (percent)
General account	11	3.4	..	..	..	..	..	..	..	..
Industrial investment special account	23	7.1	56	3.5	65	0.7	31	0.1	65	0.1
Trust Fund Bureau	168	52.2	1,064	65.6	8,211	84.4	20,029	77.5	49,910	78.0
Postal life insurance fund	50	15.5	110	6.8	1,050	10.8	2,588	10.0	8,650	16.1
Fund of surplus agricultural products	22	6.8	..	..	..	..	..	..	..	..
Government guaranteed bonds and loans	48	14.9	391	24.1	404	4.2	3,210	12.4	3,100	5.8
Total	322	100.0	1,621	100.0	9,730	100.0	25,858	100.0	53,725	100.0

.. None or negligible.
Source: Ministry of Finance (various years).

savings institution in the world. Similar postal savings systems exist in European countries, but they are smaller. Over the years, the Japanese postal savings system has developed methods to acquire deposits at a relatively small cost.

Note that the FILP is also used for purposes other than infrastructure development: in 1993 almost one-third of FILP funds went to individual borrowers for the construction of houses on preferential terms. However, infrastructure, which the FILP classifies as public amenities (water supply, sewerage, and other urban infrastructure), land conservation, disaster reconstruction, roads, transportation, and communications, has consistently captured between 30 and 40 percent of FILP funds.

The system's funds are targeted at two primary users. The first major set of users is nonfinancial project implementation institutions such as Kodan and Jigyodan. These public entities are entitled by law to borrow funds from the FILP and include the Japan Highway Corporation, the Housing and Urban Development Corporation, and the Pension Welfare Service Corporation. These public corporations rely on the FILP for a considerable share of their funds.

The second major set of users is government financial institutions, each of which has a specific policy agenda in financing the private or quasi-public sector's funding requirements. These include the Japan Development Bank; the Export-Import Bank of Japan; the Small Business Finance Corporation; the People's Finance Corporation; the Housing Loan Corporation; the Small Business Credit Insurance Corporation; the Environmental Sanitation Business Corporation; the Hokkaido and Tohoku Development Corporation; the Okinawa Development Finance Corporation; and the Agriculture, Forestry, and Fisheries Finance Corporation.

POLICY-BASED LENDING THROUGH THE JAPAN DEVELOPMENT BANK. The Japan Development Bank was established in 1951. The bank has carried out policy-based financing by supplying long-term, fixed, low-interest funds to private sector projects that complement government development objectives. Another function of the bank's financing has been to supplement and guide private financial institutions, often with so-called pump priming, that is, transmitting information from the government to induce private investment in areas considered desirable for the national economy (JDB/JERI 1993). Horiuchi and Sui (1993) found evidence of the bank's role in providing information, such as reliable signals of policymakers' intentions, which by doing so reduced operational costs for borrowing firms.

The bank has played an important role in infrastructure financing, including financing of projects related to electricity, gas, railroads, ports, and urban construction. Between the 1950s and the 1970s the bank's lending shifted from such basic industrial infrastructure as electric power; shipping; and coal, iron, and steel processing to urban infrastructure that sought to address overcrowding in urban areas and underpopulation in rural areas (for example, by constructing private railways), and then to policies for national welfare.

During the 1980s the bank further diversified its policy goals into fields such as social development to provide a better living environment and to secure a stable energy supply. In the latter half of the 1980s, government policy objectives included developing infrastructure with private initiatives and it passed a temporary act in 1986 to serve this purpose. With this legislation, a new financing program was devised to use the windfall profits accrued from the public sale of Nippon Telegraph and Telephone Corporation stock (see box 5–2), thereby mitigating the general account's decreased flexibility in allocating national funds for infrastructure.

Using this program, the bank dispersed interest free and low-interest loans to increase infrastructure construction by the private and quasi-public sectors. The bank also started financing programs related to the privatization of the national railway and telephone corporations. In 1996 the bank's main infrastructure loans were to electric power, trunk and intercity railroads (private railroad companies and privatized Japan Railways companies), urban development, and telecommunications (Nippon Telegraph and Telephone and newly established telecommunication companies). The recent administrative reform of the public institutions stresses that the bank should concentrate more on specific policy-related areas, including infrastructure financing.

Box 5–2. Profits from the Sale of Nippon Telegraph and Telephone

In 1987 the government devised a temporary, interest free lending program for specific types of infrastructure expenditures. This program was made possible by the windfall profits accrued from the public sale of the Nippon Telegraph and Telephone Corporation's stock. First transferred into the industrial investment special account through the general account, financing was then distributed to other special accounts and government institutions to promote the construction of certain types of infrastructure.

Four types of projects are eligible for the program. Type A projects are revenue generating infrastructure projects (toll roads, parking facilities) carried out by highway and other public corporations. Type B projects are infrastructure projects carried out by local governments. Type C projects are revenue generating infrastructure projects carried out by quasi-public enterprises owned jointly by the public and private sectors. Type C' projects are similar to type C projects, but are carried out mostly by private corporations. These four project groups represented about 16 percent of the total public works undertaken on the general account.

NARROWING THE COMPETITIVE ADVANTAGES OF FILP LOANS. FILP funds allow a flexibility that the general revenues do not permit. As such, the FILP has been an important and growing source of finance for infrastructure. The demands on the FILP are likely to increase as local governments commit to infrastructure of which so far not enough has been provided, for example, sewerage. Constraints on the financial capacity of local governments limit the pace of such construction. However, the competitive advantage of FILP loans has declined with financial liberalization and the sources of funds are likely to shrink in coming decades.

Until the 1980s the Trust Fund Bureau's lending rate for FILP loans was much lower than the private long-term prime rate, although the gap was gradually narrowed over time. This helped FILP agencies pursue their policy objectives at preferential interest rates. In addition, during this period the private financial system was regulated to allow private financial institutions to offer large spreads. Thus major private banks made large profits.

Since the mid-1980s, however, the competitive edge of FILP funds has narrowed and sometimes disappeared, because low nominal interest rates have proliferated (the present nominal lending rates are 2 to 3 percent per year). With financial liberalization, the rates private banks charged came under pressure, and hence the gap between the two interest rates narrowed. Sometimes FILP rates were even higher, because the rate charged by the Trust Fund Bureau had a floor specified by law.

The government was obliged to change the mechanism for setting interest rates within the FILP system to adjust to financial liberalization. In 1987 the level the bureau charged was changed from a rate regulated by law to a formula linked to the rate of newly issued national bonds. Coping with the pressure of market-based interest rates will pose a major challenge to individual FILP agencies and to the entire FILP system.

In addition, the FILP's funding prospects are not bright. In the medium and long term, the growth of funding sources will decelerate because of slower economic growth and declining saving rates as the population ages. Thus to increase efficiency, the authorities have initiated administrative reforms. Although the current measures emphasize institutional reforms, now is an opportune time to begin work on a blueprint for major modifications of the infrastructure financing process, together with a specification of desirable areas for infrastructure construction.[2] Perhaps indicative of these changes is the recent introduction of private capital into large projects, such as the Trans-Tokyo Bay Highway and the Kansai International Airport, but broader policy reform is required to ensure that delivery is efficient and that prices cover investment expenditures.

---

2. Noguchi (1994) argues that more emphasis should be given to institutional capital, in which knowledge, or human capital, plays a crucial role. Institutional capital includes such social infrastructure as education, research activities, medical care, welfare, and information-related activities.

Each Sector Funded Differently

Each infrastructure sector obtains its financing from different sources, for example:

- *Roads*. Toll roads are financed with a combination of interest bearing bonds, user fees, and loans from FILP-backed corporations. Nontoll roads are financed largely from a gasoline tax.
- *Airports*. Airport expansion is funded through a special account with money from aviation landing fees and an aviation fuel tax. Airport improvement and expansion measures have been able to accommodate a dramatic increase in passengers and cargo.
- *Ports*. Financing for the expansion and modernization of ports is mostly from the general account and local government accounts and from user fees only to a small extent.
- *Railways*. Railway bonds and bank borrowings were initially used to finance Japan National Railways. The burden of large interest payments eventually eroded the railway's profit margins, forcing its privatization into regional companies.
- *Electric power*. Power generation has been financed largely from corporate bonds and internal funds.

Roads: Rapid Development through Tolls and Taxes

After national policy began focusing on economic growth, central and local governments embarked on a vigorous effort to construct a road system that today consists of nontoll and toll roads. In 1952 the government adopted a toll road system for the construction and maintenance of expressways and other special transport links, such as bridges. In 1956 this led to the creation of the Japan Highway Corporation, which is authorized to construct and operate toll roads throughout Japan. Other public corporations were also created for specialized road links. For nontoll roads, the introduction of a gasoline tax earmarked solely for road construction and improvement had a far-reaching impact on the financing of roads.

TOLL ROADS. Most toll-road construction is the responsibility of FILP-backed public corporations. These include the Japan Highway Corporation, the Tokyo Expressway Corporation, the Hanshin Superhighway Corporation, the Honshu-Shikoku Bridge Authority, and the Trans-Tokyo Bay Highway Corporation. Among them, the Japan Highway Corporation is granted authority to administer the high-speed roads that are the backbone of the nation's road network.

One of the features of the nation's network of toll roads is the "pool system," in which money from tolls nationwide goes toward motorway construction and operating expenses. The system operates under an agreement to collect tolls for thirty years after a motorway becomes operational; the toll rate is expected to cover the full construction cost, including land acquisition. Certain subsidies are provided by the responsible governments. The toll rate has been calculated so that, after thirty years, the toll road can be transferred to the corresponding level of government free of charge. However, partly reflecting a suggestion by Miyagawa (1994), the increases in the toll rate are to be moderated and the transfer to local governments will be deferred.

NONTOLL ROADS. The government created the gasoline tax in 1949 to meet general needs in the national budget. Five years later it earmarked the tax specifically for constructing nontoll roads. The system was modeled after that used in the United States and some European countries. In 1955 the government added a local road tax to the gasoline tax. It has raised rates occasionally since then, and has introduced other taxes to supplement road construction resources, notably, an automobile weight tax in 1971. These taxes accounted for 80 to 90 percent of national government expenditure on road construction in the past decade. At the local government level, other earmarked taxes accounted for about 40 percent of road construction expenditures.

Occasionally, the revenue from these taxes exceeds road construction expenditures. On such occasions the budgeting process is inflexible, as both the users who pay the taxes and the regulating ministry firmly oppose the diversion of tax revenues. This occurred during 1983–84, when the central government capped major expenditure items, including road construction. Such instances of budgetary inflexibility have sparked debate about changing the special purpose taxes into general taxes. However, no agreement on changing the tax system has been reached.

Airports: Dramatic Volume Increases

The number of passengers and the volume of cargo have increased dramatically since Japan created its air transport system in 1951. Two main factors account for this growth: technological changes that required rapid movement of goods and economic growth. The government enacted the Airport Development Law in 1956 to facilitate airport construction and administration and to raise the necessary funds to establish the airport improvement special account. The law classifies airports into three categories. The cost of airports in class 1 is the sole responsibility of the central government through the Ministry of Transport, the New Tokyo International Airport Authority, and the Kansai International Airport Company, Ltd. Costs in classes 2 and 3 require local government participation, but the financing burden is partly offset by the transfer of part of an aviation fuel tax from the national government. In addition, the government gives class 2 airports a two-thirds subsidy and class 3 airports a 50 percent subsidy. Large cities such as Tokyo are not required to share the financing burden, even if the local return from the airport is expected to be huge.

The airport improvement special account has several sources of funds (table 5–2). Borrowing, for instance, from the FILP; airport charges, such as aircraft landing fees and air navigation facility charges; and the aviation fuel tax are the main sources of financing. Transfers from the general account contribute a little more than one-tenth of funding.

While the concept of users is limited to passengers, cargo shippers, airline companies, and enterprises in passenger terminal buildings, one could argue that the benefits of airports extend to the owners of real estate and to corporations located near airports. However, airport charges are not yet structured to make these indirect beneficiaries bear a portion of the costs. Furthermore, those who suffer an external diseconomy from an airport should be well compensated, and the airport construction budget should take such diseconomies into account.

Ports: Public Funding Provided

Japan has a steep, mountainous topography, and major economic activities take place along the coasts. Coastal maritime transportation has a long history, and the demand for port construction and improvement has been continuous since World War II. Ports were one of the areas targeted for physical infrastructure expenditure after the war ended. More recently, port expenditures have gone

Table 5–2. Sources of the Airport Improvement Special Account's Funds, 1995
(percent)

Revenue source	Share
General revenues	11.6
Aviation fuel tax	20.3
Airport charges	17.3
Miscellaneous revenues	18.6
Borrowing	32.2
Total	100.0

Source: Japan Civil Aviation Foundation data.

largely for modernization to keep pace with technological innovations, for example, containerization, and for car ferries. However, the port sector lacks a mechanism for charging beneficiaries a sufficient user fee. At the national level funds come from general revenues through the harbor improvement special account, and a considerable portion of local financing comes from the local general account. The FILP's share has been relatively small, which probably reflects the Meiji era requirement that port construction be financed solely with public money. The Port Law of 1950 stipulated that local governments act as port managers and take responsibility for harbor construction and administration. This contrasts sharply with arrangements for other types of infrastructure.

Railways: Could Not Maintain Financial Control

Japan National Railways was founded in 1949 and inherited all the railroad assets owned by the former Ministry of Railways. As early as the 1950s, it became apparent that railway facilities, especially those between Tokyo and Osaka, were operating at full capacity. To expand the rail network, the bullet train project was launched, with construction lasting from 1959 to 1964. The necessary funds came from railway bonds, bank borrowing, and World Bank funds. In 1964 the railway began suffering from managerial and financial difficulties from which it never recovered (see chapter 6 for more discussion of this topic). It was privatized in the late 1980s, when the government was forced to devolve operational and financial responsibility to seven regional railroad companies (Fukui 1992).

Several factors contributed to these financial hardships. First, proposed increases in passenger and freight rates were delayed because of political opposition. Second, the huge investment in and expansion of the road network severely affected the use of local railway lines. Third, the railway was mandated to provide services in all areas of the country, but low population densities in rural areas resulted in operating losses. Fourth, operational underinvestment and a lack of preparedness in adjusting to changing cargo transportation patterns during the era of rapid growth restricted revenue growth. Finally, difficulties with rationalizing the railway's labor force led to excessive expenditures on personnel.

Ultimately, the most significant factor was financial: the burden of large interest payments simply eroded profit margins. The government never created a special account for the railway. Most deficit financing and construction expenditures relied on funds borrowed from the FILP and private banks (table 5–3). Despite privatization in 1987, a liquidation entity, financed by FILP funds, still holds a large volume of the remaining debt of the former Japan National Railways.

Water Supply: User Fees, Local Bonds, and National Subsidies

Construction funds for water supply infrastructure come from local bonds and national government subsidies, while user fees finance operating costs. Japan's first modern waterworks were introduced in Yokohama in 1887. Since then the diffusion rate for waterworks has grown from 35 percent just before the end of World War II to 95 percent in 1990.

Municipalities, local public corporations, and syndicates are responsible for construction and management. User fees cover most of the operating costs, including the cost of depreciation. Construction funds are financed by local bonds and subsidies from the national government.

Sewerage Development: A Low Priority

The development of sewerage systems in Japan still lags far behind that in other industrial countries, partly because local government budgets account for the bulk of construction expenditures. The current diffusion rate is only about 50 percent, and about 1,900 municipalities do not have sewer systems. Development policy is targeted at conserving water quality, but the challenge of providing a nationwide sewerage system is a critical medium- and long-term policy issue.

Table 5–3. Financing of Japan National Railway, Selected Years, 1965–95

(100 million yen)

Revenue category	1965	1970	1975	1980	1981	1982	1983	1985
Profit, general account								
Operating revenue	6,341	11,457	18,209	29,637	31,730	33,130	32,989	35,528
Operating expenditure	7,571	13,006	27,444	39,643	43,254	47,749	51,401	55,728
Operating income	-1,230	-1,549	-9,235	-10,006	-11,524	-14,619	-18,411	-20,201
Liabilities outstanding,								
general account								
Long-term debt	3,946	9,455	44,069	37,696	46,760	56,589	66,682	81,476
General account	475	415	350	1,046	1,011	1,011	1,011	778
Trust Fund Bureau	3,098	7,810	40,384	28,888	35,833	44,178	53,707	67,922
Private banks				1,365	2,847	3,782	4,535	5,851
Railway bonds	7,156	16,583	23,724	53,074	61,534	70,646	79,929	100,933
Government-guaranteed								
bonds	3,481	6,706	5,110	13,788	16,203	19,288	23,075	33,171
Other	3,675	9,876	18,614	39,286	45,240	51,360	56,854	67,762
Total general account								
liabilities	11,102	26,037	67,793	90,770	108,294	127,235	146,611	182,409
Liabilities outstanding,								
extraordinary account								
Trust Fund Bureau	0	0	0	50,599	50,599	50,599	50,599	50,599
General account	0	0	0	2,622	2,622	2,622	2,622	2,602
Total special account								
liabilities	0	0	0	53,221	53,221	53,221	53,221	53,201
Total liabilities	11,102	26,037	67,793	143,992	161,515	180,457	199,833	235,610

Source: Japan National Railways, (various years).

Two financing arrangements are used for sewerage construction. One involves the central and local governments, the other involves local governments only. In both cases local financing depends heavily on the issuance of local bonds. Beneficiaries must also contribute to the financing of sewer systems. Although this direct contribution to total construction costs is small (in 1992 the share was 2 percent), beneficiaries' contribution to maintenance costs, including principal and interest repayment, is substantial (38 percent in 1992).

Electricity: Monopolies Rely on a Diverse Range of Financing

Electricity demand has increased dramatically since World War II. One of the challenges facing the electric power industry has been to raise the large amount of capital required for physical investment, especially in power generation. After lengthy debate about the form the industry should take, nine private, regional power companies were established in 1951. Each company has a monopoly in its region and is responsible for generation and distribution (see chapter 6).

During the 1950s the primary sources of long-term funds were Japan Development Bank loans and foreign capital, such as funds from the World Bank and the U.S. Import-Export Bank. During the rapid growth of the 1960s, the expansion of the private power companies gradually enabled them to raise funds from their own earnings and from private external sources, such as long-term private bank loans and bond debentures. Investment centered on thermoelectric power plants that used petroleum as fuel and on distribution facilities. Electricity rates remained relatively low, giving manufacturing industries that consumed energy a competitive edge.

The 1973 oil crisis completely changed the situation. Facing high petroleum prices, the power industry shifted its investment to other power sources (nuclear, natural gas, geothermal, and hydroelectric) to increase efficiency and to developing antipollution equipment. These efforts created a considerable demand for capital. Given their monopolistic status, the electric power companies are guaranteed a fair rate of return (currently 5.25 percent) on the value of plant and equipment. In 1980 electricity rates increased by 50 percent, making them more expensive than in any other industrial country. The easing of petroleum prices and the continued appreciation of the yen throughout the 1980s have since reduced electricity rates; however, the rates are still among the highest of all industrial countries.

The companies have made every effort to diversify their financing sources in an attempt to reduce the cost of capital and to attain long-term loans corresponding to the long service life of their equipment and structures. The most stable source of funds has been internal funds, primarily from depreciation allowances. The largest external source of funds has been corporate bonds. Bonds issued by the electric power companies have made up the largest share of the domestic bond market.

Public-Private Financing Partnerships Are Mutually Beneficial

Two infrastructure projects—the Trans-Tokyo Bay Highway and the Kansai International Airport—exemplify the willingness of Japan's government to combine private and public resources in expanding and modernizing its infrastructure base.

The Trans-Tokyo Bay Highway

The construction of the Trans-Tokyo Bay Highway is a prime example of how private and public entities can together develop social capital for infrastructure projects. In 1986 the Trans-Tokyo Bay Highway Corporation (TTB) was established as a joint stock company consisting of government capital (the Japan Highway Corporation), local governments, and private corporations. The company was established to infuse private capital into the construction of toll roads, including bridges and tunnels, between Kawasaki and Kisarazu, a distance of 15.1 kilometers.

The total cost of this project will be ¥ 1,438.4 billion, more than 80 percent of which the TTB will finance through bond issues and loans from the government, including loans from the Japan Development Bank, and from private financial institutions. Upon completion, the TTB will turn over all facilities to the Japan Highway Corporation, which is responsible for managing major toll roads, although the TTB will engage in maintenance activity. This type of build-operate-transfer scheme is one of the first major development projects conducted by the quasi-public sector in Japan.

Kansai International Airport

The Kansai International Airport project was undertaken to provide modern airport services for the Kansai area around Osaka, Japan's second largest city. In 1984 the Kansai International Airport Company was established as a joint stock company under a special law. In contrast to the scheme set up for the Trans-Tokyo Bay Highway, the Kansai International Airport Company will be responsible for all financing, construction, and operations. Total construction costs will be ¥ 1,458 billion, 30 percent of which will be financed by shareholders in both the public and private sectors. Government-guaranteed bonds, direct placement bonds, and loans from private financial institutions and the Japan Development Bank will finance the remaining expenditures. In 1994 initial demand for the airport's services was below projected levels. Thus given the project's huge construction costs and that it is financed primarily from interest bearing funds, unless demand rises rapidly, additional public funds will likely be required.

Conclusion

Since World War II various branches of the Japanese government, especially the central government, have played a pivotal role in formulating methods to finance the construction of infrastructure. Current administrative reforms are examining possible changes in the institutional aspects of the ministerial and FILP systems, including consolidation and privatization. Given that use of the FILP (except for public bonds purchases) will probably decelerate over the medium and long term, partly because of slower economic growth, and partly because of lower saving rates, now is the time to develop a blueprint for major modifications of the infrastructure financing process, along with priorities for infrastructure construction. This would require changing every aspect of the budgetary process. In addition, policymakers might want to consider altering the system of user fees, which are currently directed toward funding construction and maintenance, to a system that controls levels of service usage.

References

Aoki, Masahiko. 1988. *Information, Incentives, and Bargaining in the Japanese Economy.* Cambridge, U.K.: Cambridge University Press.

Fukui, Koichiro. 1992. *Japanese National Railways: Privatization Study—The Experience of Japan and Lessons for Developing Countries.* Discussion Paper no. 172. Washington, D.C.: World Bank.

Horiuchi, Akiyoshi, and Qing-Yuan Sui. 1993. "Influence of the Japan Development Bank Loans on Corporate Investment Behavior." *Journal of the Japanese and International Economics* 7: 441–65.

Japan National Railways. Various years. *Audit Report.* Tokyo.

JDB/JERI (Japan Development Bank and Japan Economic Research Institute). 1993. *Policy-Based Finance: The Experience of Postwar Japan.* Discussion Paper no. 221. Washington, D.C.: World Bank.

Ministry of Finance. 1996 and various years. *Monthly Statistics of Government Finance and Banking.* Tokyo.

Miyagawa, Tadao. 1994. "Highway Toll Rates Could Be Cheaper." *Nihon Keizai Shimbun,* Tokyo. (In Japanese.)

Miyazaki, Hitoshi, ed. 1962. *Public Works and Public Finance,* vol. I. Tokyo: Zaimu-Shuppan. (In Japanese.)

Noguchi, Yukio. 1989. "The Fiscal Investment and Loan Program and the Japanese Economy." In H. Uzawa, ed., *The Japanese Economy: Studies of Capital Accumulation and Economic Growth.* Tokyo: University of Tokyo Press. (In Japanese.)

_____.1993. "Development and the Present State of Public Finance." In T. Shibata, ed., *Japan's Public Sector: How the Government is Financed.* Tokyo: University of Tokyo Press.

_____. 1994. "Future Trend of Social Capital Investment." In H. Uzawa and A. Mogi, eds., *Social Overhead Capital: Cities and the Commons.* Tokyo: University of Tokyo Press.

Tachi, Ryuichiro. 1993. *The Contemporary Japanese Economy: An Overview.* Tokyo: University of Tokyo Press.

Yaginuma, H., M. Kuninori, and J. Tokui. 1987. "Research on Crowding Out: Influence of Bond Issue upon Financial Intermediation." *Economics Today* 8(1):38–111. (In Japanese.)

6

Intervention in Japan's Market for Infrastructure Services: Privatization without Full Deregulation

Tsuruhiko Nambu

After World War II Japan embarked on an industrialization program to promote economic expansion and thereby increase its international competitiveness. At the heart of the program was infrastructure development to redress critical shortages in some sectors, repair damaged equipment and facilities in others, and expand coverage overall. To control the strengthening and expansion of key infrastructure sectors, the government immediately established public corporations—known as *koshas*—in roads, airports, railways, and telecommunications. By regulating the markets of these sectors directly, the Diet ensured an environment for the *koshas* that was free of competition, theoretically enabling them to sustain their financial viability and to operate efficiently. However, two of the largest *koshas*—Nippon Telegraph and Telephone (NTT) and Japan National Railways (JNR)—ultimately deteriorated under government control. Their profitability proved untenable, and they were unable to meet the demand for services or to respond to shifts in consumption patterns.

Acknowledging these failures, the government has allowed NTT and JNR to begin operating in a privatized environment. As such, intervention in the market for the services of these two sectors—along with those of the nine regional private monopolies that constitute the electric power sector in Japan—has devolved to Japan's ministerial bureaucracy. The bureaucracy has been slow to release control under privatization, largely because its vertically integrated structure of ministries, bureaus, and sections creates bureaucratic competition over policy formulation and implementation. Analysis of the justification for the ministries' regulatory policies—based on their legitimacy and profitability—indicates mixed success. Ministerial policy seems to be justifiable in the electric power sector, cannot be justified in telecommunications, and is questionable in railways. Thus although these sectors have been privatized, they have been deregulated only to varying degrees.

Regulations Evolve from Needs

Intra- and interministerial competition is at the heart of regulatory policymaking by Japanese ministries. This competition frequently dilutes the power of regulations or gives rise to ineffective, politically motivated policy. Two criteria—the legitimacy and profitability of policy—create a matrix for assessing whether a regulation should be perpetuated.

To varying degrees, all industrial countries have bureaucratic mechanisms for regulating the provision of infrastructure services, theoretically to ensure that consumers have access to high quality, reasonably priced services. One can think of regulatory activity as market intervention, that is, control over how services are delivered and how much they cost. Bureaucracies exercise regulatory control according to their country's political framework.

In Japan the regulatory bureaucracy consists of the Diet, which enacts regulatory legislation directly, and the ministries, which formulate sector-specific policies for legislative action. The various ministries in turn comprise bureaus and, below them, sections. This structure is a vertically integrated system in which regulatory intervention in the market for infrastructure services is a function of competing interests that prevail both within and among ministries. Each ministry consists of career bureaucrats, personnel who have been selected after graduation from university as ministerial professionals who compete to become section directors, deputy directors of bureaus, and eventually, deputy ministers. Unlike the U.S. bureaucracy, in which agency heads are political appointees, deputy ministers in Japan are career professionals who theoretically have no political affiliation. They are free to pursue regulatory policies that they believe will best achieve the objectives of their respective ministries.

This competitive bureaucracy explains why none of Japan's privatized infrastructure sectors has been fully deregulated, despite evidence that regulating them is not necessary to ensure their profitability. Exactly how does this bureaucratic structure regulate the market for infrastructure services and how can one measure its effectiveness?

Regulatory Intervention: A Function of Ministerial Competition

Each ministry is allowed to intervene in the market for infrastructure services. However, the bureaucratic structure of the ministries diffuses absolute enforcement power by any specific ministry, because policymaking is a function of forces that exist both within and among the bureaucratic entities.

Within each ministry several bureaus are responsible for formulating policy toward business and industry. Policy proposals usually come up from the sections of each bureau of a ministry. If a section wishes to pass new bills, it must first go through a bill investigation committee. The committee comprises representatives of all the bureaus in the ministry, who must all agree to pass the new bills to outside ministries for consultation and discussion. A section representative must persuade the committee that the new bills capture the ministry's mandate. This process is called *intraministerial competition*.

When new proposals are authorized within the ministry, it must consult with related ministries to obtain their approval. The initiating ministry must persuade other ministries that its bills should have priority, and fierce struggles among the ministries are not unusual. These struggles are normally resolved through a series of tactical ploys by the rival ministries. This process is called *interministerial competition*. There is no guarantee that ministries compete for socially desirable policies, because the bureaucracy may be more interested in meeting its own political pressures or those from the outside.

All bills from the ministries must survive these two types of competition and, indeed, are shaped by them. But what are the key parameters for determining whether the Diet will accept policy proposals and, once it does so, whether they are effective?

Legitimacy and Profitability Define the Strength and Effectiveness of Intervention

Justification for bureaucratic intervention in the market for infrastructure services depends on both the legitimacy and the profitability of regulation. Legitimacy is a mixture of social, economic, and political forces that allow a certain market intervention policy to be authorized and continued. Strong legitimacy argues for keeping a regulatory policy in effect; weak legitimacy argues against perpetuating the regulatory intervention.

The effectiveness of a regulatory intervention is measured by the service provider's profitability. Market intervention by the government is effective only when it guarantees a firm's profitability. Thus the level of government intervention depends on the extent of policy legitimacy, whereas the demand for it depends on the strength of profit incentives or profitability (figure 6–1). The vertical axis in figure 6-1 shows the level of legitimacy and the horizontal axis shows the rate of profitability. These axes create four regions for assessing the continuity and effectiveness of market intervention by the government.

Government policies found in region 1 have continuity and are effective. They have continuity because their administrative costs are low and bureaucrats can implement (or supply) the regulatory policies with relative ease. They are effective because they enable firms to remain profitable by obeying the regulations. Policies in region 2 are made legitimate by bureaucratic strength or economic justification, but because no demand for the policies exists (that is, the policies do not ensure service providers' profitability), their effectiveness is questionable. In particular, firms will endeavor to circumvent the regulations, which will inevitably reduce the regulations' legitimacy. In region 3 policies lack legitimacy and their continuity is questionable, primarily because they hamper profitability. Finally, policies in region 4 have little legitimacy, implying that bureaucrats are reluctant to push them and are constrained from doing so by political pressures and influence. However, these policies are profitable, and thus the service providers they regulate demand them. As such, their continuity is questionable: political forces may perpetuate them despite their low legitimacy, or their low legitimacy may justify abandoning them.

The Pressures on Public Corporations Caused Them to Fail

Koshas—public corporations controlled directly by the Diet—were a key instrument of infrastructure delivery. This form of market intervention by the government was effective and legitimate as long as they were able to provide needed services. And because *koshas* had no incentive to earn

Figure 6–1. Bureaucratic Regulation in Services

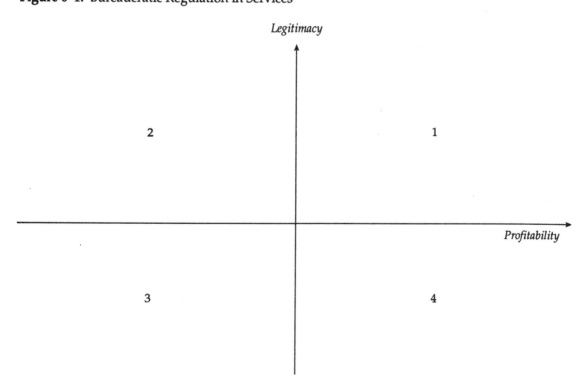

profits (that is, they needed to earn only enough money to ensure continued investment), profitability was guaranteed and market intervention was effective. However, as changes in the market for *kosha* services began emerging—in particular, technological advancements in telecommunications and shifts in the patterns of transportation use—*koshas* lost their *raison d'être* and organizational stagnation and financial distress set in. Privatization was then introduced, but continuity under the new regulatory model that governs privatization is not fully guaranteed, and its effectiveness is limited by the degree of profitability available to regulated firms.

Justification on Efficiency Grounds Dwindled

A natural monopoly is justified when inexhaustible economies of scale exist. Until the early 1970s telecommunications essentially implied no-frills voice communication. In the language of economists, this was a homogeneous service. Voices were carried over copper cables and switched mechanically or electromechanically. No technological substitutes existed for voice telephony, thereby limiting the possibilities of bypassing NTT's network. The result was a hierarchical network that called for a nationally integrated monopoly. A telephone monopoly was most efficient, because service would have been much more expensive if more than one company had established its own network, but by the early 1980s the introduction of new telephonic technology threatened NTT's existence.

In railroads the problem was not so clear-cut. Although economies of scale existed and were important to the extent that JNR provided bulk transport, for example, between Tokyo and Osaka, a nationally integrated network was not necessarily the most efficient system, because JNR faced competition from another transport mode, namely, cars. Thus the railway system could be bypassed, implying that JNR's efficiency was slipping from the start.

Justification on Income Distribution Grounds Became Questionable

The concept of universal service provision was a prominent motivation for maintaining public corporations for telecommunications and public transport. Universal service required cross-subsidization within networks, and corporations were an institutional means of providing cross-subsidies. In telecommunications, long distance telephone services subsidized local telephone services, which kept local rates low. Rural railroad rates depended on subsidies from the urban railway system.

This kind of income redistribution can be socially acceptable as long as services are homogeneous and considered essential to meet society's minimum consumption goals. Voice telephony and public transport are good examples. Without telephone service or public transit, some people may fail to join the social network and could be unduly discriminated against.

Cross-subsidization is problematic, however, when services become more heterogeneous to cater to diverse demand. Cross-subsidies might continue to be justified as long as network externalities exist. From an efficiency viewpoint some services might well be subsidized if doing so helps expand the network of services and renders benefits to all network subscribers. But when demand is not for a necessity (as with plain telephone services) but is optional, with the utility of the different services varying from one individual to another, cross-subsidies among customers can become inequitable, and hence difficult to justify.

Traditional cross-subsidization to ensure universal service can also be criticized on the grounds that keeping public prices uniformly low regardless of customers' income is economically inefficient and distributionally regressive. When the number of people who need the subsidy is limited, providing direct subsidies to them can save money. Hence, selective subsidies should be introduced when economic development enables most people to afford the cost of service.

Bureaucratic Inefficiency and Economic Disincentives Led to Organizational Stagnation

Independent bureaus within each *kosha* were responsible for different activities. Collaboration between these bureaus was often limited, and the absence of cooperative decisionmaking was the biggest obstacle to changing the economic environment. For example, NTT's headquarters could not collect customer data from regional divisions because regional independence was so strong. Compounding these bureaucratic inefficiencies was the *koshas* wage and promotion scheme: wages were based on workers' tenure rather than their productivity, and promotions were handicapped by the traditional lifetime employment system. Because employees had no incentive to reform the old system, organizational rigidity reigned.

Political Interference and Labor Unrest Undermined Control

Because the Diet supervised *koshas* directly, special committees were formed to discuss issues before the Diet implemented policy. Committee members consisted of politicians, who usually never missed the opportunity to influence a *kosha*. These politicians were known as *zoku giin* (clan members) and were liable to seek political rent. Thus the system of political intervention was introduced into *koshas'* decisionmaking. Political rent seeking was most striking when the *zoku giin* were representing local interests. The best example is the political enforcement of rail construction in local areas in the 1970s, even when the JNR had no prospect of profiting from the construction. As political pressure from the government grew greater, managerial independence was lost. Such political distortions deprived the *koshas* of their self-governing mechanism.

Labor unrest also flared up. The *koshas'* labor unions became one of the centers of the radical labor movement that characterized the protests of the 1960s and 1970s. The relationship between management and laborers was often marred by the ideological bias of labor union leaders. Especially in the JNR, factions sought to assume leadership of the labor movement to bring about a Marxist revolution.

Privatization in Practice

In response to the pressures on the *koshas*, the telecommunications monopoly—NTT—and the railways monopoly—JNR—were privatized. Today, NTT (now NTT, Inc.), JNR (now Japan Railways or JR), and the electric utilities are all regulated privatized firms. Referring to the analytical framework presented in figure 6–1:

- NTT, Inc., can be placed in region 3, where regulatory intervention in the market for services cannot be considered continuous or effective. The Ministry of Ports and Telecommunications (MPT) has worsened the financial position of NTT, whose profitability is lower than the industry average because it is not allowed to adjust its rates or collect access charges. Other policies have also undercut investment incentives.
- Railways can be placed in region 4. Although the six regional JR companies are not immensely profitable, some of them should be able to earn healthy profits in the future. However, the legitimacy of regulation by the Ministry of Transport is questionable, because competition among transportation modes exists in each region.
- The electric companies are in region 1, where market intervention is continuous and effective. The companies enjoy stable profit rates, and economies of scale justify their regulation.

From NTT to NTT, Inc.

The MPT suppresses NTT, Inc.'s profit-making incentives by encouraging competition in long distance services without allowing NTT to adjust its rates in response. Thus competitors can offer services at a lower price. The result is that as the industrial countries are now heading toward a free market approach to the telecommunications industry, the MPT's regulatory policy may keep Japan from following suit. For example, Japan is now far behind the United States in constructing a national information infrastructure because the MPT and NTT, Inc. have not been able to agree on this issue.

NTT was established in 1952 to construct the telecommunications infrastructure. Its mandate was to fulfill two objectives as quickly as possible: first, to address the backlog of demand for telephone access; and second, to construct a nationwide direct dialing system. Given these concrete objectives, NTT was efficient in an engineering sense. By the end of the 1970s it had constructed a highly reliable and modern national network, and its research and development activities were highly sophisticated and were comparable to those of American Telephone and Telegraph (AT&T) in the United States.

NTT's problems arose when new telecommunications technologies and services developed rapidly, especially in the United States. In the 1970s new competition in the telecommunications industry was on the horizon, and business customers were eager to reap its benefits, especially the low-cost technology for transmitting bulk data. But NTT was slow to adapt to these new demands from the business world and sought to forestall new competition. In addition to complaints about NTT's bureaucratic rigidities, firms sought new frontiers in the information industry and wanted to break the institutional barriers imposed by NTT. The breakup of AT&T was another impetus for deregulating the telecommunications industry.

The Second Provisional Committee on Administrative Reform was established in 1981 to assess the problem of inefficient *koshas*. Because NTT was weary of political interference from the Diet and the *zoku giin*, it favored privatization and the introduction of competition. In 1985 the Telecommunications Business Law and NTT Corporation Law were enacted, and NTT became a private firm—NTT, Inc.

Competition in long distance services has prompted a rapid increase in the number of new common carriers into the market at NTT, Inc.'s expense. The MPT's regulatory policy is biased toward these new carriers, and they are thus able to offer cheaper services. For instance, the ministry curbs price matching by NTT, Inc. and obligates the company to provide universal service, a requirement from which new entrants are exempt. Other MPT policies also have a deleterious effect. The ministry has adopted the so-called fully distributed cost method for rate setting, just as many countries have begun to examine the applicability of a price cap. Furthermore, the ministry introduced a demand and supply adjustment clause that strictly limits the number of firms in the industry, and entry or exit is impossible without the ministry's permission. Indeed, the substance of the Telecommunications Business Law came from the Electricity Business Law, which is extremely restrictive, in the spirit of the old regulatory tradition in the United States. The introduction of competition has constrained NTT, Inc.'s financial viability, and its profitability has declined continuously since its privatization.

The MPT's approach to introducing competition is unusual compared with policies in the United Kingdom and the United States. The ministry did not change the telephone rate structure, and NTT, Inc. was forced to use the old tariff scheme. When the company's long distance earnings began to suffer in the face of competition, the ministry did not allow it to raise its local telephone rate. In addition, the MPT made no arrangement for access charges (interconnection fees), so customers of the new common carriers only have to pay the local rate in addition to NTT's long distance rate. That contrasts with policy in the United States, where an access charge was imposed on old common carriers, and with the policy in the United Kingdom, where rate rebalancing was approved with the introduction of a price-capping formula. In the United States long distance carriers must pay an extra tax in the form of an access charge to subsidize local telephone deficits. In the United Kingdom British Telecom could raise local rates so long as the average increase was within the ceiling of the price-capping formula. The only rationale for Japan's strategy was that NTT had been an inefficient bureaucracy, and it could finance the necessary deficit of local telephone service internally by cutting its organizational costs. After NTT, Inc. had eliminated its organizational inefficiency, it still faced a structural deficit in local telephone service, and it will stay this way until rate rebalancing is introduced or an access charge plan is implemented (Nambu 1994; box 6–1).

As NTT, Inc.'s profitability continued to fall throughout the early 1990s, the company reached an agreement with the MPT to introduce an access charge in 1994, although the problem of insufficient access lines was not discussed at that time. Even though competition has created a long distance surplus for consumers, the fixing of local rates has had serious side-effects. First, it has become a significant barrier to local telephone service. Whereas technological competition is becoming increasingly important in the United Kingdom and the United States, Japan is far behind in this area because of its strict regulatory policy. Second, NTT, Inc.'s financial difficulties have deprived it of an ambitious investment plan, and Japan has become a late starter in developing a national information infrastructure.

The problem of interconnection between NTT, Inc. and new entrants has become an urgent policy issue. NTT, Inc. proposed opening up its local network, which required an appropriate interconnection rate charged to competitors in local and long distance markets. As a result—as in the United Kingdom and the United States—the network architecture has been broken up and fees for interconnection are based on the use of specific network elements. Open network architecture is an internationally recognized standard that has been developed to realize efficient interconnections between local operating companies and long distance telephone carriers. It is the basis of engineering models to calculate interconnection costs based on the dismantling of networks into pieces. This divisible network is expected to help new entrants find opportunities to compete with NTT, Inc. Another problem for the company is that its inherited (and inflexible) rate structure impedes the development of Internet services. In an effort to provide better services at lower rates, NTT, Inc. is developing a new service, the Open Computer Network.

Despite these reforms, Japan's deregulation lags behind efforts in the United Kingdom and the United States on several fronts, for example: incentive pricing schemes have not been introduced, fully distributed cost pricing remains intact, the Type I and Type II classification of carriers prevents the emergence of an active provider of wireline for leasing, and NTT, Inc. cannot enter the international market. Public concern about the MPT's regulatory approach is increasing, and the Economic Planning Agency recently proposed more extensive deregulatory measures.

Box 6–1. Privatization Should Be Profitable

NTT and British Telecom were both privatized in the mid-1980s. The privatization of these two giant carriers was similar in a number of ways: neither was broken up into local and long distance entities, the number of entrants into the long distance market was limited (three new common carriers in Japan and one in the United Kingdom), and both companies had been criticized for their inefficient management. Based on these similarities, one might expect the two to exhibit similar economic performances after deregulation. The reality is the opposite. NTT, Inc.'s profit rate declined during 1988–92, whereas British Telecom's was essentially stable—and high. This disparity can be explained by differences in the two governments' style of regulating telecommunications carriers.

In Japan neither rate rebalancing nor arrangements for introducing access charges existed. NTT, Inc. was obliged to provide universal service, as it did before privatization. The MPT chose to foster competition in the long distance market by allowing price differences to continue until recently (NTT, Inc.'s services were 15 to 20 percent higher than those of the new common carriers). This situation contrasts with that in the United Kingdom, where price capping was introduced at the start and British Telecom could easily raise its local rates. The Japanese ministry adopted its policy because it thought that NTT, Inc. could overcome this financial disadvantage by downsizing, which it has done, but the ministry's policy is fundamentally flawed, because it ignores the signaling function of prices. The deficit of the local network implies negative profitability for entrants into this market. Without any rate rebalancing (until 1994) the local market was not attractive for entrepreneurs. The subsidiaries of electricity companies that entered the local market lost money without exception. Elsewhere, innovations in telecommunications technology have fostered competition among local telephone companies, particularly in the United Kingdom and the United States. Japanese-style telephone regulation has now become the highest entry barrier to local telephone markets.

JNR's Failure and Its Rebirth as Japan Railways

Two factors hastened JNR's demise: the emergence and proliferation of private vehicle use during the 1960s, and inflationary pressures during the 1970s, which forced the government to freeze railway prices. JNR quickly became a financially distressed and organizationally bloated institution. The government decided to privatize JNR in 1987, breaking the monopoly up into six regional companies and one freight company.

So far, this breakup has been more successful than expected. The increasing demand for JR's services is striking, especially compared with other private railways. Although this trend can be partly attributed to economic expansion in the late 1980s, two other factors are key: JR's tariff rate has remained constant and self-management in each organization has been revived. Perhaps most crucial to JR's success, however, is the smooth relationship between labor unions and the railways. A vigorous power struggle took place during JNR's final days, with many union members and management staff arguing against privatization, but the provisional committee and Minister Nakasone were determined to privatize JNR. Thus they removed many dissidents from top management and the labor union, thereby eliminating the friction between management and labor. The fundamental problem now is whether regulation should continue to be imposed on the railways. Given the size of JR in each region, regulation might be justified for the purpose of fair competition, but the possibility always exists that JR can be bypassed, and competitive pressure is great enough to invite more deregulation into the railway industry.

JNR started as a railroad monopoly and was able to maintain a profitable status while trucking and airline industries were in their infancy and the use of private vehicles was still limited, but as these sectors began maturing in the early 1960s, JNR faced increasingly difficult financial circumstances. The company earned a profit until 1963, and in 1964 experienced only a slight loss, but during the late 1960s, when Japan experienced inflation and the government was eager to control the rise of public prices, JNR's railway rates were essentially frozen. Adding to JNR's financial woes was the absence of technological advances to lower costs and a sharp increase in wages in the face of inflation. JNR's breakdown was also a result of organizational problems. By the late 1970s JNR could no longer be rescued from its financial breakdown: the relationship between management and the labor union was too poor to enter into constructive negotiations, and the labor union itself was split into factions; JNR faced frequent labor strikes and worker malpractice; it could not resist political pressure to build unprofitable new lines; the ratio of costs to labor was unusually high when compared with other industries; and the number of employees was excessive.

The Diet appointed the Provisional Committee on Administrative Reform in 1981 to review the economic performance of the public service sector. The committee focused particular attention on JNR's efficiency. This committee, which had strong political influence, decided to privatize JNR in 1987. JNR was split into six passenger transport companies and one freight transport company. The main purpose behind the breakup was to revive the old JNR, which still had superb human capital and a geographical advantage inherited from its monopoly standing. At the same time, it created a new body to manage JNR's huge long-term debt so that the new companies could achieve organizational efficiency and managerial performance could be reviewed from the outside. The body, JNR Settlement Corporation, inherited debt of ¥ 25 trillion.

In an extensive study of JNR's privatization, Fukui (1992) provided ten lessons about the experience. Three are particularly important. First, the huge debt the JNR Settlement Corporation inherited has not yet diminished, partly because of the recession. Second, regional differences exist between JR on the mainland and JR on the islands, primarily because of Japan's economic structure, which is geographically biased. JR on the islands may never become financially independent and could remain as special companies that cannot raise capital in the market. Third, JR retained an excessive labor force, which could trigger cost increases. Good labor-management relationships and motivational incentives will be essential for truly efficient organizations.

Pension refunding is another difficulty facing JR. The ratio of recipients to the members of JR mutual pension funds is extremely high, which has created a critical situation since 1992. In 1984 the government decided to integrate public pension funds. Ongoing implementation of that effort should help stabilize JR's pension funds.

Electricity Regulation Is Limiting Competition

The nine electric power companies are treated as local monopolies. They are regulated by the Ministry of International Trade and Industry and are subject to the following regulations:

- Tariffs must be cost based. Customers are required to pay the full cost of electrical service.
- Electric companies must always supply electricity, meeting peak demand and providing universal service.
- Profits cannot exceed the fair rate of return, which is determined by the Electricity Business Law.
- Companies cannot diversify into unrelated fields, so as to prevent cross-subsidies that might be a source of unfair competition.

Despite these strict regulations, the local monopolies have grown into some of the largest corporations in Japan. Their size is impressive: Tokyo Electrical Power Corporation is the second largest electric company in the world. Yet some economists argue that economies of scale are no longer important in power generation, and that the legitimacy of regulation should be questioned, particularly given that independent power producers in the United States and competitive power providers in the United Kingdom are thriving. But even if competition is introduced in the power market, the basic status of Japan's electric firms will remain unchanged, simply because transmission and distribution networks will still exhibit economies of scale and scope.

In 1951 nine electrical power companies were created under the supervision of the General Headquarters, the central body for managing the reconstruction of Japan's postwar economy. These companies were fully integrated to provide electrical services in demarcated regions. Until World War II a public monopoly had provided generation and transmission, and nine private companies were responsible for distribution in specific regions. These distribution companies are now local monopolies, entitled to deny any entry into electrical service. But two other categories are important here: wholesalers who can generate power to supply these local monopolies, and electricity customers who generate power for their own use. Thus there are three sources of electric power supply: nine common carriers, wholesalers, and self-generators, but the first two account for almost 90 percent of power production.

Japan's local monopoly system was an experiment in the market supply of electrical service. In discussions about reconstructing the prewar electricity supply system, the authorities agreed that a regional division was more efficient than a national monopoly and that vertical integration was necessary to provide stable and reliable service. Although each company is a local monopoly, it must face an objective evaluation of its economic performance based on a comparison of its performance with that of other local utilities, thus employing the so-called yardstick competition. Ito and Miyazone (1994) suggest that many efficiency indicators—such as the thermal efficiency of steam power, the loss ratio of transmission, and the distribution or blackout times per customer—have converged in the past twenty years. If this phenomenon is interpreted as representing the existence of rivalry among electric utilities, the yardstick competition may be effective.

Price of Electricity Is High, but Quality Is Good

The price of electricity is much higher in Japan than in other industrial countries. Japan's electricity is not exportable, and one must use caution when making direct comparisons, but Japanese manufacturers are competing with foreign manufacturers who are paying much less for electricity, and electricity is a large operating expense. At the same time, high prices must be balanced against the quality of services.

The quality of electricity is measured by four indexes:

- *Thermal efficiency of steam power.* The average efficiency of the nine companies is almost 40 percent, which is the highest internationally.
- *Loss ratio of transmission and distribution.* This ratio has been constantly decreasing.
- *Blackout hours per customer.* The average blackout time is twenty minutes per customer per year, or about one-fifth of the time in the United States.
- *Dependence on atomic power.* The utilization rate of the atomic power plant is about 70 percent, which is the highest among industrial countries.

Self-Generated Electricity Might Threaten the Profitability of Common Carriers

Large users prefer to generate their own electricity when it is economical to do so to avoid buying power from common carriers. These users are eager to increase their self-reliance, because the normal tariff for business customers is relatively high compared to prices abroad and because firms must cut their energy costs to compete internationally. Self-generation capability can also increase buyers' negotiating position when trying to obtain a special discount from the normal tariff. Although power generating industries are restricted by economies of scale, technological advances and lower oil prices have permitted firms to produce electricity more economically. The recent development of self-generated electricity threatens common carriers and has spurred discussion about introducing more competition into the electricity industry.

Economies of Scale in Power Generation Recently Refuted

Until recently Japanese economists generally believed that the electricity industry enjoyed huge economies of scale in production and could be defended as a natural monopoly. This argument has now become less convincing for two main reasons. First, the construction of power plants has created environmental problems that usually incur a huge social cost. Even if the engineering cost of power generation still exhibits economies of scale, these cost savings can be negated by the increase in environmental costs. The opportunity cost of constructing new plants has been increasing, because sites have become more distant, usually located well away from residential centers, and more scarce. In addition, electricity companies must also spend huge sums to win over those who are against the construction of power generation plants.

Second, technological developments have allowed small electricity users to engage in self-generation. Cogeneration technology is one example, although it depends on oil prices. If small users can satisfy their demand without high production costs, they can compete with common carriers. In this case the justification for a natural monopoly is no longer valid. The lack of evidence about economies of scale invites discussion about introducing competition in power generation. In the United Kingdom and the United States competition in power production is already common. In Japan the process of deregulating electricity generation is moving slowly.

Move toward Full Deregulation Faces Obstacles

The most difficult problem facing electric companies in Japan is the high price of electricity. Although new technology should foster competition in power generation, the problem is complicated by the fact that the nine local monopolies operate in different regional markets. The common carriers located in the largest cities (Tokyo, Osaka, and Nagoya) welcome competition because it may help them to meet peak demand by increasing supply capacity and lowering generation and transmission costs. Other carriers hope to avoid competition because they fear losing their markets. This divergence of opinion has made the formulation of deregulation policy difficult. Besides, the government cannot easily disregard the opinions of the electric companies, because their size and economic importance in each regional economy make them politically strong.

In 1992 the electric companies agreed to buy excess power from nonelectric companies, such as cogenerators, but this new institutional framework has not worked well, mainly agreeing on prices has proven difficult. The electric companies fear the emergence of cream skimmers who may not take responsibility for providing stable power. Nevertheless, the carriers face obligations to meet peak demand and are thus forced to depend on outside suppliers, whether or not they are reliable.

Service quality also may impede competition. In general, the optimal quality will be found by a competitive process through trial and error, but if quality is regulated uniformly by the Ministry of International Trade and Industry, this process is not allowed to work, and poor quality may result.

In 1995 the Japanese government introduced deregulation as a cornerstone of its economic policy. It revised the Electricity Bidding Law in 1996, liberalizing entry into wholesale electricity distribution. Nine electricity companies have been licensed to buy power from independent generators under an open bidding scheme. The result of bidding was made public in March 1997. According to reports, 10.8 gigawatts worth of bids were received, which is almost quadruple the scheduled bid. Most bidder are giant companies like Shin Nippon Steel, Kobe Steel, Osaka Gas, Showa Denka, and Hitachi Manufacturing, which could be powerful new entrants as independent power producers in Japan. The bidding was also successful because helped reduce the costs of generating power. In the case of Tokyo and Osaka electricity, the bid price was almost 25 percent less than the upper limit price proposed by each electricity company.

Conclusion

Public corporations—*koshas*—helped expand infrastructure networks and service coverage, but ran into economic constraints that were compounded by political interference. In the telecommunications and railways sectors, the government responded by initiating privatization. Along with the traditionally private power sector, a substantial segment of Japanese infrastructure is now in private hands, but experience with privatization has been mixed. Pricing policies have hamstrung NTT, Inc. Certain privatized segments of the railways are profitable, others are not. Even in the power sector, which has maintained a long and successful record of private delivery, new technologies and customer demands for diversified sources of power are creating pressures for entry by competitors.

References

Fukui, Koichiro. 1992. *Japanese National Railways Privatization Study: The Experience of Japan and Lessons for Developing Countries*. Discussion Paper no. 172. Washington, D.C.: World Bank.

Ito, N., and T. Miyasone. 1994. "The Yard Stick Competition." In M. Uekusa, ed., *Electric Power Generation, Transmission, and Distribution*. Tokyo: NTT Publishing (in Japanese).

Nambu, Tsuruhiko. 1994. "A Comparison of Deregulation Policies." In Eli Noam, Seisuke Komatsuzaki, and Douglas A. Conn, eds., *Telecommunications in the Pacific Basin: An Evolutionary Approach*. New York: Oxford University Press.

7

How Infrastructure Agencies Motivate Staff: Canal Irrigation in India and the Republic of Korea

Robert Wade

This chapter analyzes one of the most common canal irrigation designs—the gravity-fed, high-response system—and discusses how canal agencies in two countries, India and the Republic of Korea, have been structured to operate and maintain the system. As similar operations and maintenance functions can be organized in different ways, determining which organizational designs are most effective at motivating workers to take the goals of the agency as the basis for their own actions is a useful endeavor.

In India the organization has no way to reward behavior that is in line with the organization's goals or to punish behavior that is contrary to those goals; the organization's large size discourages identification with the irrigation department as a whole; frequent job transfers discourage positive peer pressure and identification with smaller work units; and problem solving in the field is solely the responsibility of engineers and supervisors, yet the organization is too large, individual staff are too scattered, and information monitoring costs are too high to enable these personnel to address problems effectively. This system is not compatible with the Irrigation Department's objectives.

Compare this to Korea's system. The reward system combines seniority with both subjective judgments of current performance and objective indexes of competence. In this way a link is established between individual's efforts and material rewards. However, individually targeted incentives are also structured to encourage teamwork. Teamwork-related qualities are factored heavily into the formula that assesses annual performance among the operator grades, and special awards to organizational units are factored into the individual promotion scores of unit heads, giving them a direct incentive to motivate their teams. At least as important as the reward system is the basic organizational structure, which encourages group identification and peer monitoring. The salary of canal irrigation staff depends on the farmers' water payment, and hence on the general prosperity of agriculture in the area. Salary differentials within the organization are relatively small, facilitating collective identification. Stringent monitoring by principals at the top of the structure reinforces a collective sense of duty. Recruitment and promotion rules select people for the organization who have a strong local identification, and the density of staff in the field is much higher than in India's system, again facilitating peer monitoring. Other organizational devices help reinforce the sense of teamwork, such as contests between field stations and other organizational divisions and the dissemination of symbols of collective entity, such as badges, pennants, and brochures.

Of course, building up a sense of teamwork in a government agency is no guarantee that staff will be motivated to carry out the agency's objectives. The agency could become instead a cozy

The budget for this research was supported by a grant from the Ford Foundation. The author thanks Program Officer John Ambler. The Korean data are from 1979 and the Indian data are from 1975–82.

rental haven in which spoils are shared. This is a greater danger in Korea, which lacks independent farmer advocates, independent media, and local elected politicians. What checks this tendency in Korea, however, is the monitoring from above by multiple independent agencies and the dependence on farmers' water payments as a source of revenue, that is, in effect, discipline from above and below. The contrast between the two countries is striking: India's organization for maintaining and operating irrigation canal systems has virtually no incentives for conscientious work; Korea's organization is full of both individual and collective incentives.

The Agency Problem in Organizations

The relationship between the principals (or management) of an agency and its agents (or workers) influences on-the-job performance. Whether this relationship is strong or weak, and thus whether employees perform their jobs effectively or poorly, is predicated on a set of incentives established by the agency to encourage workers to pursue the agency's goals.

Modern economics identifies an incentive deterrent in organizations called the principal-agent problem, or the agency problem for short. An agency problem exists when an economic actor (the principal) employs one or more others (the agents) to undertake certain tasks on the principal's behalf, where it is difficult for the principal to monitor the agents' behavior and enforce performance standards. The danger of this problem is that it can lead to moral hazard, meaning that the agent shirks job responsibilities, subverts organizational procedures, or behaves opportunistically. This approach is contrary to the common sociological assumption that most people conform to expectations, keep promises, follow social norms, and obey organizational rules. It assumes instead that individuals comply with organizational expectations only if doing so benefits their own objectives.

The issue for organizational analysis is to determine the incentives to which principals and agents respond and the degree of compatibility between these incentives and what is required to meet organizational objectives. The challenge for public policy is to design a set of organizational arrangements that creates a compatible association between the incentives to which people respond and those that elicit the behavior necessary to achieve organizational objectives. Arrangements that reward people for behavior in line with organizational objectives are incentive compatible; those that do not are incentive incompatible.

How do officials ensure that their subordinates work conscientiously and competently on behalf of the organization in exchange for a salary?[1] The literature on organizations identifies four broad methods for tackling the agency problem: authority, rewards, identification, and peer pressure (Simon 1991).

Authority is the canonical method. Employees agree to do what they are ordered to do (within limits) in return for a wage or salary and other benefits. Employees are generally not commanded to perform every action that is specific to their job. Rather, they are ordered to apply discretion or to secure a certain result, but the details of how they do so are left to them. The challenge here is to ensure that employees use their discretion in ways that advance organizational objectives.

Rewards are the method the new institutional economics favors. Employees are induced to use their discretion to advance organizational objectives by being offered a salary, bonus, or promotion tied to their performance as assessed by management. This method has limited practical application, in that it can be used only to the extent that performance indexes measure performance appropriately (for example, capture both the quality and quantity of work) and identify individual contributions properly. The more interdependent the work of individuals in organizations, the more difficult it is to measure individual contributions. This point is not minor, because the basic rationale of

---

1.   Another equally important facet of the agency problem is how subordinates ensure that their superiors act on behalf of organizational objectives, but this facet is less easily accommodated in principal-agent analysis, except in a strictly formal way.

organizations is to exploit intense interdependencies. Thus the relationship between the organization's goals and the material rewards employees receive is indirect and weak in most organizations.

Identification with the organization—individuals' inclination to use the goals and authority of the organization as the basis for their own actions—is an important, and often neglected, source of motivation. Identification with the organization is rooted in something more than the link between an organization's overall success and the monetary rewards given to its employees. The strength of organizational identification varies from one society to another, as well as according to the structure of the organization.

Peer pressure is a related but distinct source of motivation. It also depends heavily on the organization's structure, including the extent to which individual reward depends on the performance of the entire group. As such, it also depends on the ease with which group members can monitor and motivate each other's activities.

The Agency Problem in Canal Irrigation

In canal irrigation the principal-agent relationship is complicated by the nature of the facility itself. First, canal systems are hostage to terrain and to weather. Second, the agents—canal patrollers and their immediate supervisors—are highly dispersed and are beyond direct supervision and peer group pressure. Management cannot easily monitor their actions and results cannot be readily attributed to individual action or inaction. Third, agents interact closely each day with clients beyond the organization's bureaucratic reach and have much discretion in shaping this interaction. This factor complicates the agency problem, because it introduces a third actor in the principal-agent relationship: the farmer as client.

The Role of Water Availability and Topography

Climate is a major determinant of the size of the gap between the supply of and demand for irrigation water, and in turn determines the extent to which canal operators must deny farmers water. The demand for irrigation is a function of the difference between precipitation and evapotranspiration, which is a function of temperature. When average precipitation is equal to or greater than evapotranspiration during the growing season, only a small amount of irrigation is needed and the stress placed on the system by excess demand for water is slight. When precipitation is much less than evapotranspiration (as in a desert), without irrigation farmers can grow only meager crops or no crops. Water demand is thus predictable. This means that it is possible to design physical facilities so that, within large subunits of the canal command, the hardware—the network of channels and outlets—allocates constant shares of the given water supply without intervention by system operators. The stress on the system from fluctuating, and sometimes excess, demand for water can be slight if the design of the physical structures is accommodating.

The most difficult climate for irrigation is when average precipitation is somewhat less than average evapotranspiration and precipitation is highly variable. In such conditions crops can be brought to harvest with little irrigation when rainfall is normal, but when a drought strikes, even if only for a few weeks, farmers all want extra water at once, placing great stress on the system.

Another factor that affects the agency problem in irrigation canals is topography. Whether flat or hilly, topography affects how large a system is. Where land is flat, water may have to be supplied from a reservoir many miles away (perhaps hundreds of miles), and the larger the system, the more difficult it is for local groups of farmers—or even the system operators—to understand the system as a whole. Hilly country makes it easier and more necessary to have multiple reservoirs, which in turn make it easier for local groups of farmers to understand the system that affects their supply. Topography also affects the need for drainage, which influences the system's design and operations.

The Role of Operations and Maintenance

The second set of factors affecting the agency problem in irrigation systems pertain to how job responsibilities are defined, how operations are financed, and where decisionmaking authority is situated. Each of these factors affects the inclination of staff to cooperate in achieving organizational goals and, in turn, the relationship between the organization and its clients.

CONSTRUCTION OFTEN TAKES PRIORITY OVER OPERATIONS AND MAINTENANCE. The relationship between operations and maintenance activities and construction activities has a major bearing on how staff functions are divided in an organization. For example, construction and maintenance require skills that differ from those needed to operate the system. The skill requirements would argue for separating operations from construction and maintenance, but operations and maintenance are ongoing activities within a system, while construction is not, and the information required for executing operations and maintenance activities overlaps substantially, suggesting that operations and maintenance activities should be kept together and construction should be kept separate. Budgetary considerations reinforce the case for separating operations and maintenance from construction. Because the budget for construction is likely to dwarf the budget for operations and maintenance, and because the number of officer-level posts in construction is likely to be much larger than the number in operations and maintenance (particularly when, as in most countries, the irrigated area is expanding fairly rapidly), the organization tends to define its mission as being construction. When irrigation staff are trained only in engineering, this pushes them in the same direction. In these conditions operations and maintenance are eclipsed as a serious professional activity.

DECENTRALIZING OPERATIONS AND MAINTENANCE CAN BE BENEFICIAL. Whether canal operations and maintenance are governed by a single, centralized hierarchy or by decentralized agencies with circumscribed geographical boundaries also affects the agency problem. Although scale advantages are often associated with a single organization, a number of motivational and informational advantages argue for geographically separate agencies. However, within a set of decentralized agencies, another issue is determining how much power the agencies should wield, that is, whether their powers constitute only a delegation of state power without a legally defined transfer of political power, or whether they are a legally defined devolution of state power that weakens the power of the center.

OPERATIONS AND MAINTENANCE SHOULD BE SELF-FUNDING. The agency problem is also affected by whether the budget for operations and maintenance comes from user fees or from a grant from the state treasury. A grant from general revenue allows operations and maintenance claims to be weighed against other claims and allows governments that are seeking to boost irrigation coverage to subsidize farmers easily. However, grants orient the operations and maintenance organization toward the core of government and away from farmers. If the organization's revenues are based on farmers' water payments, it is likely to be more strongly oriented toward serving the farmers. In addition, given that operations and maintenance expenditures are recurrent and fairly stable, this mitigates the advantage of grants of allowing all expenditure claims to be weighed against each other.

The Agency Problem in India and Korea

The climate and topography of India and Korea place different demands on their canal agencies, and thus on their staff. In general India's lower, but still substantial, average rainfall and vast geographical area make operating canals and monitoring job performance more difficult. Nevertheless, three factors make canal irrigation systems in Korea more effective, even after its climatic and topographical advantages are accounted for, namely:

- Korea has a decentralized organizational structure for operating and maintaining its canal systems and a centralized organization for designing and constructing them.
- Korea funds its canal irrigation systems predominantly from user fees, making them more cost-responsive and their staff more diligent about revenue collection.
- Korea has a more sophisticated field communications network, thereby enabling workers to recognize and respond to field problems more rapidly and effectively.

India at a Disadvantage because of Climate and Topology

Korea has more rainfall than evapotranspiration throughout the year; India has less rainfall than evapotranspiration for nine months of the year. The stress on canal systems is correspondingly greater in India. India also has large tracts of flat plains and large rivers. Water, rather than irrigable land, is the binding constraint. Korea has broken valleys and hills, with small rivers. Irrigable land, rather than water, is the main constraint.

The differences in climate and topography have important consequences. One is that Korea does not suffer from one of the major difficulties of India's irrigation systems: overextended command areas. Canal facilities in India are commonly built to service a much larger area than the water supply is capable of servicing. This design leaves a large number of farmers toward the tail end of the system to compete with one another for limited supplies. Another consequence is that system operators in Korea do not have to ration water resources to meet the crop water requirement for the irrigated area, whereas operators in India must be more conservative. In other words, the opportunity cost of a given amount of irrigation water at the margin is relatively low in Korea, at least in normal times, and is generally high in India.

Differences in climate and topography also affect the size of the irrigation systems. Canals in India are typically larger than those in Korea. Only 18 percent of Korea's canal systems have an irrigated area of more than 5,000 hectares; only three systems irrigate more than 20,000 hectares. India also has plenty of canals of this size, but most of India's canal-irrigated areas are fed from canals that are at least five times—and often more than ten times—larger than the largest canal in Korea.

These climatic and topographical differences mean that operating and maintaining an irrigation canal, that is, keeping water in the crop root zone at close to optimal levels, is more difficult in India than in Korea. Irrigated rice yields in Korea are about twice as high as in India, and it is fair to assume that this difference is due in part to the fact that water in the crop root zone is maintained at optimal levels (IRRI 1985). (More daylight during the growing season, heavier use of fertilizer, and other factors also help explain Korea's higher yields.) However, because meeting this condition is much easier in Korea than in India for climatic, topographical, and system size reasons, one cannot assume that Korean irrigation canals are operated and maintained more effectively. Nevertheless, if the two systems were subject to the same degree of water stress, with holding size and other physical parameters constant, Korea's system would be more efficient operationally because of its superior organization (figure 7–1).

Korea's Decentralized Structure Makes Operations and Maintenance More Effective

In India the national Irrigation Department is responsible for designing, constructing, operating, and maintaining canals. Thus the same organization that designs and constructs canals is responsible for their operation and maintenance. Therefore the chain of command stretches from the chief engineer in the capital down to scattered field offices. In the state of Andhra Pradesh alone, this hierarchy employs about 40,000 people. The organization is not responsible for providing agricultural extension or for collecting water payments from farmers; both tasks are the responsibility of separate and similarly organized government departments.

Figure 7–1. The Organization of Canal Irrigation in India   and Korea

India (national level)

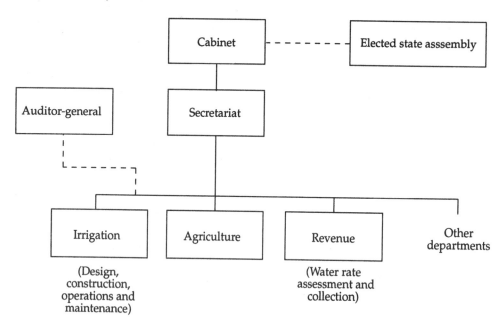

Korea

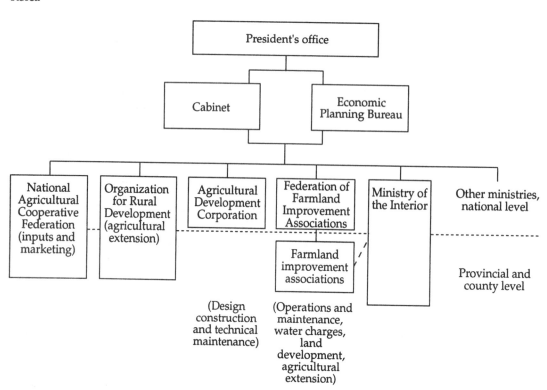

In Korea the organization for canal operations and maintenance is separate from the organization responsible for design and construction. One organization carries out design and construction activities for the entire country (equivalent in scale to an Indian state). This organization—the Agricultural Development Corporation—has the status of a public corporation, responsible to, but legally separate from, the Ministry of Agriculture. Its status allows the corporation to buy and sell land, machinery, and other items on its own account and to sue and be sued.

Decentralized agencies called farmland improvement associations (FLIAs) carry out canal operations and maintenance based on watershed boundaries. These agencies also have the status of public corporations. Beyond normal operations and maintenance functions, staff also provide agricultural extension; assess and collect water charges from farmers; and undertake land development by leveling fields, rectangularizing boundaries, and constructing a grid-shaped network of field channels and drains. Canal operations and maintenance personnel in India perform none of these tasks.

The FLIAs are responsible to the Ministry of Agriculture and also to the administration of the province in which they are located, which is part of the Ministry of the Interior's hierarchy. The Ministry of Agriculture sets detailed budget, accounting, staffing, administrative, and technical parameters within which the FLIAs must operate. The ministry must approve FLIA budgets in advance, and the minister of agriculture appoints the presidents of the larger associations. The FLIAs' separate legal status enables them to buy and sell land and machinery on their own account, but the associations have delegated, not devolved, powers: authority remains concentrated in the central government and the associations have operational and administrative discretion within limits set from the center.

As a new canal starts to supply irrigation water, it is first operated by the staff of the canal construction agency, the Agricultural Development Corporation (ADC). At the same time, an FLIA is formed if one does not already exist in the watershed and gradually starts to expand its staff and take over operational responsibilities from ADC staff. For the first several seasons after the canal is completed, formal authority for operations and maintenance continues to rest with the corporation. A handing over procedure then takes place during which the staff of the FLIA agree that the canal is in good working order. In this way the ADC avoids being responsible for designing canals without being able to operate them. Moreover, the relationship between the corporation and the FLIAs does not end at the handing over ceremony; the corporation remains the associations' main source of technical assistance.

Korea's Graduated User Fee System Distributes Operating Costs More Equitably

In India the Irrigation Department's budget comes in the form of a grant from the national treasury. User fees are a small part of general national revenue. In Korea about three-quarters of the ordinary (noncapital) budget of the FLIAs comes from user fees, and commissions for various agricultural services account for much of the rest. Water charges are based on a division of costs among the beneficiaries, not on the quantity of water used. Charges must cover 30 percent of capital costs. Water charges must also cover a portion of land development costs. The state pays 71 percent of such costs and the farmers whose land has been developed pay 29 percent, half of which can be, and often is, in labor time. The government also provides a 70 percent subsidy for construction work (reservoirs, main conveyances, and drainage structures) and gives cheap, long-term loans (3.5 percent over thirty-five years) for the remaining 30 percent.

Charges for each farmer are not the same within any one FLIA. A complex formula is used to ensure that farmers who gain more pay a higher share of costs than those who gain less. First, farmers under a reservoir (because of the hilly terrain any system may have several reservoirs) are treated as a separate accounting unit. They share in the general administrative costs of the entire

FLIA, but do not share in the costs that are specific to other accounting units, including those for pumps and pumping and for land development. Second, all land is classified according to its use before the irrigation facilities were constructed: the lower its previous productive value, the higher its current water charge. Third, some land is identified as having a substantially worse water supply than other land, and farmers on this land pay 30 percent less than the average charge in that district. Fourth, land that produces less than 2 tons of produce per hectare in a given year receives a discount, the level of which depends on how much less than 2 tons it produces, based on a scale set by the Ministry of Agriculture. Within any one FLIA the average water charge for each of its districts may vary by 20 percent or more.

Korea's Field Communication Network Is More Sophisticated

The communications infrastructure of the two countries also differs. Korea has a much denser network of roads, an abundance of motorized transport, and good radio communication. Irrigation staff in Korea move about in jeeps or motorcycles and can communicate at a distance by radio. In India more than 80 percent of irrigation staff move about the canals on bicycles or on foot. Communication is maintained through a main-trunk telephone network or a single-wire relay telephone along the main canal; both devices are slow and unreliable. Response time in India's irrigation systems, that is, the length of time it takes the appropriate person to learn about a problem and initiate action in the field, is thus much longer than in Korea.

The Agency Problem and Canal Design

The predominant canal irrigation system in both India and Korea is the gravity-fed, high-response design, one that gives workers great discretion over water allocation. The resulting agency problem is a large part of the reason that these systems tend to perform more poorly than do other canal designs, in the sense that a larger gap exists between design performance and actual performance and that rates of return on investment at current and expected future cereal prices are lower (Burns 1993).

To analyze the agency problem in India and Korea in detail—specifically, to discuss how organizations induce operators to work toward organizational objectives and how the relationship between the organization and its clients (farmers) plays out—this chapter compares two specific canal systems in India and Korea. The Indian system is called here the MN Canal and the Korean one is called the SY FLIA (both MN and SY are pseudonyms). Although these canals are not unusual for their respective countries as concerns design, crops, or organization, the MN Canal is in the average range of the size of major canals in India, and the SY FLIA is in the top 5 percent of canals in Korea, but is still less than a tenth the size of MN Canal. Table 7–1 shows other differences between the two canals.

Both these systems are gravity-fed, high-response designs. This is the most common of three irrigation systems used throughout the world. The other systems are the gravity-fed, low-response design and the drainage and lift design (box 7–1).

The gravity-fed, high-response design tends to intensify the severity of the agency problem for two reasons. First, under this design operators and higher-level staff have much more discretion in water allocation. Consequently, attempts to capture economic rents—the difference between what the farmer must officially pay and what the water is worth—are likely to be more intensive than under the other two designs. When a farmer plants irrigated crops on the assumption that rainfall will meet 70 percent of the water requirement, and drought occurs, the value of the irrigation may be close to the value of the crop. Official water charges to farmers in developing countries are seldom more than 25 percent of the value of the water and are generally much less, thus the rent is at least 75 percent of the value of the water (Repetto 1986). Farmers compete to get this rent, and

Table 7–1. Key Features of India's MN Canal and Korea's SY FLIA Canal

Feature	MN Canal	SY FLIA Canal
Gross irrigated area (hectares)	128,000	11,200
Water source	Single diversion from nonperennial river and upstream storage in single reservoir	Four main reservoirs and 13 small reservoirs
Means of water delivery	Gravity (no conjunctive use of ground water)	Mostly gravity, supplemented by pumps for lifting surface water (little conjunctive use of groundwater)
Length of main canals (kilometers)	300	27–36
Time of construction	1860–90; extensively modernized, 1955–60	Four main reservoirs 1961–72; small reservoirs mostly 1940–60
Main crops	First season: paddy Second season: paddy, sorghum groundnut, cotton	First season: paddy Second season: none
Average irrigated area under each outlet (hectares)	160	14
Staff	258 patrollers, 150 others	109 patrollers, 177 others
Irrigated area per patroller (hectares)	496	103

irrigation staff may not be indifferent to the fact that what they are allocating is worth much more to the farmers than what the farmers must pay. Thus irrigation workers may also compete to get some of the rent in the form of bribes and extortion.

India's MN Canal

The MN Canal is one division—the chief executing unit—of the Andhra Pradesh Irrigation Department. The division is headed by an executive engineer (box 7–2). Divisional headquarters are located in a town within the command area and contain three main sections: one for administration, one for finance, and one for technical affairs (mainly drafting).

The MN Canal division has an irrigated area of 128,000 hectares a year. The division consists of four subdivisions, each headed by an assistant engineer. The gross irrigated area of a subdivision is 30,000 to 35,000 hectares, three times the irrigated area of SY FLIA. Each subdivision has a small office, normally with a staff of five or six clerks, draftsmen, and drivers. The office is located in a town or village near its command area. The subdivision has four or five sections, each headed by a supervisor who supervises four foremen, each of whom supervises four patrollers.

Box 7–1. Three Irrigation Canal System Designs

Gravity-Fed, High-Response Design

The most common irrigation canal design is the publicly owned and operated, gravity-fed, extensively gated canal. Rainfall and snow in hills and mountains supply rivers and then storage facilities, which in turn serve conveyance and distribution networks in the plains and valley bottoms. For water to flow by gravity in open channels from the source to the fields, the channels must "command" the fields, that is, the water level in the channels must be raised above the level of the surrounding terrain. Doing so requires raised embankments for carrying the water and gates at various points in the network to control the flow.

Gates are used extensively when rainfall in the command area is highly variable, so most outlets serving an area of 100 hectares or less have a gate. Gates allow the water supply to be adjusted in line with rainfall. These systems thus require many gate operators. Data from the Food and Agriculture Organization of the United Nations suggest that publicly owned and operated systems of this type account for 60 to 70 percent of the irrigated areas in the developing world.

Gravity-Fed, Low-Response Design

The other two design types are found in more extreme climatic and topographical conditions. The gravity-fed, low-response design is a variant of the high-response system. It also works by gravity, but it is not extensively gated. Control structures are concentrated at higher levels of the network, serving much larger areas (thousands of hectares). Within these areas water allocation is determined by the shape and size of the conveyance channels and the outlets. The main difference between this design and the high-response design is that it gives system operators much less discretion about where the water goes. This factor greatly reduces its susceptibility to agency problems.

The low-response design is well suited to desert conditions, where topography and soils are uniform and precipitation is so much less than evapotranspiration that rainfed agriculture is barely possible. Here the demand for irrigation water is high and stable. Under these conditions water can be allocated through the network with a high degree of regularity, using the equivalent of a mass production assembly line.

Drainage and Lift Design

The third design is found in the great river deltas of Asia (the Ganges-Brahmaputra, Yangtze, Chao Phya, Mekong, and the Saga plain of Japan). Rainfall is heavy in these areas and flooding is a problem. The irrigation network both gets water in during the dry season and gets floodwater out during the wet season into a network of channels. For the channels to function as drains they must be excavated deep enough that the water level remains below the level of the surrounding land. With floodwaters controlled and diverted in this way, rice can be grown in the wet season primarily with rainfall. During the dry season the water in these excavated channels is lifted by pumps to irrigate a second crop. Thus the canal network provides storage between wet and dry seasons, and the system has a physical break between the conveyance of water to the excavated channels and the distribution of water to the fields. Distribution is done using private pumping; users must pay in proportion to the amount of water they use. (This is rare in gravity systems.) Figures from the Food and Agriculture Organization of the United Nations suggest that 20 to 30 percent of the irrigated area in developing countries is under this type of system. The share may be higher in monsoon-prone areas of Asia.

Source: Burns 1993; Moore 1989.

Korea's SY FLIA

Korea's organization is much more complicated, reflecting its wider range of activities (see figure 7–1 and box 7–2). Several features of SY FLIA's structure are of interest. First, the headquarters consists of three main bureaus, one each for management, administration, and land development. Second, the management bureau deals with canal operations, maintenance, and agricultural affairs.

Box 7–2. Employee Hierarchy of India's MN Canal and Korea's SY FLIA

Rank	Number of employees
MN Canal	
Executive engineer (divisional officer)	1
Assistant engineer (subdivisional officer)	4
Supervisor (section officer)	20
Foreman	73
Patroller	258
Other (clerk, draftsman, driver)	52
Total	408
SY FLIA	
Grade 1a (president)	1
Grade 1b (manager)	1
Grade 2 (bureau chief)	4
Grade 3 (section chief)	15
Grade 4	32
Grade 5	46
Permanent employee	46
Temporary employee	29
Patroller	109
Total	283

Operations and maintenance within this bureau are the responsibility of separate sections, and the operations section also does agricultural extension. In India the same unit performs canal operations and maintenance, but not agricultural extension. Korea's grouping reflects the orientation of the entire irrigation organization toward agriculture; India's organization reflects its origins in and orientation toward construction. Third, most of the staff is based in field station offices scattered throughout the command area. The organizational separation between operations and maintenance is maintained at the field station level, with one officer for operations and agricultural affairs and another for maintenance.

Canal Patrollers as Agents

Canal irrigation patrollers are responsible for guarding and monitoring the banks of the canal, opening and shutting water gates, and performing other operations and maintenance. They are at the bottom of the organizational hierarchy (in both countries men always fill this position). India's rules minimize identification between the patroller and the locality, and—at least in theory—maximize identification with the Irrigation Department. Korea's system instills a common bond between patrollers and farmers, increasing responsiveness and accountability. Of all the work functions in canal operation, those of the canal patroller are most directly comparable across the two countries.

The contrast in the employment rules for patrollers in the two countries is clear. In India the patroller
- Must be a full-time employee and cannot farm more than a marginal amount of land
- Is selected by the engineer-manager responsible for the subdivision in which he works
- Is employed permanently after serving a probationary period
- Must be rotated to another post within six years
- Must not be posted in the jurisdiction in which his native village is located.
  In Korea the patroller
- Must be part-time and a farmer the rest of the time
- Is selected by the chiefs of the villages within his jurisdiction and approved by the irrigation hierarchy
- Must be renominated by the village chiefs each year

- Is not transferred from one place to another
- Must live and farm within his own jurisdiction.

India's system seeks to increase patrollers' compliance with instructions that filter down the hierarchy and to reduce incentives to accede to the wishes of local farmers seeking preferential treatment. Korea's system seeks workers who themselves suffer irrigation difficulties similar to those other farmers in their jurisdiction experience, who are connected to those other farmers in a larger structure of social networks, and who are explicitly accountable to farming leaders. By tying the workplace to the residence and by enlisting other farmers (especially village chiefs) as supervisors and monitors, Korea's rules make the patrollers less susceptible to shirking and subversive behavior. (Of course, the relatively small size of Korea's system and its relatively abundant water supply are also relevant in this connection.)

Recruitment and Promotion

India and Korea apply different recruitment and promotion standards to their canal work force. Recruitment in India is not based on competency and job performance is almost never a criterion for promotion. Korea's recruitment and promotion system is a mix of subjective and objective criteria. Recruitment is based on the results of a fair examination, and although the Korean system allows the president and senior managers some influence over the order of promotion, it also contains several more objective elements, some based on length of service, others on examination scores, and others on merit scores given by people outside the set of hierarchical superiors. Korea's recruitment and promotion rules create a much stronger link between staff and the workplace, combining incentives for conscientious individual performance and in-service training with incentives for teamwork.

India's Recruitment and Promotion System Distinguishes Sharply between Officers and Subordinates

In India officers are promoted, subordinates are not. Junior engineers are recruited from universities after they complete a four- or five-year degree in civil engineering and can expect to be promoted to senior positions in the department. (Box 7-2 does not show junior engineers because they are not normally posted to canal operations and maintenance. They appear in the hierarchy between assistant engineer and supervisor.)

Supervisors must have a diploma in civil engineering from a two- or three-year program following high school. They can be promoted to assistant engineer only near the end of their careers. Below the supervisors are foremen and patrollers. Both are closed cadres in the sense that there is no promotion from them: once a foreman, always a foreman; once a patroller, always a patroller. Foremen must have a high school diploma; patrollers must be literate. Thus more than 90 percent of the staff running Indian irrigation canals do not have any prospect for promotion, and the 6 percent who are supervisors have some chance for promotion only toward the end of their career.

Holders of degrees in civil engineering are recruited to the officer ranks by the national-level Public Service Commission. The commission sets its own entry examinations for the different departments and conducts oral interviews with candidates. Given the number of candidates, the oral interviews normally take five minutes or less. Nevertheless, the examination and interview do give a modest meritocratic element to officer recruitment. The executive engineer of the division in which vacancies exist recruits patrollers and foremen without any type of testing. Thus most staff of India's irrigation canals are recruited without any objective test of competence.

Promotion within the officer cadre depends solely on seniority, not on any judgment of merit. Officers are recruited to the department in batches of 100 or more every few years. All those in one batch are senior to those in later batches. Seniority within each batch is assigned by the Public Service

Commission on the basis of the initial examination, referee reports, and the interview. Officers carries this ranking with them for the rest of their careers. Rarely is someone promoted out of order, and performance is almost never a criterion for promotion. India's system provides almost no in-service training of any kind, thus also precluding any objective basis for judging current performance.

Korea's Recruitment and Promotion System Is More Complicated and Meritocratic

In Korea FLIA staff are divided into graded categories: professional staff, who are graded from 5 (lowest) to 1, in which promotion is possible and expected; permanent employees, who perform semiskilled clerical or technical work; temporary employees, who perform the same work as permanent employees, but who are hired on a yearly contract basis and are paid a daily wage; and patrollers, who are employed for the six-month irrigation season each year and are paid a daily wage.

In SY FLIA professional staff account for 35 percent of the staff and permanent employees for another 17 percent. Thus the organization makes a long-term commitment to just over half of its employees, while India's organization makes a long-term commitment to the vast majority of its employees after they serve a probationary period. Yet only about 2 percent of India's operations and maintenance employees have promotion prospects, while in Korea 35 percent of professional staff have promotion prospects within the ranks, and the others gain these prospects by passing an examination at entry into grade 5, the lowest level of the professional hierarchy. Anyone can take the examination and no minimum educational qualifications are required. (Note that none of the professional staff has a university degree, in contrast to the Indian organization.) In practice, candidates for the grade 5 examination are either those who have worked for several years as permanent or temporary employees or those who have recently graduated from a technical college.

The senior positions of each FLIA are filled almost entirely by promotion from within. Other than the president, outsiders are rarely recruited for senior positions. (The exceptions are mainly for technical positions, such as head of the land development bureau.) The president is appointed by the Ministry of Agriculture, or in small FLIAs by the provincial governor. The president is normally a Ministry of Agriculture official near retirement age who resigns from the ministry to take the position (the retirement age from the FLIA is several years beyond the retirement age from the ministry) and remains as the ministry's representative in the FLIA.

The method for determining promotion is complex and highly codified, and it marries incentives for individual performance with incentives for teamwork. This system is worth examining, because conventional wisdom says that this marriage is unlikely under real-world civil service conditions. The same system used for irrigation parastatals is used throughout Korea's civil service.

Each professional staff member has a "promotion score" that weighs heavily in promotion decisions. The score is the sum of a length of service formula and a merit score. Length of service points are accumulated according to the following formula: a person must stay in each grade for a stipulated minimum period (one year in grade 5, two-and-a-half years in grade 4, and so on). Each month after this minimum period earns 0.13 points, up to twenty-four months; each month for the following twenty-four months earns 0.09 points. Staff stop earning points beyond forty-eight months after the minimum period and must accumulate additional promotion points by increasing their merit scores.

Merit scores have three subcomponents. First, individuals' hierarchical superiors—the bureau chief, the manager, and the president—write annual performance assessments. Superiors score performance under several headings and their verdicts are averaged. Scores for grades 5 and 4 are weighted toward diligence and cooperativeness; scores for grade 3 (the first management grade) are weighted toward knowledge, leadership, and willingness to take responsibility. The superiors' judgment is, of course, subjective, but weighting grade 5 and 4 scores toward teamwork does help make their overall judgment more likely to conform to peer judgment. In promotion systems that are not weighted explicitly toward teamwork in the lower grades, superiors' judgment may diverge more widely from peer judgment, thus reinforcing tendencies toward conflict and low-trust supervision.

The second subcomponent of the merit score is in-service training. The Ministry of Agriculture bureau that supervises FLIAs arranges with the counterpart supervisory office of the provincial administration to provide in-service training courses for FLIA staff that can last anywhere from a morning to two weeks. The longer courses culminate in an examination. The percentage score in this examination is weighted by 0.02 and added to the merit total.

The third subcomponent includes other sources of merit, such as special prizes for valor, public service (charity work or political work), or outstanding job performance. For example, when the national government mounted a campaign to promote agricultural mechanization, the president of Korea awarded certificates of outstanding performance to the heads of the agricultural machinery sections of FLIAs whose agricultural mechanization showed rapid progress. Special awards, which feed directly into the promotion score, are scored according to who confers them. One from the president of Korea is worth 3 points, one from the prime minister 2.5 points, one from the minister of agriculture 2 points, one from the provincial governor 1.5 points, and one from the president of the FLIA 1 point. When an award is made not to an individual, but to a team (such as an FLIA's agricultural mechanization section), the points count toward the promotion score of the team head.

An individual's overall promotion score consists of the merit score weighted by 0.4 and the length of service formula weighted by 0.6. The score earned by staff at one grade cannot be carried forward at promotion.

Individuals are supposed to be promoted according to the rank order of scores, but in practice the president and manager have some discretion about who is promoted and when. In addition to gaining promotion points, staff who are seeking promotion from grade 4 to grade 3 (the first management grade) must pass a special examination set and marked by the provincial administration (not by the FLIA), but the president of the FLIA can decide who is allowed to take the examination.

Employee Transfers

India's personnel rules require that staff at all levels of the irrigation hierarchy be transferred to other regions at regular intervals and that they not be posted to their native villages. Korea's system allows staff to remain in their native localities, and transfers are largely made within, not beyond, regions. Korea's system thus fosters a lasting relationship between workers and farmers. These two disparate transfer systems can be viewed as the difference between single-shot and repeated games. As game theory suggests, cooperation is more likely when interactions are more frequent and habitual than when they are not.

The frequency and distance of transfers in India vary according to rank. Most engineers average between two and three years at a posting. A new posting generally means a change in residence. Officers who enters the Irrigation Department at age twenty-five will have changed residence, on average, twelve to fourteen times by the time they retire at fifty-eight. The normal tenure of executive engineers in operations and maintenance posts is between twenty and twenty-four months, and they can be transferred anywhere in the state. Assistant engineers average 2.5 years at a post and can also be sent anywhere in the state. Supervisors average 3.7 years at a post and tend to spend most of their careers within their (four-district) region. Foremen average 4.3 years a post and normally remain within 100 miles of their native villages. Patrollers average 6.4 years at a post and their transfers are normally within fifty miles of their native villages.[2]

---

2.   The data come from the author's survey of irrigation staff.

In Korea staff are rotated from post to post within each FLIA (excluding patrollers), but the small size of the systems means that changes in residence are rare, and there is almost no movement of staff among FLIAs.

Salary Scales

In India salaries are based disparately on staff rank, reflecting the irrigation system's emphasis on hierarchy. In Korea they are based largely on length of service, giving FLIA workers a huge incentive to remain with their agency. Appropriate salary scales contribute to the efficiency of any public sector enterprise.

FLIA salary scales are weighted heavily toward length of service. The weight is such that a grade 5 worker with more than ten years of service will earn more than a grade 4 worker with six years of service. More dramatically, a grade 5 operator with twenty-one years of service will earn more than a rapidly promoted grade 3 manager with ten years of service. Permanent employees receive only a slightly lower salary than grade 5 staff when length of service is held constant.

Thus the salary difference between ranks is relatively small. When length of service is held constant, the ratio between an operator's (grade 5) salary and a section chief's (grade 3) salary is 1:1.6; the ratio between an operator's salary and that of a manager (grade 2, the position directly below the president) is 1:2.2. The salary of the FLIA president depends on the area of the FLIA, as stipulated by a Ministry of Agriculture.

Compared with the salary scale of central government civil servants, the FLIA scale gives more weight to length of service than to rank. However, FLIA staff receive a salary that is higher than the salary of central government staff of equivalent rank for grade 3 and below when length of service is held constant. FLIA staff of grade 2 and above receive less than their central government counterparts. FLIA staff receive the same medical, retirement, and holiday benefits as central government employees. Thus, up to the level of central government bureau chief, FLIA staff are well paid in relation to central government staff. The system's emphasis on length of service gives FLIA workers a strong incentive to stay with the FLIA, and small salary differentials by rank equalize pay scales. These organizational features help to build identification between the individual and the organization.

As shown below, salary differentials in India are about twice as large as those in Korea:

Korea:	Grade 5 (operator): grade 3 (section chief) = 1:1.6
India:	Foreman: supervisor = 1:2.6 to 1:3.7
Korea:	Grade 5 (operator): grade 1b (manager) = 1:2.2
India:	Foreman: assistant engineer = 1:3.7 to 1:4.6
Korea:	Grade 5 (operator): grade 1a (president) = 1:2.7
India:	Foreman: executive engineer = 1:5.5 to 1:6.7

The much larger salary jumps between ranks in India could provide a stronger material incentive for conscientious performance than does Korea's organization, but as noted earlier, in India promotion from one rank to another is determined largely by seniority, not by current performance. Conversely, the relatively flat salary profile in Korea is consistent with the argument that a steep salary profile is not necessary if staff are motivated by other means.

Supervision

Literature on organizations suggests that in the absence of trust such characteristics as conscientiousness and initiative are impaired and that, conversely, shirking or other types of opportunistic behavior are encouraged to the extent that the risk of being detected is small (Blau and Scott 1962; Fox 1974; Heginbotham 1975; Leonard 1977; March and Simon 1958). In India low-trust management discourages conscientiousness and problem solving. The concern, rather, is ensuring that superiors do not find fault or that they are not angered. Trying to improve procedures and performance in this system can be risky, because doing so may create nonroutine situations that are unacceptable to superiors. Workers can avoid trouble simply by maintaining existing levels of performance. Interpersonal relationships are where high trust management is evident in Korea's SY FLIA. The harsh, authoritarian style common in India is not in evidence. There is also less emphasis on rank differences, for example, staff wear the same types of clothes and senior managers eat lunch with junior employees.

Administration in India Based on the Assumption That Subordinates Are Not to Be Trusted

Supervision in India's canal systems is geared more toward discovering grounds for punishment than toward identifying problems. This pattern seems to be pervasive throughout India's bureaucracy; indeed, it may be a pattern in pre-industrial bureaucracies generally. Low-trust management methods and the wide gulf in power between officers and field staff in India is a legacy of the relationship between the British colonial administration and the natives.

Thus expenditure rules concentrate control tightly in the hands of the executive engineer who oversees the canal system. Assistant engineers—who manage subdivisions of 20,000 to 40,000 gross irrigated hectares—have little budgetary discretion. Lack of trust is expressed more directly in the generally harsh and coercive style that superiors use with their subordinates, especially employees more than one rank below them. The discretion of assistant engineers and supervisors is frequently curtailed by orders from superiors, and their security is threatened by the punitive and authoritarian stance of those superiors. In turn, assistant engineers and supervisors exhibit even less trusting attitudes and behavior to their field staff.

The tendency of bureaucratic superiors to use coercive supervisory techniques prompts subordinates to shirk or subvert compliance when they believe that the risk of being detected is small, and given the size of the systems and the primitive means of communication, the risks of detection are often minimal. For example, an assistant engineer on patrol may receive a telegram from the executive engineer ordering him to attend a meeting at headquarters. Despite receiving the telegram in time, and despite the urgency of the telegram, he may well not go. The assistant assumes that the executive will not be able to determine when he received the telegram.

The effect of this institutionalized lack of trust is most evident when a canal breaches. If the breach is small the patrollers and foremen can fix it without using laborers from outside the department. If they need outside laborers, the rules dictate that the assistant engineer obtain the permission of the executive engineer before incurring any expenditures, even though it is often not possible to contact the executive engineer on short notice. If the assistant engineer waits, the breach will deteriorate and the risk of field and crop damage increases, and he may then be faulted for inefficiency. If the assistant goes ahead and employs outside workers, the executive may not believe that he used as many laborers as he claimed, on the assumption that he pocketed the difference. Strictness about granting pre-expenditure permission for work varies among executive engineers; nevertheless, most assistant engineers are inclined to play it safe, allowing the breach to deteriorate until they can contact their superior.

Korea's Supervisory System Makes Workers More Accountable

The FLIAs are under intensive scrutiny from above. Not only must the Ministry of Agriculture approve budgets, but the associations are also subject to annual, separate inspections by officials from the Ministry of Agriculture's FLIA bureau, assisted by auditors from another part of the ministry; by the national Board of Audit; and by the provincial administration, which is part of the

Ministry of Home Affairs. Each inspection team consists of three to five persons who spend up to a week checking records, operations, materials, and property. In addition, surprise inspections can be made at any time (SY FLIA had three surprise inspections in a five-year period during the 1970s).

Such intensive supervision could create the same type of environment that prevails in India, but this effect seems to exist to only a limited extent in Korea. Rather, the intensity of inspections and the diversity of inspecting organizations is meant to make large-scale falsification difficult. Multiple monitors also mitigate against collusion between the FLIA and an inspection team.

One striking supervisory difference pertains to the patrollers. In India four to six patrollers with geographically contiguous beats are supervised by a foreman; four to five foremen are supervised by a supervisor; and so on in a neatly tiered arrangement, whereas in Korea employees in all parts of the organization (including the administrative section) supervise one or two patrollers in addition to their other duties. Supervisors must travel to their patrollers' area once or twice a week at irregular intervals (using motorcycles provided by the FLIA) to ensure that they are on the job and assess whether they have encountered any problems. This one-to-one supervisory arrangement complements the collective responsibility of each field station for all patrollers in its area. While it is certainly time-consuming for staff and entails high travel costs, it also ensures that FLIA staff are constantly traveling throughout the command area, obtaining information on the condition of crops, water supply, physical structures, and so on. Staff also have frequent contact with farmers, with whom they stop to talk along the way. Information on crops and farmers thus comes into the FLIA at all levels, rather than upward through a hierarchy as in India.

Organizational Devices Can Improve the Agency-Worker Relationship

Korea combines its incentive structure with other organizational devices to encourage workers to identify with the organization, thereby improving productivity and worker satisfaction. India's administrative system does little to foster a sense of group purpose among the staff who operate and maintain a particular canal.

The common goals of Korea's canal workers are reinforced in myriad ways: the canal irrigation agency holds monthly staff assemblies, addressed by the president and manager; on Friday mornings staff perform calisthenics in the courtyard of the headquarters' building; and units organize sports teams to compete against each other in closely followed competitions, and the FLIA sends teams to compete with other local organizations. These activities are meant to build a sense of the group. Similarly, FLIAs promote group identity using more tangible mechanisms: brochures that explain the history and facilities of each FLIA, pennants printed with the name and symbol of the FLIA, and certificates of achievement conferred by higher authorities (such as the provincial governor or the minister of agriculture).

Contests among work units are used to help workers achieve FLIA goals. For example, a Ministry of Agriculture campaign to encourage farmers to use more organic and less chemical fertilizer might lead to the organization of a competition within each FLIA to see which field station can induce the farmers in its area to make the most organic fertilizer. Contests may also be held for canal maintenance, pest and disease control, water distribution, or the adoption of higher yielding varieties. The prizes are primarily certificates of achievement from the president of the FLIA, which earn valuable promotion points for the head of the field station and add to the general reputation of individuals and field stations.

By contrast, India does nothing to foster a sense of professional pride: canal officers receive training in general civil engineering; which department they join after graduation (irrigation, roads and buildings, or public health) depends primarily on which department has vacancies; the Association of Engineers has few active participants and is open to any civil or mechanical engineer who works for the government; and the Irrigation Department publishes little promotional literature on its projects. In short, irrigation engineers' identification with the Irrigation Department as a whole is weak, and is even weaker with the part of the department that runs the canal on which they are, for the moment, working. Their main motivation comes from material incentives.

Relationships with Farmers

The level of cooperation that canal irrigation staff elicit from their clients influences the staff's ability to perform their jobs conscientiously, the extent to which staff are perceived as performing their jobs conscientiously, and their legitimacy in the eyes of farmers. India's highly bureaucratic and inflexible organizational structure discourages open, productive relationships between workers and farmers. Korea's structure is more fluid, largely because staff at all levels interact with farmers.

Conflicts between Workers and Farmers over Water Access in India

The organizational structure of India's irrigation staff increases the likelihood that the farmers they deal with will be uncooperative and antagonistic or will seek to offer bribes. Because most canals operate on gravity alone, a gate or earthen embankment is often all that stands between farmers and water in the channel. It is the staff's job to ration water during shortages, which means denying farmers the full amounts that they want. Furthermore, the command area is often overextended in the sense that it is too large to provide more remote areas with water reliably. (Recall that in India water, rather than irrigable land, is the binding constraint. Canal designers "lift" the constraint by including more irrigable land than the water supply can cover, often because of bribes or political pressure.) This overextended network means that, during shortages, farmers compete against farmers elsewhere in the system for water. Acquiring water often requires influencing staff or damaging physical structures.

Similarly, the farmers served by the canal are not organized to gain institutional access to the canal organization, for example, there is no farmers' representative council. Neither do farmers have information about the water supply in the system as a whole, the timing of agricultural operations in different parts of the command area, and so on, that is, information that might help local groups of farmers estimate their future water supply.

Access by farmers to the supply organization is highly bureaucratic. Any local group normally has contact with one or two patrollers, with the foreman in charge of those patrollers, with the supervisor in charge of the foreman, and sometimes with the assistant engineer in charge of the supervisor. To influence the higher ranks farmers must enlist the help of elected members of the district council or state assembly.

Much of the contact between farmers and staff involves negotiations about the precise conditions for water access. Although the staff are supposed to have exclusive authority over water releases, in reality they must negotiate with local farmers. Keeping the farmers in the dark about the general water supply greatly strengthens the staff's position in these negotiations, especially if the farmers are not confident that they will receive water unless they comply. This may help explain why irrigation departments have not shown much interest in keeping farmers informed about the system, in involving them in decisions about systemwide issues, or even in computerizing water release schedules under large canals.

Not surprisingly, India's irrigation departments maintain a large-scale and well-organized system of corruption in which irrigation staff, primarily at the officer level, reacquire some of the rents that they allocate. In 1980 irrigation officers and clerks in Andhra Pradesh received between 25 and 50 percent of their maintenance budget in the form of kickbacks from private contractors. Adding together the illicit income obtained from maintenance contracts with that obtained from the illicit sale of water (or sale of the promise not to cut off water), officers at the assistant engineer level in

1980 were commonly obtaining a net illicit income equal to at least two-and-a-half times their official annual salary. Estimates indicate that at the executive engineer rank the illicit income was at least seven times their annual salary, while at the superintending engineer rank it was much more (Wade 1982).[3]

Corruption gives irrigation engineers strong incentives that are absent in the formal employment system. However, these incentives are contrary to the public goals of the Irrigation Department. They encourage "blind eye" supervision of maintenance work, and they make farmers insecure about when they will obtain water. The absence of other incentives for work and the difficulties of close supervision give these corruption incentives much force.

Supervision of Patrollers in Korea Key to Effective Worker-Farmer Relationships

As in India, farmers in Korea do not assume a formal role in running the public irrigation systems. Even though the FLIAs are referred to as associations, they have no farmers' councils, and unlike India, Korea has no local politicians to provide channels of access and no independent media.

Yet farmers are better informed about and have better access to the irrigation organization than their Indian counterparts. This difference is partly a function of the much smaller size of Korea's systems, but the arrangements for supervising patrollers are also important. With staff from all levels of the organization frequently traveling the canals to or from their patrollers' jurisdictions, contact is easily initiated by either side. The type of contact—between a single staff member and a small group of farmers—is thus quite different from contact involving representatives of farmers and of the FLIA (as in a joint governing council). It leaves the balance of power firmly in the hands of the association, but it also means that staff at many levels are informed about the farmers' thinking on such issues as water charges and spending patterns.

Farmers also receive information that helps them make their decisions about such issues. Each FLIA publishes a monthly newsletter for all farmers. Most of the items are reproduced from the pages of the provincial daily newspaper, with little information on the inner workings of the FLIA or on events of specific interest to FLIA farmers. However, the newsletter does give FLIA-specific financial information, including the budget for the previous and following years, thus farmers can easily know how their water payments are being spent.

Korea's Charging and Collection System Fosters Effective FLIA-Farmer Interactions

An organization tends to pay close attention to its source of revenue. India's irrigation departments focus on those who can influence the allocation of grants from the state treasury. Korea's FLIAs focus more on farmers, whose water fees support their salaries and operating budget. The design and implementation of procedures are targeted to ensure that farmers pay.

One part of the strategy is to calibrate water charges to the value of water on the land of each farmer, where value is determined by the productivity of the land before and after irrigation, as well as by current yields and other factors. This strategy is meant to maximize perceived fairness or to minimize the grounds for farmers' complaints about the unfairness of their charges.

The other part of the strategy is meant to ensure that farmers pay quickly by offering significant incentives for quick payment and imposing stringent penalties for slow payment. Farmers can use the speed of payment as a signal of their satisfaction with the quality of water service. A troubled FLIA with unhappy farmers would show a slower than normal collection rate, signaling to higher level FLIA monitors that something was wrong. FLIAs, of course, are anxious to avoid sending this signal.

---

3. Net illicit income is gross illicit income minus the cost of buying the transfer to that post (Wade 1982).

The main collection strategy is contests between villages designed to impose peer pressure on recalcitrant farmers. Substantial monetary prizes are given to villages in which all farmers quickly pay their assessed water charges. For this purpose the FLIA is divided into small districts (1,000 hectares or less), each with its own competition. (These districts are even smaller than those used for calculating water charges.) In this way the number of villages competing against each other is small (ten to twenty) and the intensity of the incentive is high. The total value of the prizes depends on the total amount to be collected from the district; between 0.5 and 1.0 percent of the total is common. The prize money is normally divided into six prizes: one first, two second, and three third prizes. The money is spent on some public good, such as bridge or road maintenance, or perhaps a festival, at the discretion of the villagers.

The FLIA also arranges contests for its field stations to be first to have all farmers paid up. The winning field station receives a certificate of commendation from the president and a cash award. The prize money is usually spent on a feast for field station staff and prominent farmers. The commendation adds to the promotion score of the head of the field station.

These efforts are meant to speed up collection to within thirty days of water charge assessments being sent out. If irrigators have not paid within thirty days, they are sent a letter that informs them that if they pay within fifteen days, they are liable for a 10 percent surcharge, and that the police will levy possessions worth the amount of the arrears if they fail to pay within fifteen days thereafter. Not surprisingly, 99 percent of water charges are collected in the first thirty days. In practice no one fails to pay eventually, and no attempts are made to cut off water to nonpayers.

The intensity of these collection procedures reflects the fact that the water charge is the issue that farmers are most concerned about; it forms the basis of their relationships with the FLIA. FLIA staff know that they will have to justify any increase in rates to the farmers, and here the supervisory arrangements for the patrollers are useful, because they allow ample opportunity for staff to talk to groups of farmers. In addition, staff are well informed about farmers' feelings toward current water rates. FLIA staff have, on occasion, opposed proposals from the Ministry of Agriculture for higher salaries on the grounds that these changes would necessitate higher water charges.

Maintenance Activities Are a Joint Responsibility in Korea

Another vital area of FLIA-irrigator interaction is canal maintenance. As in India, canals in Korea are state property, but Korean farmers, unlike their Indian counterparts, see the canals as being partly their own. This sense of ownership is manifested in their contributions to canal maintenance. Whereas private contractors, supervised by the Irrigation Department, undertake maintenance in India, in Korea the staff of the irrigation agency undertake it with the help of farmers. The role of private contractors is limited to the leasing of heavy machinery. Most farmers contribute one or two days of work a year in this way.

Several factors reinforce the agency's reliance on farmers for maintenance labor. One is that the agency pays farmers a daily rate, but less than the prevailing rate for agricultural laborers, and provides generous quantities of rice wine. Another is that a farmer who refuses to participate could be subject to a wide range of informally instituted penalties at the hands of local government bodies, given the wider authoritarian structure of the state. Beyond this, farmers recognize an obligation to help with the work stemming from the sense that the canals are partly theirs.

Success Ultimately Rests on Interdependent Factors

The contrast between the organizational arrangements of the two countries is stark: India's organization for maintaining and operating canal systems contains virtually no incentives for conscientious work, while Korea's is replete with individual and collective incentives. The organizational differences identified in this chapter are also found in other bureaucracies of the two countries. To the extent that this is so, any infrastructure organization in Korea would be more effective than its counterpart in India. Thus recommending that India adopt elements of Korea's (or East Asia's) organizational designs could be tempting, but this conclusion is too simple for reasons that pertain to the interdependence between technology and organizations.

This chapter discusses one type of canal design: the gravity-fed, high-response system. Much the same organizational arrangements as those described here are used to operate the gravity-fed, low-response systems of northwest India, yet these canals operate with a high level of efficiency (Malhotra, Raheja, and Seckler 1984; Wade 1985). The key difference is that the northwest systems give little discretion in water allocation to field-level staff and give farmers few incentives to interfere in the system to improve their water supply. This, in turn, reflects the fact that the northwestern canals did not have to be designed to accommodate fluctuating rainfall.

However, the gravity-fed, high-response systems that account for most of India's (and Asia's) canal irrigation are located in areas where heavy rainfall is a key factor in canal operations. As long as irrigation systems remain gravity-fed, and as long as there are no local reservoirs into which water can be deposited by the conveyance organization and then distributed by the farmers' organization, canal staff must use discretion in varying the amount of water that goes to different localities. It is this design—which puts the entire task of rationing on the supply side (government officials)—that is especially sensitive to issues of organizational structure and motivation.

This argument suggests that countries might improve the performance of canal irrigation systems by introducing technological changes in system design that reduce the discretion of staff and the incentives of farmers to intervene. The argument also shows that small variations in physical design can have important organizational implications, and it thus suggests a flaw in current proposals for improving canal performance. Current literature on canal management tends to be categorized into technological, pricing, managerial, and organizational strategies, but one cannot presume that one set of solutions will be more effective than another. In some designs the bureaucratic incentive issues discussed herein are rather minor. In other designs they are central.

References

Blau, Peter, and W. Scott. 1962. *Formal Organizations*. San Francisco: Chandler.

Burns, Robert. 1993. "Irrigated Rice Culture in Monsoon Asia: The Search for an Effective Water Control Technology." *World Development* 21(5):771–89.

Fox, A. 1974. *Man Mismanagement*. London: Hutchinson.

Heginbotham, Stanley. 1975. *Cultures in Conflict: The Four Faces of Indian Culture*. New York: Columbia University Press.

IRRI (International Rice Research Institute). 1985. *World Rice Statistics*. Los BaZos, Philippines.

Leonard, David. 1977. *Reaching the Peasant Farmer: Organizational Theory and Practice in Kenya*. Chicago: University of Chicago Press.

Malhotra, S., S. Raheja, and D. Seckler. 1984. "A Methodology for Monitoring the Performance of Large-Scale Irrigation Systems: A Case Study of the Warabandi System of Northwest India." *Agricultural Administration* 17(4):231–59.

March, James, and Herbert Simon. 1958. *Organizations*. New York: John Wiley.

Moore, Mick. 1989. "The Fruits and Fallacies of Neoliberalism: The Case of Irrigation Policy." *World Development* 17(11).

Repetto, Robert. 1986. *Skimming the Water: Rent-Seeking and the Performance of Public Irrigation Schemes.* Research Report no. 4., Washington, D.C.: World Resources Institute.

Simon, Herbert. 1991. "Organizations and Markets." *Journal of Economic Perspectives* 5(2):25–44.

Wade, Robert. 1982. "The System of Administrative and Political Corruption: Canal Irrigation in South India." *Journal of Development Studies* 18(3):287–327.

_____. 1985. "Canal Performance in Northwest India: Is It So Bad?" *Economic and Political Weekly* 20(50):204.

8

Advanced Infrastructure for Time Management: The Competitive Edge in East Asia

Ashoka Mody and William Reinfeld

Advanced infrastructure is a range of transportation and communications systems that is enhanced through the use of information technology and delivered by innovative providers. Used for moving cargo, managing ports and airports, and transferring documents electronically, such infrastructure is part of the system of modern time management techniques that allows users to reduce costs, improve services, and enhance their market competitiveness. Both companies and governments worldwide are recognizing these benefits of advanced infrastructure. In contrast to basic infrastructure, which has been biased toward achieving quantitative physical targets, advanced infrastructure is more demand oriented and consists of innovative applications designed to meet an array of specific user needs. Products and markets that benefit from advanced infrastructure have one or more of the following characteristics: they have high value added, they compete in terms of time to market (particularly to the United States and Europe), or they are linked to extensive global operations.

Advanced infrastructure is now diffusing to the newly industrialized economies of Asia, a development that, along with prevalent low wage levels, will make these economies attractive to global firms as they make decisions about locating regional headquarters and production and sourcing operations. Based on in-depth interviews with the top management of twenty leading firms in Hong Kong, Singapore, and Taiwan (China) between December 1992 and February 1993, this chapter documents the growing use of advanced infrastructure. Support for advanced infrastructure is best provided by skilled manpower and a regulatory approach that permits competitive entry by innovative service providers. Incentives to adopt advanced infrastructure arise from the sophistication of customers, the degree of market competition, the pace of product development, the need to streamline and to globalize operations, and the extent of marketing by service providers.

The governments of Hong Kong, Singapore, and Taiwan (China), in particular, have recognized the importance of advanced infrastructure, especially as they seek to enhance their roles as regional hubs for global manufacturing and service industries. Each government has taken a different approach to expanding and promoting advanced infrastructure services:

- In Hong Kong the government has taken a laissez faire approach to encouraging advanced infrastructure development, and firms have been comparatively slow to adopt it, particularly in the manufacturing sector. Responsibility for advanced infrastructure services is thus left to third-party providers, who have been quite active.

The conclusions reached and views expressed in this chapter are those of the authors and should not be attributed to the World Bank or to Andersen Consulting.

- In Singapore both the government and the private sector have vigorously supported advanced infrastructure development. The government itself is an active provider of services.
- In Taiwan (China) pockets of development exist within the advanced infrastructure industry, but the government has not yet undertaken the policy reforms required for successful advanced infrastructure development. Although the government is unable to provide the diversity of services needed, it has not permitted easy entry by new providers. Third-party service providers are thus not as active as they are in Hong Kong and Singapore

The different government approaches in part reflect, but also reinforce, the types of industrial activity undertaken in the three economies. In some cases advanced infrastructure and advanced management techniques have not been incorporated into industries or firms because their standards and language requirements have not been made compatible with local operations. However, other Asian economies that still rely on their less expensive labor forces to compete in worldwide markets are beginning to realize that they are lagging behind Hong Kong, Singapore, and Taiwan (China) in development. For these countries, where basic communications infrastructure is underdeveloped, the development of advanced infrastructure is an additional burden that is being imposed before they can compete successfully even in traditional industries, which are well on their way to global integration.

Advanced Infrastructure: Changing How Business Is Done

Twenty years ago East Asian economies were attractive for their low costs. With rising wages and soaring land costs, governments and firms located in the region are seeking new strategies for maintaining their competitive edge. Advanced infrastructure is a key component in the emerging economics of international competitiveness. Those engaged in international business as investors or exporters are increasingly looking at the availability of advanced infrastructure when deciding where to establish headquarters and produce and source their products. Based on the in-depth interviews mentioned earlier, this chapter identifies the factors responsible for increased use of advanced infrastructure and the implications of such use for location and sourcing decisions in the region.

In parallel with advanced infrastructure, this chapter also considers the use of logistics management techniques. While not part of infrastructure in a conventional sense, logistics management techniques—such as just-in-time and quick-response production—have a growing relationship with advanced infrastructure based on information technology. Thus, although advanced infrastructure specialists are key to coordinating the distribution of goods and services, the distinction between the producer and distributor blurs with the increasing use of time management, as production and distribution strategies mesh (Suri 1995).

The enhanced physical facilities and value-added service applications of advanced infrastructure significantly augment the moving of cargo and information. By exploiting synergies among information technology, logistics management, and transportation and communications technology, advanced infrastructure has given industries the opportunity to reduce their costs, decrease production and product development cycles, and compete more effectively through improved service and reliability. Taken together, these changes have radically altered ways of doing business, particularly among firms in industrial countries (Peters 1992). As manufacturers increasingly focus on reducing product cycle times and improving customer service, the use of advanced infrastructure becomes more important.

To demonstrate the growing influence of advanced infrastructure beyond industrial countries to regions that have traditionally competed on the basis of low wages, this chapter focuses on labor-intensive products—certain electronics products, automobile parts, and garments and footwear—where timeliness and user responsiveness considerations are increasingly crucial for successful competition.

Advanced Infrastructure Takes Many Forms

In international commerce advanced infrastructure may be applied to three activities: cargo flow and freight movement, terminal and facility operations, and inter- and intra-industry communications. While the construction of physical infrastructure is often an element of advanced infrastructure, it is the value added services overlaying the basic infrastructure that are of greatest interest. Innovative providers of value added services who use modern information technology to manage the flow of goods and information are key to the success of effective advanced infrastructure delivery. Of course, they often choose to provide advanced infrastructure services because their users demand them. Table 8–1 shows specific examples of such services.

Cargo Flow and Freight Movement

One of the best examples of advanced infrastructure is integrated transport logistics systems. These systems incorporate various forms of enhanced physical infrastructure and provide a range of services, starting with sourcing, continuing in some cases with inventory management, and extending through warehousing and ultimate distribution of the finished product. Logistics systems such as these integrate numerous forms of advanced infrastructure: air express cargo movement, automated warehousing, and computerized tracking of the flow of goods. Taken together, the various components of the logistics infrastructure allow goods to move in the fastest, most reliable way, minimizing total logistics costs and strengthening users' strategic position.

Various service providers who previously concentrated primarily on specific steps in the process, such as airlines or freight forwarders, now offer integrated transport logistics systems. As a consequence of information technology and policy reforms that have reduced traditional service distinctions and associated entry barriers, some of these companies are now providing services that not only integrate the disparate components of cargo flow, but also include cargo tracking; document

Table 8–1. Examples of Advanced Infrastructure Networks in East Asia

Type of operation	*General examples*	*Specific examples*	*Service providers*
Cargo flows and movement	Integrated transport logistics	Flex (Fritz)	Airlines, air freight express companies, freight forwarders, warehouse and distribution companies
	Time-definite, door-to-door, express service	International priority service (Federal Express)	
Terminal, facility, and modal operations	Electronic data interchange applied to cargo clearance at terminals	TradeVan (Taiwan, China) TradeNet (Singapore) TradeLink (Hong Kong)	Terminal operators, integrated service providers, government agencies, steamship companies
	Intelligent warehousing	CDS/Tait facility (Taiwan, China)	
	Integrated intermodal transport systems	HACTL facility (Hong Kong)	
Inter- and intra-industry communications	Electronic data interchange applied to procurement and production systems	OrderLink (Singapore); EasyLink/iNet (Hong Kong); Center Satellite Factory (Taiwan, China)	Value-added network vendors, government agencies

processing; customs clearance; and time-definite, door-to-door, and express pickup. The service providers generally use a combination of public conveyances, their own conveyances, public and proprietary data networks, and systems that have been tailor-made for the customers.

According to service providers, these developments are market-driven. End users are finding the use of one-stop services increasingly advantageous and are demanding that suppliers tailor services to meet their total needs. With all their logistics needs supplied by one vendor, shippers can enjoy savings from fewer errors, lower transport costs, lower capital costs for warehousing and maintaining inventory, and the elimination of redundancy in time and effort. They are also finding that revenues increase as a result of greater customer satisfaction and faster, more reliable delivery.

The impact of these services on a company's business depends on the economics of its product and the characteristics of its market. The benefits typically include reduced distribution or inventory costs. For example, an international air express service can provide door-to-door, break-bulk service from Hong Kong, Singapore, or Taiwan (China) to any major city in the United States in three to four days. This service includes separation and boxing (by store) at point of pickup, preparation of all necessary accompanying documentation, cartage to port of departure, air transport, customs clearance, delivery, and tracking and tracing of every package. The same steps by traditional services take ten days by air and thirty days by ocean vessel. Total distribution costs vary according to the nature of the products shipped. According to service providers, the savings in costs between traditional air cargo and the integrated air service can be anywhere from 10 to 25 percent. When inventory costs are significant, the time savings of integrated air express service over ocean service can be a much more critical factor.

Terminal and Facility Operations

Another area in which advanced infrastructure can potentially benefit the manufacturing sector is the application of electronic data interchange to cargo movement through ports. The enhanced physical infrastructure used in this case centers around telecommunications, principally an integrated services digital network. The enhanced value added services are the electronic data interchange applications, which are prepared by service suppliers referred to as value added network services (or VANS) suppliers. Benefits from this example of advanced infrastructure result from computerized systems that link shippers, shipping agents, freight forwarders, couriers, and cargo agents into an electronic information network that allows them to make declarations of relevant trading documents more efficiently.

The most common use of this system is for handling customs documents. However, more sophisticated systems, such as those developed in Singapore, allow users to take advantage of this standardized data network to communicate information about their shipments to both upstream and downstream elements in the trading process, such as banks, insurance agents, other manufacturers, distributors, and retailers (Tan and others 1992). (For more details on the Port of Singapore, see chapter 4.) These electronic transactions allow users to reduce the paperwork resulting from repeated keying of the same trade data. The significance of such savings can best be appreciated from studies in the United States and Europe, where investigators found that this type of paperwork can cost between 4 and 7 percent of the value of goods freighted in international trade.

Considerable savings are also realized from expedited customs clearance procedures. In Singapore, for example, average cargo clearing time has been reduced from a day or more to thirty minutes. Users have increased their productivity by 20 to 30 percent, and savings in nonvalue added manpower are estimated at up to 50 percent.

Several of the major ports in Asia provide such systems, including those in Japan, the Republic of Korea, Singapore, and Taiwan (China). Hong Kong is currently working on developing a system. While each system has certain basic similarities, Singapore's TradeNet is the most comprehensive.

Other applications of advanced infrastructure in terminal operations may be found in intelligent warehouse facilities. Such facilities are now being operated in Hong Kong, Singapore, and Taiwan (China); however, their effectiveness depends on how much operational flexibility the government allows. Potentially, these facilities offer users considerable savings as a result of enhanced storage and handling capabilities, which along with intensive use of information technology permits rapid processing of and access to goods. These warehouses only reach their full potential value if the goods also pass rapidly through customs clearance, which is often impossible because of policy, not technology, restrictions.

Inter- and Intra-Industry Communications

Another family of advanced infrastructure applications is the set of technologies and services that facilitates the integration of firms' business, engineering, and manufacturing with relevant activities of other companies in the value chain, that is, those involved in design, production, distribution, and sales. These communications applications are based largely on value added network capabilities that support the exchange of information (data, text, graphics, image, voice) between dispersed components within an organization and between different organizations.

Various applications of electronic data interchange to procurement and production allow manufacturers, within the same or related industries, to integrate their information bases to take better advantage of available advanced infrastructure. Asian industries—other than those in Japan—are still relatively behind their counterparts in more industrialized parts of the world in applying electronic data interchange techniques, but they are beginning to see the advantages and are starting to develop systems.

Singapore, with systems such as OrderLink, is probably the most advanced in electronic data interchange applications. In Hong Kong Hutchison Telecom, a private value added network operator, has joined with American Telegraph and Telephone to provide EasyLink, an interindustry electronic mail and facsimile service. In Taiwan (China) pilot studies are under way to develop interindustry electronic data interchange systems for automobile manufacturers and grocery stores. These systems will allow companies to manage their inventories better and to speed new product development.

Time Management Tools Used or Not Used for a Number of Reasons

The extent to which a firm uses advanced infrastructure depends on the sophistication of its business and whether its government takes an active role in promoting advanced infrastructure. A firm's decision to use advanced infrastructure is driven by the demands of its customers, the time it takes to develop products, the competitive forces it faces in its market, and the operational structure of its facilities.

The intent of the survey conducted was to examine how the economics of industries are changing in response to the new opportunities advanced infrastructure provides. Of the twenty firms in which we interviewed managers, eight were in Hong Kong, four were in Singapore, and eight were in Taiwan (China). The distribution among industries was seven in clothing and footwear, seven in electronics, and six in automobiles and auto parts.

The sample is small. Our strategy was not to study a wide cross-section of firms, but to focus on relatively large firms with a strong international orientation. Each of the firms interviewed has factories throughout the region, and about half have factories around the world. They all export to markets both in the region and outside. They vary in size from multinational giants (with regional headquarters in one of the three economies) to medium-size firms (by Asian standards) with at least US$50 million in annual sales. All are well established and successful and all are considered forward-looking.

We used a questionnaire in the interviews to guide the discussion. Discussions focused on issues about which the interviewee was particularly knowledgeable or with which he or she was most comfortable. Our strategy was to interview the firm's top management to get their insights into the dynamic relationship of advanced infrastructure and operational decisions, including strategies for locating various firm activities.

Which Types of Firms Are Most Likely to Use Time Management Tools?

Table 8–2 presents a profile of the firms interviewed and whether or not they employed time management techniques. We asked whether the firm employed logistics management—using techniques such as just-in-time or quick response—or whether it was tied into any electronic data interchange networks. This question was used to determine both a firm's familiarity with issues surrounding time-sensitive management criteria and its use of information technology in production and distribution management. All twenty firms interviewed were familiar with logistics management and electronic data interchange. Half were relatively experienced users. Use was most extensive in electronics, where five of seven firms were experienced users, followed by three users of five in automobiles and auto parts and two users of five in clothing and footwear. Even though the techniques were used least in clothing and footwear, even these firms were beginning to use some form of time management.

The sectoral differences also appear in the relationship between the extent of usage and the location of the firm interviewed. For instance, in Singapore, where information technology and advanced infrastructure are relatively well developed and the government actively supports these developments, all four firms interviewed were actively using these techniques. At the same time, three of the four firms interviewed in Singapore were in electronics and none were in clothing or footwear. In Hong Kong, where, according to the director general of the Federation of Hong Kong Industries, more than 40 percent of the manufacturing sector has relocated its factories (mostly to nearby sites on mainland China in search of cheap labor) and where the government has taken a less active role in promoting information technology and advanced infrastructure, the split between novices and active users was six to two. The usage pattern also reflects the relatively high concentration of garment firms in Hong Kong. Taiwan (China) lies in between, with the number of novices and experienced users split evenly. There the efforts to promote information technology

Table 8–2. Extent of Use of Time Management Tools in Surveyed Firms, by Sector

Location	Clothing or footwear	Electronics	Automobiles or auto parts	Total
Hong Kong	5	2	1	8
Singapore	0	3	1	4
Taiwan (China)	2	2	4	8
Total	7	7	6	20

Using logistics management or electronic data interchange

Location	In place	Starting to use	In place	Starting to use	In place	Starting to use	In place	Starting to use
Hong Kong	1	4	1	1	0	1	2	6
Singapore	0	0	3	0	1	0	4	0
Taiwan (China)	1	1	1	1	2	2	4	4
Total	2	5	5	2	3	3	10	10

Source: authors' research.

and advanced infrastructure have been started and the manufacturing sector is actively seeking to retain its competitiveness, yet the government has been less progressive than in Hong Kong and Singapore in reforming the regulatory environment. Thus a combination of supply and demand factors appears to influence the use of time management tools.

What Are the Advantages of Time Management Tools?

From a review of the responses to the questionnaires and the views expressed in the interviews we can gain further insights into what the managers of these firms believe are the important determinants of the extent to which their firms employ logistics management and other management tools based on information technology. Table 8–3 summarized the importance that the managers interviewed assigned to external requirements for employing tools such as just-in-time and quick-response production. Table 8-4 provides a further breakdown by industry.

According to the manufacturers, the availability of value added services ranks as the most important requirement, external to the firm, for employing modern logistics management techniques. In this connection note that both just-in-time and quick-response are time-sensitive activities that require efficient communications with a variety of suppliers, customers, and intermediaries along the distribution chain. We thus can see the emerging link between the management tools that firms adopt and the information technology-based infrastructure available to them. This relationship is noteworthy, because such tools, especially just-in-time, can be usefully adopted to manage internal work processes so as to reduce costs and improve quality even in the absence of sophisticated communications technologies. Other important considerations for adopting logistics management include the availability of qualified human resources, followed by physical infrastructure.

An interesting finding was that the appropriate regulatory environment was considered highly important by only two of the manufacturing respondents and moderately important by eight of them. By contrast, the value added services providers whom we also interviewed (and whom these same manufacturers find essential to the successful deployment of logistics management) thought that the appropriate regulatory environment was among the most important requirements for them to be able to offer the kinds of services manufacturers require.

As one might have expected, all the interviewees in Singapore acknowledged government support as highly important. The government's involvement was assigned a low weight in Hong Kong, and Taiwan was in between. These results reflect the different levels of government involvement and effectiveness in the three economies and the private sector's comfort and confidence in government support.

Although the three types of industries surveyed are quite different from one another and the extent of adoption of logistics management and advanced infrastructure varies, they did not vary significantly in their responses to questions concerning the reasons for adopting logistics management and advanced infrastructure (table 8–4). As a result, making generalizations about industries is difficult. Although all firms viewed advanced infrastructure as potentially important, differences in the degree of use stem from the precise nature of the products made and markets served by individual firms. Such variations exist not only across, but even within, the industries studied. Relevant aspects of products and markets include customer sophistication, degree of competition, importance of rapid product development, and the need to streamline international operations. Marketing efforts by value added service suppliers also influence decisions to adopt advanced infrastructure services.

SOPHISTICATION OF CUSTOMERS. Eleven of the twenty firms said their use or intended use of advanced infrastructure greatly depends on the demands of their customers. Even in the clothing and footwear industry, for example, firms indicated that time-to-market was critical to customers in high fashion or trendy markets. Such customers presented the firms with precise production and

Table 8–3. Factors Contributing to the Adoption of Logistics Management Techniques (number of firms)

Factor	Hong Kong			Singapore			Taiwan (China)			Total				
	High	Medium	Low	High	Medium	Low	High	Medium	Low	High	Medium	Low	Score	Rank
Advanced infrastructure														
Physical infrastructure	5	3	0	2	2	0	3	5	0	10	10	0	80	3
Value added services	7	1	0	4	0	0	6	2	0	17	3	0	94	1
Support														
Regulatory environment	0	2	6	1	1	2	1	5	2	2	8	10	34	6
Human resources	4	4	0	3	1	0	5	3	0	12	8	0	84	2
Government assistance	1	1	6	4	0	0	2	5	1	7	6	7	53	4
Other	0	6	2	0	4	0	0	5	3	0	15	5	45	5

Note: Score based on firms' rankings of factors as being of high, medium, or low influence. Score = (number of high responses x 5) + (number of medium responses x 3).

Table 8–4. Factors Contributing to the Adoption of Logistics Management Techniques by Industry (number of firms)

Industry and factor	Hong Kong			Singapore			Taiwan (China)			Total responses		
	High	Medium	Low	High	Medium	Low	High	Medium	Low	High	Medium	Low
Clothing and footwear												
Advanced infrastructure												
Physical infrastructure	3	2	0	n.a.	n.a.	n.a.	2	0	0	5	2	0
Value added services	4	1	0	n.a.	n.a.	n.a.	2	0	0	6	1	0
Support												
Regulatory environment	0	1	4	n.a.	n.a.	n.a.	0	2	0	0	3	4
Human resources	2	3	0	n.a.	n.a.	n.a.	1	1	0	3	4	0
Government assistance	1	1	3	n.a.	n.a.	n.a.	0	2	0	1	3	3
Other	0	3	2	n.a.	n.a.	n.a.	0	2	0	0	5	2
Electronics												
Advanced infrastructure												
Physical infrastructure	1	1	0	2	1	0	0	2	0	3	4	0
Value added services	2	0	0	3	0	0	2	0	0	7	0	0
Support												
Regulatory environment	0	0	2	0	1	2	0	0	2	0	1	6
Human resources	2	0	0	2	1	0	1	1	0	5	2	0
Government assistance	0	0	2	3	0	0	1	1	0	4	1	2
Other	0	2	0	0	3	0	0	1	1	0	6	1
Automobiles and auto parts												
Advanced infrastructure												
Physical infrastructure	1	0	0	0	1	0	1	3	0	2	4	0
Value added services	1	0	0	1	0	0	2	2	0	4	2	0
Support												
Regulatory environment	0	1	0	1	0	0	1	3	0	2	4	0
Human resources	0	1	0	1	0	0	3	1	0	4	2	0
Government assistance	0	0	1	1	0	0	1	2	1	2	2	2
Other	0	1	0	0	1	0	0	2	2	0	4	2

n.a. = Not applicable.
Note: Score based on firms' rankings of factors as being of high, medium, or low influence. Score = (number of high responses x 5) + (number of medium responses x 3).
Source: authors' research.

delivery specifications attainable only through advanced methods. Another example, mentioned in the electronics and auto components industries, was the extent to which the product they produced was tied into global linkages with other components of larger systems. The movement of specific items in these industries required extensive coordination and timely deliveries.

MARKET COMPETITIVENESS. Firms, particularly in Taiwan (China), became interested in logistics technology because of increased industry competition. If advanced infrastructure techniques enable them to cut prices and gain a competitive edge over other firms, they are keenly interested in trying them, especially if the initial investment is not too great. However, these same firms mentioned that for lower value added goods these techniques were less likely to make a significant difference.

Firms producing higher value added goods, particularly in the electronics industry, also stressed the goal of keeping inventory costs down, while still being responsive to customer needs. While quantifying cost reductions achieved was not possible (nearly all of them confessed that they did not know the extent of these savings), they all agreed that advanced infrastructure can produce significant net savings.

PRODUCT DEVELOPMENT. The more progressive firms in each of the three industries are looking to advanced infrastructure to reduce their product development time cycle. As noted, the firms interviewed had extensive global links with other firms. New product development occurs within the dispersed subsidiaries of the firm or in collaboration with allied firms, such as subcontractors or vendors. As such, an individual enterprise may be called on as part of a global team to help design, develop, test, and deliver a new product to the market as quickly as possible. Cutting this product development time cycle by even a small percentage (whether measured in months, weeks, or even days, depending on the industry and the product) can mean considerable market advantages.

STREAMLINED OPERATIONS. The large multinational firms interviewed indicated that an important reason for stepping up their use of advanced infrastructure was that their firm, globally, was becoming a "paperless" operation and that all offices and plants throughout the world would have to follow procedures established by headquarters. In a number of these cases corporate rather than customer requirements were the main determinant for employing advanced infrastructure.

MARKETING BY SERVICE PROVIDERS. Several of the firms in Hong Kong mentioned the initiatives taken by value added service providers as an important factor leading to their use of advanced infrastructure. The rapidly growing number of value added service providers see a vast array of opportunities to apply advanced infrastructure and other business logistics techniques to improve firms' productivity. Given the opportunity, these providers will aggressively market their services and generate large benefits for their clients.

Why Are Many Industries Not Investing in Time Management Tools?

The interviews also provided insights into why advanced management techniques and advanced infrastructure may not be widely used or fully developed in some places or in certain industries. In addition to the more obvious reasons, such as not being totally convinced that these technologies will make a difference at this time given the nature of their products and markets, manufacturers cited a number of other reasons for not being more active users of advanced infrastructure.

INCOMPATIBILITY OF THE SYSTEMS OR THE TECHNOLOGY. Because most of the service-related activities associated with advanced infrastructure were developed in Western environments, and because services' usefulness depends heavily on being user sensitive, firms have encountered difficulties in introducing the techniques and technologies into local operations. For instance, a number of the basic application systems, such as electronic data interchange, have been developed for English-speaking (or at least Western alphabet) users and for accounting and bookkeeping systems that are not used in certain economies. This makes assimilating these techniques and technologies difficult, particularly among smaller firms or in places where English is not a principal language.

Similarly, databases are sometimes not compatible with these systems or often are not as complete as the systems require. Also, while international standards are available, such as the Electronic Data Interchange for Administration, Commerce, and Transport (EDIFACT) for electronic data interchange, they are not universally accepted. Japan, for example, has its own electronic data interchange system. Reconciling such situations can be a costly and lengthy procedure.

LACK OF STRONG INDUSTRY ASSOCIATIONS. Industry associations are important for establishing standards; sharing activities common to specific industries, such as research and development and lobbying for policy reform; and enabling the diffusion of information. The restricted development of industry associations in many East Asian economies limits diffusion of new technologies. In many cases the slow rate of adopting advanced infrastructure seems to result from insufficient information about the power and success of these techniques. More information about the costs and benefits of logistics management, advanced infrastructure, and other technologies in contexts that are relevant to specific local conditions needs to be developed and widely disseminated.

Governments Can Actively Endorse—and Facilitate—Advanced Infrastructure

Advanced infrastructure development is a function of both the rate of technological development and the rate of deregulation. The application of information technology and other technologies and services is often limited by outdated regulations restricting their application. For the forward-looking governments, establishing a regulatory framework that supports advanced infrastructure development is a must.

Government policy should not restrict the entry or operations of qualified international service providers. Often these companies may be the most qualified to serve local interests, particularly in their international operations. In Taiwan (China), for instance, the Telecom Authority has had an ongoing battle with the legislature to restrict value added networks from operating in the local market, claiming that private providers pose security risks. This kind of action breeds frustration and undermines the communication between government agencies and private users that is needed to upgrade and enhance physical infrastructure.

Beyond creating a level playing field for advanced infrastructure service providers, governments must also provide a policy environment that actively supports the use and applications of advanced infrastructure. This includes removing policy obstacles that hinder the use of advanced infrastructure. For example, consider the automated warehouse established by Tait in Taiwan (China). Despite the speed and efficiency with which the warehouse can track and deliver goods, operations are hindered because it cannot access customs officials on a twenty-four-hour basis. This arcane policy indirectly affects advanced infrastructure, because it slows service capacity. Other examples of indirect policy obstacles might include restrictions on owning a truck line, on having a private warehouse at an airport, or on granting a private radio frequency.

An important example in this regard has been the aborted attempt by Federal Express Corporation to establish its Asia-Pacific hub in Taiwan (China) (Reinfeld 1992). The so-called hub and spoke system, pioneered and perfected by Federal Express, establishes the central location or facility (the hub) within an air cargo shipping network, at which sorting and loading activities are performed on freight moving between various origins and destinations (the spokes). The regional hub that the company wished to establish in Taiwan (China) was to be the primary routing for all intraregional flights in Asia and, therefore, the principal facility for sorting and transloading all air cargo within the region. Under the proposed plan this hub was to be linked to almost every address in Pacific Rim and Organization for Economic Cooperation and Development countries within thirty hours, and to nearly every other city worldwide within forty-eight to seventy-two hours.

For Federal Express to be able to proceed with its plans, it required approvals from the government in several areas. In terms of space and facilities at the airport, these approvals included parking for their aircraft; adequate maintenance and storage facilities; and sufficient warehouse, office, and canopy space. In terms of operations these approvals included full access to a dedicated on-airport bonded warehouse and freight processing facility, full rights to conduct aircraft support and warehouse operations, airport and customs clearance services available twenty-four hours a day year round, efficient and unencumbered customs clearance procedures, freedom to operate its own radio dispatch and mobile data communications systems, and liberalization of international intermodal trucking restrictions. Although the benefits of the hub appeared overwhelming, it proved difficult for Taiwan (China) to grant the approvals required by Federal Express to proceed with its plans.

As we have seen, effective delivery of advanced infrastructure requires the operator to embrace the notion of customer service. This is not a natural function for a government agency to undertake. The government of Singapore appears to be an exception. All the government-run facilities and value added services in Singapore have been extremely progressive in serving their markets. Even in Singapore, however, the importance of private initiative for advanced infrastructure services has been recognized. Singapore Network Services (SNS) is a private, for profit, value-added network service provider that the government set up and initially supported to develop systems applications for physical infrastructure. SNS was responsible for developing TradeNet, and has now developed a host of other systems, such as AutoNet (for manufacturing), PortNet, OrderNet, and many others. SNS was privatized after it developed some of the more important value added services. Moreover, while SNS operates a variety of electronic data interchange networks for local industries, it has a cooperative relationship with foreign operators for international services.

Governments may intervene selectively by providing assistance to small firms or those without industry associations, or by supplementing the high research and development costs of private firms. Because of the predominance of small firms with insufficient resources to develop the techniques themselves, governments have been a source of support, especially in the pilot phases of developing or testing management tools or systems applications. The worldwide experience of such government support has, at best, been mixed. However, it may be appropriate for a government to become involved through providing general funding support; taking on initial development at one of its own institutes; or contracting with nongovernmental organizations, such as polytechnics, to undertake the research and development. For example, the National Computer Board in Singapore (Wong 1992) and the Institute for Information Industries in Taiwan (China) have initiated a large number of information technology projects to help local industries become more sophisticated in the use of advanced infrastructure and, hence, more competitive. As many private companies in Singapore and Taiwan (China) are not large enough to take on such projects or lack the resources to employ outside consultants, these government-funded agencies have played an important role in developing and then transferring technology and applications to private operators.

In the case of Taiwan (China), the automotive industry lacks the kind of competitiveness that would drive manufacturers to develop electronic data interchange on their own. Nevertheless, manufacturers benefit by having automobile suppliers linked to an electronic data interchange system. Because the local private value added service providers did not have strong incentives to develop electronic data interchange in this fragmented market, for the government to develop the service was both appropriate and useful. As in the Singapore example, however, the system can be handed over to the private sector or to an industry association after a suitable gestation period. Consider also the experiences with TradeNet in Singapore and TradeLink in Hong Kong. In Singapore the government took the lead in organizing representatives of the shipping community, the software industry, large import and export manufacturers, the relevant government agencies, and so on. The system has been operating successfully for several years. In Hong Kong TradeLink was left in the hands of the private sector and has been unable to muster the cooperation needed to develop the project. However, drawing a general lesson from this example for other countries where the quality of government delivery cannot match that of Singapore would be imprudent.

Outside government, international institutions can help set the standards needed to operate advanced infrastructure facilities and applications. For example, electronic data interchange systems generally use EDIFACT standards, a system established by the United Nations. Local and regional representatives meet regularly to modify and refine EDIFACT standards to make them more applicable for use in a particular industry or region. A variety of other international organizations also help set the standards needed for advanced infrastructure applications to function as efficiently as possible. These include the International Association of Travel Agents, the International Standards Organization, Intelsat, and many others. Without the objective oversight and coordination from these kinds of organizations, service applications would quickly become bogged down in conflicting computer languages or incompatible formats that would undermine the efficiency gains these applications are intended to deliver.

Access to Advanced Infrastructure Affects Location Decisions

The availability of advanced infrastructure is an important consideration for firms as they make expansion and location decisions. The survey's findings indicate that advanced infrastructure is the most or second most important determinant of where a firm locates its regional headquarters, production sites, and delivery systems. During the interviews we asked several questions about the role of advanced infrastructure in a firm's future expansion or relocation decisions. We distinguished among investments in regional headquarters and service centers, factories, and sourcing operations. We wanted to determine how the relative importance of advanced infrastructure and other factors decisionmakers normally take into account in such evaluations might be changing. Table 8–5 summarizes the results of the survey according to each firms' major activity, and table 8–6 breaks the information down by industry. Locational decisions are surprisingly similar across the three industry groups, and so are not reported here.

Before reviewing these results, note that important issues such as intellectual property protection, level of corruption, and political stability or national security were not included among the factors we asked the respondents to evaluate. We assumed that these considerations are always of great concern, and we wanted to focus on the tradeoffs that firms would make on economic factors, assuming that the social-political conditions were acceptable.

In choosing locations for regional centers—whether headquarters, service, or design—firms assigned the most importance to advanced infrastructure, with a close second being the availability and skill of the work force (table 8–5). The other factors were not assigned much importance, except by two electronics firms who felt that ordinary infrastructure was very important, and a clothing manufacturer who felt that the headquarters should be close to the market.

Firms mentioned a couple of other noteworthy criteria as important in choosing regional headquarters, both of which are implicit in advanced infrastructure. These were availability of a well-developed information technology infrastructure and a policy framework that allowed critical information to be transmitted internationally without any delays or interference.

In choosing production sites, the firms said that they assigned the greatest importance to the cost of labor. While sixteen of the twenty firms rated this factor as very important, nearly all indicated that the availability of advanced infrastructure was already or would soon become the first or

Table 8–5. Factors Contributing to Firms' Location Choice by Major Activity

Activity and factor	Very important	Moderately important	Score	Rank
Regional headquarters and service				
Advanced infrastructure	9	0	45	1
Ordinary infrastructure	2	0	10	4
Cost of labor	0	2	6	6
Other costs	0	0	0	7
Manpower (availability and skill)	5	6	43	2
Distance from market	1	2	11	3
Entry to local market	0	0	0	7
Other	2	0	10	4
Production				
Advanced infrastructure	11	6	73	2
Ordinary infrastructure	0	3	9	8
Cost of labor	16	3	89	1
Other costs	3	9	42	5
Manpower (availability and skill)	9	5	60	4
Distance from market	2	6	28	6
Entry to local market	9	6	63	3
Other	3	0	15	7
Sourcing				
Advanced infrastructure	8	5	55	2
Ordinary infrastructure	1	5	20	4
Cost of labor	0	0	0	5
Other costs	11	6	73	1
Manpower (availability and skill)	0	0	0	5
Distance from market	2	8	34	3
Entry to local market	0	0	0	5

Note: Score based on firms' rankings of factors. Score = (number of "very important" responses x 5) + (number of "moderately important" responses x 3).
Source: authors' research.

second most important location consideration. Again, depending on the particular product or market, the tradeoff between labor costs and logistics and communication can vary significantly. The important point is that as value of service and time-related criteria—product development cycle and time to market—become increasingly important competitive factors, the relative importance of labor costs will diminish.

Respondents mentioned several criteria other than advanced infrastructure as important in selecting future production locations. These included consideration of the regulations and restrictions on importing capital goods and replacement parts, the availability of suitable and compatible local partners, and (in the case of the clothing industry) the situation regarding quotas.

Finally, according to the firms interviewed, in making sourcing decisions the cost of what is being sourced is the most important location consideration. Advanced infrastructure received a high score for this activity as well, however, particularly from firms for which reliability and time-definite delivery are considered essential. One respondent in the automobiles and auto parts industry said, "In the future, not having twenty-four-hour freight delivery, say for fuel injection systems, will not just be a limiter in choosing a place from which to source, but a knockout."

Table 8-6. Factors Contributing to Firms' Location Choice by Industry

Factor	Clothing and footwear			Electronics			Automobiles and auto parts		
	Very important	Moderately important	Score	Very important	Moderately important	Score	Very important	Moderately important	Score
Regional headquarters and service									
Advanced infrastructure	4	0	20	5	0	25	n.a.	n.a.	n.a.
Ordinary infrastructure	0	0	0	2	0	10	n.a.	n.a.	n.a.
Cost of labor	0	2	6	0	0	0	n.a.	n.a.	n.a.
Other costs	0	0	0	0	0	0	n.a.	n.a.	n.a.
Manpower (availability and skill)	3	1	18	2	5	25	n.a.	n.a.	n.a.
Distance from market	1	0	5	0	2	6	n.a.	n.a.	n.a.
Entry to local market	0	0	0	0	0	0	n.a.	n.a.	n.a.
Production									
Advanced infrastructure	4	1	23	4	2	26	3	3	24
Ordinary infrastructure	0	2	6	0	1	3	0	0	0
Cost of labor	7	0	35	3	3	24	6	0	30
Other costs	0	3	9	0	4	12	3	2	21
Manpower (availability and skill)	4	1	23	5	2	31	0	2	6
Distance from market	0	3	9	2	3	19	0	0	0
Entry to local market	0	2	6	3	4	27	6	0	30
Sourcing									
Advanced infrastructure	2	3	19	4	1	23	2	1	13
Ordinary infrastructure	1	1	8	0	2	6	0	2	6
Cost of labor	0	0	0	0	0	0	0	0	0
Other costs	4	1	23	4	2	26	3	3	24
Manpower (availability and skill)	0	0	0	0	0	0	0	0	0
Distance from market	0	0	6	2	3	19	0	3	9
Entry to local market	0	0	0	0	0	0	0	0	0

n.a. = Not applicable.
Note: Score based on firms' rankings of factors. Score = (number of "very important" responses x 5) + (number of "moderately important" responses x 3).
Source: authors' research.

Conclusion

Companies worldwide are recognizing the benefits they can derive from advanced infrastructure: lower inventory costs, greater productivity, shorter time to market, and faster product design cycles. Forward-looking governments are also acknowledging these trends and recognizing that advanced infrastructure will be necessary for them to maintain global competitiveness. Government strategies vary from the direct provision of services to the elimination of restrictions on private provision.

Although the need for rapid advanced infrastructure development is recognized in each of the economies discussed here by both the private sector and the government, the responses vary greatly. In Singapore both the government and the private sector vigorously support the development of advanced infrastructure. In Hong Kong only certain segments of industry show much interest in advanced infrastructure. While pockets of advanced infrastructure development do exist in Taiwan (China), the government has yet to undertake the policy reforms required for comprehensive development.

Other Asian economies are beginning to recognize the need to be integrated with global networks, but they trail considerably in the development of advanced infrastructure. For all countries, the ability to compete in global markets now rests on the successful development not only of basic infrastructure, but also of advanced infrastructure.

References

Peters, Hans. 1992. "Service: The New Focus in International Manufacturing and Trade." Policy Research Working Paper no. 950. Transport Division, Infrastructure and Urban Development Department, World Bank, Washington, D.C.

Reinfeld, William. 1992. "Benefits to the Republic of China of an Air Cargo Transportation Hub." White Paper presented to the Republic of China by Federal Express.

Suri, Rajan. 1995. "Common Misconceptions in Implementing Quick Response Manufacturing." *Journal of Applied Manufacturing Systems* 7(2):9–20.

Tan, Boon Wan, Eric Liu, Chu Wah, and Loh Chee Meng. 1992. "The Use of Information Technology by the Port of Singapore Authority." *World Development* 20 (2):1785–96.

Wong, S. H. 1992. "Exploiting Information Technology: A Case Study of Singapore." *World Development* 20 (2):1817–28.

Distributors of World Bank Publications

Prices and credit terms vary from country to country. Consult your local distributor before placing an order.

ARGENTINA
Oficina del Libro Internacional
Av. Cordoba 1877
1120 Buenos Aires
Tel: (54 1) 815-8354
Fax: (54 1) 815-8156

AUSTRALIA, FIJI, PAPUA NEW GUINEA, SOLOMON ISLANDS, VANUATU, AND WESTERN SAMOA
D.A. Information Services
648 Whitehorse Road
Mitcham 3132
Victoria
Tel: (61) 3 9210 7777
Fax: (61) 3 9210 7788
E-mail: service@dadirect.com.au
URL: http://www.dadirect.com.au

AUSTRIA
Gerold and Co.
Weihburggasse 26
A-1011 Wien
Tel: (43 1) 512-47-31-0
Fax: (43 1) 512-47-31-29
URL: http://www.gerold.co/at.online

BANGLADESH
Micro Industries Development
Assistance Society (MIDAS)
House 5, Road 16
Dhanmondi R/Area
Dhaka 1209
Tel: (880 2) 326427
Fax: (880 2) 811188

BELGIUM
Jean De Lannoy
Av. du Roi 202
1060 Brussels
Tel: (32 2) 538-5169
Fax: (32 2) 538-0841

BRAZIL
Publicações Tecnicas Internacionais Ltda.
Rua Peixoto Gomide, 209
01409 Sao Paulo, SP.
Tel: (55 11) 259-6644
Fax: (55 11) 258-6990
E-mail: postmaster@pti.uol.br
URL: http://www.uol.br

CANADA
Renouf Publishing Co. Ltd.
5369 Canotek Road
Ottawa, Ontario K1J 9J3
Tel: (613) 745-2665
Fax: ...

GERMANY
UNO-Verlag
Poppelsdorfer Allee 55
53115 Bonn
Tel: (49 228) 212940
Fax: (49 228) 217492

GREECE
...otirou S.A.
...potinou S.A.
...mara Str.
...hens
...4-1826
...8254

Infoenlace Ltda.
Carrera 6 No. 51-21
Apartado Aereo 34270
Santafé de Bogotá, D.C.
Tel: (57 1) 285-2798
Fax: (57 1) 285-2798

COTE D'IVOIRE
Center d'Edition et de Diffusion Africaines (CEDA)
04 B.P. 541
Abidjan 04
Tel: (225) 24 6510;24 6511
Fax: (225) 25 0567

CYPRUS
Center for Applied Research
Cyprus College
6, Diogenes Street, Engomi
P.O. Box 2006
Nicosia
Tel: (357 2) 44-1730
Fax: (357 2) 46-2051

CZECH REPUBLIC
National Information Center
prodejna, Konviktska 5
CS – 113 57 Prague 1
Tel: (42 2) 2422 9433
Fax: (42 2) 2422-1484
URL: http://www.nis.cz/

DENMARK
SamfundsLitteratur
Rosenoerns Allé 11
DK-1970 Frederiksberg C
Tel: (45 31) 351942
Fax: (45 31) 357822

EGYPT, ARAB REPUBLIC OF
Al Ahram Distribution Agency
Al Galaa Street
Cairo
Tel: (20 2) 578-6083
Fax: (20 2) 578-6833

The Middle East Observer
41, Sherif Street
Cairo
Tel: (20 2) 393-9732
Fax: (20 2) 393-9732

FINLAND
Akateeminen Kirjakauppa
P.O. Box 128
FIN-00101 Helsinki
Tel: (358 0) 121 4418
Fax: (358 0) 121-4435
E-mail: akatilaus@stockmann.fi
URL: http://www.akateeminen.com/

FRANCE
World Bank Publications
66, avenue d'Iéna
75116 Paris
Tel: (33 1) 40-69-30-56/57
Fax: (33 1) 40-69-30-68

Culture Diffusion
5, Rue Capois
C.P. 257
Port-au-Prince
Tel: (509 1) 3 9260

HONG KONG, MACAO
Asia 2000 Ltd.
Sales & Circulation Department
Seabird House, unit 1101-02
22-28 Wyndham Street, Central
Hong Kong
Tel: (852) 2530-1409
Fax: (852) 2526-1107
E-mail: sales@asia2000.com.hk
URL: http://www.asia2000.com.hk

INDIA
Allied Publishers Ltd.
751 Mount Road
Madras - 600 002
Tel: (91 44) 852-3938
Fax: (91 44) 852-0649

INDONESIA
Pt. Indira Limited
Jalan Borobudur 20
P.O. Box 181
Jakarta 10320
Tel: (62 21) 390-4290
Fax: (62 21) 421-4289

IRAN
Ketab Sara Co. Publishers
Khaled Eslamboli Ave.,
6th Street
Kusheh Delafrooz No. 8
P.O. Box 15745-733
Tehran
Tel: (98 21) 8717819; 8716104
Fax: (98 21) 8712479
E-mail: ketab-sara@neda.net.ir

Kowkab Publishers
P.O. Box 19575-511
Tehran
Tel: (98 21) 258-3723
Fax: (98 21) 258-3723

IRELAND
Government Supplies Agency
Oifig an tSoláthair
4-5 Harcourt Road
Dublin 2
Tel: (353 1) 661-3111
Fax: (353 1) 475-2670

ISRAEL
Yozmot Literature Ltd.
P.O. Box 56055
3 Yohanan Hasandlar Street
Tel Aviv 61560
Tel: (972 3) 5285-397
Fax: (972 3) 5285-397

R.O.Y. International
PO Box 13056
Tel Aviv 61130
Tel: (972 3) 5461423
Fax: (972 3) 5461442
E-mail: royil@netvision.net.il

Palestinian Authority/Middle East
Index Information Services
P.O.B. 19502 Jerusalem
Tel: (972 2) 6271219
Fax: (972 2) 6271634

EBSCO NZ Ltd.
Private Mail Bag 99914
New Market
Auckland
Tel: (64 9) 524-8119
Fax: (64 9) 524-8067

NIGERIA
University Press Limited
Three Crowns Building Jericho
Private Mail Bag 5095
Ibadan
Tel: (234 22) 41-1356
Fax: (234 22) 41-2056

NORWAY
NIC Info A/S
Book Department
Postboks 6512 Etterstad
N-0606 Oslo
Tel: (47 22) 97-4500
Fax: (47 22) 97-4545

PAKISTAN
Mirza Book Agency
65, Shahrah-e-Quaid-e-Azam
Lahore 54000
Tel: (92 42) 735 3601
Fax: (92 42) 758 5283

Oxford University Press
5 Bangalore Town
Sharae Faisal
PO Box 13033
Karachi-75350
Tel: (92 21) 446307
Fax: (92 21) 4547640
E-mail: oup@oup.khi.erum.com.pk

Pak Book Corporation
Aziz Chambers 21
Queen's Road
Lahore
Tel: (92 42) 636 3222; 636 0885
Fax: (92 42) 636 2328
E-mail: pbc@brain.net.pk

PERU
Editorial Desarrollo SA
Apartado 3824
Lima 1
Tel: (51 14) 285380
Fax: (51 14) 286628

PHILIPPINES
International Booksource Center Inc.
1127-A Antipolo St.
Barangay, Venezuela
Makati City
Tel: (63 2) 896 6501; 6505; 6507
Fax: (63 2) 896 1741

POLAND
International Publishing Service
Ul. Piekna 31/37
00-677 Warzawa
Tel: (48 2) 628-6089
Fax: (48 2) 621-7255
E-mail: books%ips@ikp.atm.com.pl
URL: http://www.ipscg.waw.pl/ips/export/

PORTUGAL
Livraria Portugal
Apartado 2681
Rua Do Carmo 70-74
1200 Lisbon
Tel: (1) 347-4982
Fax: (1) 347-0264

Licosa Commissionaria Sansoni SPA
Via Duca Di Calabria, 1/1
Casella Postale 552
50125 Firenze
Tel: (55) 645-415
Fax: (55) 641-257
E-mail: licosa@ftbcc.it
Url: http://www.ftbcc.it/licosa

JAMAICA
Ian Randle Publishers Ltd.
206 Old Hope Road
Kingston 6
Tel: (809) 927-2085
Fax: (809) 977-0243
E-mail: irpl@colis.com

JAPAN
Eastern Book Service
3-13 Hongo 3-chome, Bunkyo-ku
Tokyo 113
Tel: (81 3) 3818-0861
Fax: (81 3) 3818-0864
E-mail: orders@svt-ebs.co.jp
URL: http://www.bekkoame.or.jp/~svt-ebs

KENYA
Africa Book Service (E.A.) Ltd.
Quaran House, Mfangano Street
P.O. Box 45245
Nairobi
Tel: (254 2) 223 641
Fax: (254 2) 330 272

KOREA, REPUBLIC OF
Daejon Trading Co. Ltd.
P.O. Box 34, Youida
706 Seoun Bldg
44-6 Youido-Dong, Yeongchengo-Ku
Seoul
Tel: (82 2) 785-1631/4
Fax: (82 2) 784-0315

MALAYSIA
University of Malaya Cooperative
Bookshop, Limited
P.O. Box 1127
Jalan Pantai Baru
59700 Kuala Lumpur
Tel: (60 3) 756-5000
Fax: (60 3) 755-4424

MEXICO
INFOTEC
Av. San Fernando No. 37
Col. Toriello Guerra
14050 Mexico, D.F.
Tel: (52 5) 624-2800
Fax: (52 5) 624-2822
E-mail: infotec@rtn.net.mx
URL: http://rtn.net.mx

NEPAL
Everest Media International Services (P)Ltd.
GPO Box 5443
Kathmandu
Tel: (977 1) 472 152
Fax: (977 1) 224 431

NETHERLANDS
De Lindeboom/InOr-Publikaties
P.O. Box 202
7480 AE Haaksbergen
Tel: (31 53) 574-0004
Fax: (31 53) 572-9296
E-mail: lindeboo@worldonline.nl
URL: http://www.worldonline.nl/~lindeboo

Compani De Librarii Bucuresti S.A.
Str. Lipscani no. 26, sector 3
Bucharest
Tel: (40 1) 613 9645
Fax: (40 1) 312 4000

RUSSIAN FEDERATION
Isdatelstvo <Ves Mir>
9a, Lolpachniy Pereulok
Moscow 101831
Tel: (7 095) 917 87 49
Fax: (7 095) 917 92 59

SINGAPORE, TAIWAN, MYANMAR, BRUNEI
Asahgate Publishing Asia Pacific Pte. Ltd.
41 Kallang Pudding Road #04-03
Golden Wheel Building
Singapore 349316
Tel: (65) 741-5166
Fax: (65) 742-9356
E-mail: ashgate@asianconnect.com

SLOVENIA
Gospodarski Vestnik Publishing Group
Dunajska cesta 5
1000 Ljubljana
Tel: (386 61) 133 83 47; 132 12 30
Fax: (386 61) 133 80 30
E-mail: belicd@gvestnik.si

SOUTH AFRICA, BOTSWANA
For single titles:
Oxford University Press Southern Africa
P.O. Box 1141
Cape Town 8000
Tel: (27 21) 45-7266
Fax: (27 21) 45-7265

For subscription orders:
International Subscription Service
P.O. Box 41095
Craighall
Johannesburg 2024
Tel: (27 11) 880-1448
Fax: (27 11) 880-6248
E-mail: iss@is.co.za

SPAIN
Mundi-Prensa Libros, S.A.
Castello 37
28001 Madrid
Tel: (34 1) 431-3399
Fax: (34 1) 575-3998
E-mail: libreria@mundiprensa.es
URL: http://www.mundiprensa.es/

Mundi-Prensa Barcelona
Consell de Cent, 391
08009 Barcelona
Tel: (34 3) 488-3492
Fax: (34 3) 487-7659
E-mail: barcelona@mundiprensa.es

SRI LANKA, THE MALDIVES
Lake House Bookshop
100, Sir Chittampalam Gardiner Mawatha
Colombo 2
Tel: (94 1) 32105
Fax: (94 1) 432104
E-mail: LHL@sri.lanka.net

SWEDEN
Wennergren-Williams AB
P.O. Box 1305
S-171 25 Solna
Tel: (46 8) 705-97-50
Fax: (46 8) 27-00-71
E-mail: mail@wwi.se

Librairie Payot Service Institutionnel
Côtes-de-Montbenon 30
1002 Lausanne
Tel: (41 21) 341-3229
Fax: (41 21) 341-3235

ADECO Van Diermen Editions Techniques
Ch. de Lacuez 41
CH1807 Blonay
Tel: (41 21) 943 2673
Fax: (41 21) 943 3605

TANZANIA
Oxford University Press
Maktaba Street
PO Box 5299
Dar es Salaam
Tel: (255 51) 29209
Fax: (255 51) 46822

THAILAND
Central Books Distribution
306 Silom Road
Bangkok 10500
Tel: (66 2) 235-5400
Fax: (66 2) 237-8321

TRINIDAD & TOBAGO, AND THE CARRIBBEAN
Systematics Studies Unit
9 Watts Street
Curepe
Trinidad, West Indies
Tel: (809) 662-5654
Fax: (809) 662-5654
E-mail: tobe@trinidad.net

UGANDA
Gustro Ltd.
PO Box 9997, Madhvani Building
Plot 16/4 Jinja Rd.
Kampala
Tel: (256 41) 254 763
Fax: (256 41) 251 468

UNITED KINGDOM
Microinfo Ltd.
P.O. Box 3
Alton, Hampshire GU34 2PG
England
Tel: (44 1420) 86848
Fax: (44 1420) 89889
E-mail: wbank@ukminfo.demon.co.uk
URL: http://www.microinfo.co.uk

VENEZUELA
Tecni-Ciencia Libros, S.A.
Centro Cuidad Comercial Tamanco
Nivel C2
Caracas
Tel: (58 2) 959 5547; 5035; 0016
Fax: (58 2) 959 5636

ZAMBIA
University Bookshop, University of Zambia
Great East Road Campus
P.O. Box 32379
Lusaka
Tel: (260 1) 252 576
Fax: (260 1) 253 952

ZIMBABWE
Longman Zimbabwe (Pvt.)Ltd.
Tourle Road, Ardbennie
P.O. Box ST125
Southerton
Harare
Tel: (263 4) 6216617
Fax: (263 4) 621670

04/29/97